HANDBOOK OF
ORGANIZATIONAL
MEASUREMENT

HANDBOOK OF ORGANIZATIONAL MEASUREMENT

JAMES L. PRICE
UNIVERSITY OF IOWA

D. C. HEATH AND COMPANY

Lexington, Massachusetts   Toronto   London

Portions of pp. 60–65, 84–89, 103, 104 (Table 12-1)–106 are reprinted with permission of The Macmillan Company from *The Community General Hospital* (pp. 242–243, 258, Table 27, 279–284, 512–513) by Basil S. Georgopoulos and Floyd C. Mann. © 1962 by The Macmillan Company, New York.

Table 19-1 (p. 166) and Table 19-2 (p. 167) are reprinted with the permission of Rand McNally & Company from *The Measurement of Satisfaction in Work and Retirement* (Tables 4.3 and 4.8) by Patricia Cain Smith, Lorne M. Kendall, and Charles L. Hulin. © 1969 by Rand McNally & Company, Chicago.

To my children, Jimmy and Wanda

ACKNOWLEDGMENTS

It is from one's colleagues that a researcher expects critical analysis of his work. I am indebted to the following, who amply fulfilled my expectations: George R. Boynton, Robert T. Golembiewski, Jerald T. Hage, Richard H. Hall, David J. Hickson, and Stanley H. Udy, Jr. Unfortunately, I cannot hold them responsible for the final version of this handbook!

The Graduate School of the University of Iowa awarded me a research assignment which considerably facilitated research for this handbook. This award was greatly appreciated, especially since the regular funding agencies of the Federal Government and the private foundations were massively unwilling to support this type of *nonempirical research.*

It is impossible, as many before me have noted, to indicate exactly the source of one's ideas. However, I can state that Allen H. Barton's pioneering work on organizational measurement[1] helped me to see the need for a handbook of organizational measurement and was the source of many thoughts concerning the compilation of such a book. A stimulating paper by William M. Evan further encouraged me to undertake the project.[2]

The Department of Sociology of the University of Iowa generously provided me with that most basic of all research resources, a full-time assistant. Phil Day admirably filled this role for two years.

Joe Mansfield labored diligently, and often in vain I fear, to translate the original manuscript from Sociologese into "plain" English. Mrs. Jane Snow is responsible for converting my small, printed script into a neatly typed bundle of papers. Their assistance is appreciated.

My wife Lee wonderfully endured many high-sounding lectures on the subject "The Importance of Standardizing and Improving Organizational Measurement," a topic hardly calculated to warm a woman's heart! Her encouragement was profound.

---

[1]Allen H. Barton, *Organizational Measurement* (New York: College Entrance Examination Board, 1961).
[2]William M. Evan, "Indices of the Hierarchical Structure of Industrial Organizations," *Management Science*, 9 (April, 1963), 468–477.

CONTENTS

HANDBOOK OF
ORGANIZATIONAL
MEASUREMENT

INTRODUCTION

STATEMENT OF PURPOSE

There is little standardization of the measures used in studying organizations. Although there are no systematic studies of the extent to which different researchers use the same measure when studying the same concept—the definition of standardization used in this handbook—various researchers have commented upon the lack of standardization with respect to selected concepts used in the field.[1, 2]

This lack of standardization hinders the development of organizational theory. Standardization of measures makes it easier for findings to be compared. Different researchers studying the same phenomena often obtain different findings and, without standardization, there is the problem of determining whether the differences reflect actual differences in the phenomena studied or are the result of different measures.[3] When measures are standardized, one source of the differences—the measures used—is controlled and the likelihood increases that the different results reflect actual differences in the phenomena.

The comparison of findings is important because it is the means whereby theory is generated and verified. Generalizations with respect to different phenomena—an essential characteristic of theory—cannot be generated and verified unless the findings obtained by studying the different phenomena can be compared. Without the comparison of findings, there would be no theory.[4] Standardization promotes the development of theory because it facilitates the comparison of findings.

The primary purpose of this handbook is to promote standardization of the measures used in the study of organizations. If existing measures are compiled in a compact, orderly, and precise manner, then it will be easier to use them, and this greater ease should increase the likelihood that researchers will use the same measure when studying identical concepts. This handbook is intended to be such a compilation.[5]

The level of organizational measurement could be significantly improved, to state the matter charitably. Many—perhaps most—organizational measures are based on a single piece of information rather than on combinations of different pieces of information. In short, the typical organizational measure is an indicator rather than an index.[6] Or again, most measures are accompanied

1

by no information that explicitly discusses their validity and reliability.[7] Given the low level of organizational measurement, an exclusive focus on standardization would result in the standardization of a set of inferior measures! A secondary purpose thus informs this handbook.

The secondary purpose of this handbook is to promote the improvement of the measures used in the study of organizations. This improvement should come about in two ways. First, the mere compilation of organizational measures reveals obvious deficiencies that require correction. For example, the neglect of the problems of validity and reliability is dramatic. Most organizational measures are accompanied by no information which explicitly discusses their validity and reliability. The paucity of measures associated with widely used organizational concepts is also evident. Second, specific suggestions for the improvement of these measures are advanced at different places in this handbook. The most extended discussion of these suggestions is found in the final chapter; however, the Comments that accompany the measures often contain specific suggestions for their improvement.

Two exclusions from this handbook should be noted. First, it does not focus on organizational theory. Consider, for example, the concept of effectiveness. This handbook discusses the conceptualization and measurement of effectiveness; however, it does not present a theory about the determinants of effectiveness.[8] Second, this handbook is not a compendium of factual information.[9] Factual information is contained in the handbook; however, this information is sketchy and always subordinate to the compilation of measurement data. The reader who is searching for theory and facts had best direct his attention elsewhere.[10]

ORGANIZATION AND MEASUREMENT

To standardize and improve the measures used in the study of organizations—the purposes of this handbook—is to make assumptions about the nature of organizations and the nature of measurement. These assumptions will now be made explicit.

Organization. Organizations are social systems with specific goals.[11] Examples of organizations are government agencies, business firms, schools, hospitals, prisons, military units, trade associations, professional societies, fraternal orders, churches, and trade unions. Other terms often used to designate organizations are "complex organizations," "formal organizations," "bureaucracies," "large-scale organizations," and "associations." Lest the reader come to the conclusion that organizations are all encompassing, it should be noted that families, communities, peer groups, and societies are examples of social systems that are not organizations.

Administrative organizations are sometimes distinguished from voluntary associations. The distinction between these two types of organizations can be made in terms of the time-commitments of their members. Administrative organizations are primarily composed of full-time members, whereas voluntary associations are primarily composed of part-time members. Government agencies, business firms, schools, hospitals, prisons, and military units are examples of administrative organizations, whereas trade associations, professional societies, fraternal orders, churches, and trade unions are examples of voluntary associations.[12]

Most of the measures in this handbook are used in the study of administrative organizations. Some of these measures can be readily used in the study of voluntary associations, but many—perhaps most—apply exclusively to administrative organizations. The reason for this imbalance is that good measures in the literature that focus on voluntary associations are hard to find. This focus on measures of administrative organizations is thus a reflection of a measurement emphasis in the study of organizations.

Measurement. Measurement is the assignment of numbers to data according to a set of rules.[13] Four levels of measurement are commonly distinguished: nominal, ordinal, interval, and ratio.[14] Nominal measures are classifications of data. An example of a nominal measure is the psychiatric system for classification of the mentally ill ("schizophrenic," "paranoid," "manic-depressive," and "psychoneurotic"). Ordinal measures are rankings of the classifications of data. An example of an ordinal measure is the measurement of social class developed by Warner and his colleagues ("upper upper class," "lower upper class," "upper middle class," "lower middle class," "upper lower class," and "lower lower class"). Interval measures are rankings of the classifications of data about which the distances between the classifications are of a known size. An example of an interval measure is the Fahrenheit scale for the measurement of temperature. Ratio measures have all the characteristics of interval measures, plus a true zero point. An example of a ratio measure is pounds used to measure weight.

Almost all of the measures in this handbook are nominal and ordinal measures. The reason for this is that interval and ratio measures have not generally been developed for the concepts used to study organizations. The handbook's almost exclusive focus on nominal and ordinal measures is thus a reflection of the level of measurement used in the study of organization.

The validity and reliability of measures is a constant concern of this handbook. "The commonest definition of validity," according to Kerlinger, "is epitomized by the question: Are we measuring what we think we are measuring?"[15] Most organizational research, as previously indicated, does not explicitly deal with the problem of validity. Most of the research, however, has data that are relevant to validity. These data primarily consist of predictions that are confirmed, findings that are in agreement with current knowledge, and correlations between concepts that have not been predicted and about which there is some uncertainty as to their agreement with current knowledge. Reliability is the accuracy of a measuring instrument.[16] Most organizational research does not have data that are relevant to reliability. When the problem of reliability is confronted by organizational researchers, it is typically by means of test-retest coefficients and split-half coefficients.

The assignment of numbers to data according to a set of rules—the definition of measurement used in this handbook—must be distinguished from the means of data collection. The data to measure "satisfaction" (often termed "morale") can be collected by means of surveys, documents, or observations. Once the data are collected, numbers are assigned. The two operations—data collection and assignment of numbers—must be distinguished.

This handbook provides information about the means of data collection *and* the assignment of numbers to the data collected. The reason for providing both types of information is to make it possible for a researcher to use the measures in this handbook without having to consult the primary source materials. Researchers are more likely to use the measures contained in this handbook, thereby increasing standardization, if the measures are easy to use, and a single source compiling information about both the means of data collection and the assignment of numbers to the data collected is easier to use. However, a list of the primary source materials is provided in case the researcher prefers to consult them.

The measurement of organizational concepts can be based on subjective data, that is, on the questioning of individuals, or on objective data, the study of documents and the use of observations.[17] For example, the concept of "centralization" can be measured by questioning the individual members of an organization as to their perceived influence in the decision-making process or by the distribution of monetary compensation in the organization. Information about monetary compensation is best obtained from the payroll records.[18]

Most of the measures in this handbook are based on data obtained through questioning individuals. The reason for the reliance on this type of data is that the best organizational research uses this method. Most of the researchers using this method are trained either as psychologists or social psychologists. This handbook's neglect of measures based on documents and observations is thus a reflection of the neglect of this type of measure in the study of organizations.

SELECTION OF MEASURES

There are two major problems involved in the selection of measures to be included in this handbook. First, the literature to be reviewed must be selected; second, specific measures within the reviewed literature must be selected. These two problems will now be discussed.

Literature Selection. The selection of the literature could be determined by some type of objective procedure, such as the review of a specific number of journal articles over a specified number of years. An example of this type of objective procedure is provided by the work of Bonjean and his colleagues.[19] To construct a handbook[20] of sociological measurement, Bonjean and his colleagues reviewed all the articles that appeared between January, 1954 and December, 1965 in the *American Sociological Review*, the *American Journal of Sociology*, *Social Forces*, and *Sociometry*.

Unlike the work of Bonjean and his colleagues, this handbook does not use an objective procedure to select the literature to be reviewed because no relatively simple procedure could be devised for selecting a sample representative of the universe of organizational research. Bonjean and his colleagues probably obtained a representative sample of sociological measurement by their objective procedure because of the importance of the four journals they reviewed and the length of time used (a decade). However, the study of organizations is undertaken by researchers who are based in five different disciplines (sociology, psychology, social psychology, political science, and economics) and three main professional schools (business, education, and public administration). Their findings are published in a large number of journals and books. Therefore, a relatively simple objective procedure would ignore too much that is valuable in organizational measurement.

The selection of literature to review is based on the author's knowledge of the field of organizational study. It does not take a profound grasp of organizational literature to discover that the measure developed by Smith and her colleagues for "satisfaction" (the "Job Descriptive Index") is outstanding, or that the research undertaken during the past two decades by Tannenbaum and his colleagues with respect to the measurement of "centralization" (the "control graph") is exceptional.[21] Especially helpful in the selection of literature in the early stages of work on this handbook was a series of reviews of organizational literature.[22] This type of subjective procedure for the selection of literature has its limitations. The sociological background of the author predisposes him to select some types of literature more often than others. However, the author believes that this subjective procedure yields more representative data with less expenditure of resources than a relatively simple objective procedure.[23] The test of the selection procedure is whether or not this handbook has excluded any significant organizational measures. This is a test the reader can make.

Measures Selection. Seven guides are used in the selection of the measures.

(1) Preference is given to measures that use the organization as the unit of analysis. Since the concepts used to describe organizations are also used to describe other types of social systems, the measures for a concept could have different units of analysis. This handbook is interested in the development of organizational theory; therefore, its preference is for measures that use the organization as the unit of analysis.[24] A further preference is for measures that are applicable beyond a specific type of organization. In short, the preference is for general measures within a limited class of social systems, organizations.

(2) Preference is given to measures that are used in an empirical study. Researchers, when discussing a concept, will often advance valuable suggestions about its measurement.[25] However, suggestions of this type are not

included in this handbook because, although they may appear valuable at first glance, empirical use of the suggested measures often reveals that they are unusable. The selection of measures that are used in an empirical study increases the likelihood that the measures selected are at least appropriate to empirical research.

(3) Preference is given to measures that present data about their validity and reliability. Acceptable levels of validity and reliability is seldom a problem because few studies explicitly discuss these issues.

(4) Preference is given to simple measures. Some organizational measures, for example, are long and difficult to score. There is likely to be greater standardization of simple measures than of complex measures. Many organizational researchers, for example, are interested in a series of concepts and thus must have short measures to keep their instruments of data collection within manageable lengths.

(5) Preference is given to multiple measures of a concept. In short, indices, rather than indicators, are preferred.[26] Multiple measures are preferred because they yield higher validity than single measures. The problem of random measurement error is, of course, more adequately dealt with by multiple measures.

(6) Preference is given to published measures. Published measures have been subject to more collegial review, and thus should generally be of higher quality than unpublished measures. It is also considerably easier to obtain published measures since professors are not always the most willing correspondents when asked to supply detailed information about their measures.

(7) Preference is given to measures that are related to precisely formulated concepts. There are some sophisticated organizational measures whose conceptual referents are not at all apparent.[27] If the conceptual referent for a measure was not apparent, it was difficult to classify the measure and thus to include it in this handbook.

Two points must be emphasized about these guides. First, the guides are of most assistance when there is an abundance of good measures for a concept, and this is an infrequent occurrence. The usual problem is that of locating a reasonably adequate measure rather than in screening out a series of good contending measures. Second, the guides are not viewed as absolutes. If inclusion of a measure appears to promote the purposes of this handbook—the standardization and improvement of organizational measures—the measure is included, whether or not one or more of the guides are violated.

Use of these seven guides to select the measures means that the work of many important organizational scholars is not represented in the selections in this handbook. If a scholar has conducted no empirical research, his work will not appear in this handbook, no matter how eminent. The more theoretically and methodologically sophisticated the research, the greater the likelihood of inclusion. The emphasis of this handbook is thus on empirical research. However, some scholars whose work is not represented in the selections are included by virtue of their distinguished theoretical work. This type of representation occurs most frequently in connection with the frame of reference, the next topic of this introductory chapter.

FRAME OF REFERENCE

The statement of purpose notes that this handbook attempts to compile existing organizational measures in a compact, orderly, and precise manner. Such a compilation requires a system of classification: to classify organizational measures properly is to arrange them in a compact, orderly, and precise manner. A proper system of classification must provide classes for all possible measures and allow unambiguous assignment.

The set of concepts (frame of reference) used to study organizations should constitute the requisite system of classification. (These concepts are variously labeled: "characteristics," "attributes," "dimensions," "properties," and "variables.") The problem is that there is no set of concepts agreed upon by all—or even a large majority—of organizational researchers. Different researchers study different components of organizations and no one has yet devised an agreed-upon frame of reference to direct this research. This conceptual diversity is to be anticipated because, as previously indicated, the study of organizations is undertaken by researchers who are based in five different disciplines and three main professional schools.

There is, however, a fair degree of agreement among researchers concerning what it is about organizations that should be studied. In short, there is some agreement on the frame of reference. Research published within a single discipline or applied area (the concern of the professional schools) is widely read outside the discipline or applied area. This means that the different researchers within a discipline or applied area are probably benefiting from research performed elsewhere. These benefits would not be experienced unless there was some agreement concerning what it is about organizations that should be studied.

This handbook classifies its measures by those concepts about which there is the greatest degree of agreement among organizational researchers.[28] The assumption is that the concepts about which there is the greatest degree of agreement are the most significant concepts for organizational analysis. The experts—the organizational researchers—may be in error; some concepts thought to be significant, that is, to be related systematically to other concepts, have been shown by subsequent research to be of little value. However, given the long-term objective of constructing organizational theories, it seems that one has little choice but to accept the current judgment of organizational researchers as to what ultimately will be the significant concepts in these theories.

There seems to be a fair degree of agreement among organizational researchers concerning the importance of the 28 concepts within this handbook's frame of reference. Measures could be located for 22 of these concepts; these measures constitute chapters 2 through 22 of this handbook. Measures could not be located—strange as it may seem—for six of these concepts; these are discussed in the concluding chapter of this handbook.

There is little agreement among organizational researchers regarding the set of terms or labels to be used to refer to the frame of reference. The same term may refer to different concepts or different terms may refer to the same concept. However, there is some agreement on this matter. This handbook seeks to use those terms about which there is the greatest degree of agreement, because standardization of measures should be accompanied by standardization of the terms used to refer to the measures. It seems as if this standardization of terms is best promoted in this way.

The question arises as to how this handbook determined the concepts and terms about which there is the greatest degree of agreement among organizational researchers. There is, of course, no scientific academy that places an imprimatur on a single set of concepts and terms. It is difficult to answer this question meaningfully. It is not terribly enlightening—although it is true—to state that recognition of these areas of agreement concerning concepts and terms emerged slowly during the research process. The important question, however, is not how these concepts and terms were selected, but whether or not this handbook has in fact delineated the concepts and terms about which there is the greatest degree of agreement among organizational researchers. The important question is thus empirical rather than procedural. The degree to which this handbook is used by organizational researchers will be, ultimately, an approximate indication of this handbook's success in determining those points of agreement among organizational researchers.

A number of deviations from the "agreement approach" will be noted throughout this handbook. There are, for example, some concepts whose meaning does not appear to be adequately caught up by the currently agreed-upon set of terms. Where there seems to be a serious discrepancy between the meaning of a concept and its currently agreed-upon set of terms, this handbook attempts to reformulate the terms used to indicate the concept. There are also some widely used terms that result in awkward formulations. In these situations, this handbook suggests the use of simpler terms. The current agreement with respect to concepts and terms is thus not an absolute to be conformed to at the expense of critical analysis. However—and this is crucial— departures from the points of agreement are justified in this handbook.

Treatment of these conceptual issues requires space. The introductory comments with which each chapter begins generally devote more space to conceptual issues than to measurement issues. The amount of space devoted to these conceptual issues may appear excessive; however, the ultimate resolution of these conceptual issues is basic to the improvement of organizational measurement. The most intractable problem in compiling this handbook of organizational measurement was the theoretical one of obtaining a frame of reference with which to classify the measures. No claim is made that the problem of constructing an adequate frame of reference has been solved. An attempt, however, has been made to confront squarely the conceptual problems·

Some organizational researchers construct classifications for the concepts contained in their frame of reference. Pugh *et al.*, for example, classify their concepts (which they term "variables") into four classes: contextual, activity, structural, and performance.[29] On the other hand, Hage and Aiken use two classes for their concepts (which they term "dimensions"), structure and performance.[30]

This handbook provides no classification of the concepts selected for the frame of reference. Given the purposes of this handbook, there seems to be no advantages to be gained by the construction of a system for the classification of concepts.

There is great variation in the quality of the available measures for the different concepts in this handbook. For some concepts, such as satisfaction, a set of extremely impressive measures is available; for other concepts, such as dispersion, there are almost no measures. This handbook, of course, cannot modify this characteristic of organizational research, but can merely compile what is currently available.

The statement of purpose noted that this handbook does not focus on organizational theory. This means that the concepts used to classify the measures are not systematically related, either as propositions or as theories, within this handbook. There is some presentation of propositions, mostly in connection with the validity of the measures. However, this handbook makes no attempt to relate systematically the 28 concepts in its frame of reference.

THE AUDIENCE AND THE USE OF THIS HANDBOOK

This handbook is intended for scholars and students in the field of organizational study. The scholars will most likely be professors from the five disciplines and the three main professional schools that specialize in the study of organizations. The students will most likely be students of these professors. This handbook is written in such a manner that it will be comprehensible to students, undergraduate or graduate, who are beginning to study organizations. It was not designed for managers. The lack of a theoretical focus means that managers will find very little guidance from this handbook in the solution of their problems.

It is intended that this handbook be useful in research and teaching. The researcher, be he professor or graduate student, will probably consult those sections of this handbook that contain measures relevant to his research. The student, undergraduate or graduate, will probably consult this handbook to clarify concepts and to become acquainted with some of the better empirical studies in the field.

There is little likelihood that this handbook will be read and studied like a research report, that is, straight through from the first chapter to the last. Each chapter constitutes a unit and the chapters can be read with little or no reference to each other. When the same research is used for different concepts, which is sometimes the case, the research is described completely for each concept, thus making it unnecessary for the reader to refer to previous descriptions. (Consecutive reading of the chapters would reveal a fair amount of repetition.) The assumption is that this handbook is more like a dictionary than like the typical research report. The average reader will probably consult different chapters at different times, in no particular sequence.

HANDBOOK OUTLINE

The concepts of the frame of reference are arranged in alphabetical order with a chapter devoted to each concept. Within each chapter, there is first a general discussion of each concept's definition and measurement. Following the general discussions, different measures appropriate to the concept are described. The measures are arranged alphabetically, by author. When there are multiple authors, the first author is selected as the basis for the alphabetical listing. In some instances, a literature has developed dealing with the different measures; this literature is listed after the measures are described. The final part of each chapter consists of additional measures which were examined, but which, for various reasons, were not selected for inclusion within this handbook.

NOTES

1. Brayfield and Crockett comment upon the lack of standardization for satisfaction (which they term "morale"); a hospital study conducted by the Public Health Service makes similar comments with respect to succession (which is termed "turnover" in the study); and Watkins and his colleagues note the lack of standardization with respect to absenteeism. See Arthur H. Brayfield and Walter H. Crockett, "Employee Attitude and Performance," *Psychological Bulletin*, 52 (September, 1955), 396–424 (esp. p. 409); Public Health Service, *Hospital Personnel* (Washington, D.C.: Public Health Service Publication No. 930–C–9, U.S. Government Printing Office, October, 1964), esp. p. 3; and Gordon S. Watkins, Paul A. Dodd, Wayne L. McNaughton, and Paul Prasow, *The Management of Personnel and Labor Relations* (New York: McGraw-Hill, 1950), pp. 376–377.

2. The degree of measurement standardization in organizational research must be checked by the type of study reported in Charles M. Bonjean, Richard J. Hill, and S. Dale McLemore, *Sociological Measurement* (San Francisco: Chandler, 1967), pp. 1–16.

3. Comparison of findings can, of course, be made without standardization. If different measures of the same concept can be demonstrated to be equivalent, then the results of the different measures can be compared. The use of equivalent measures is especially significant in cross-cultural research. The equivalence of measures is discussed in Patricia C. Smith, Lorne M. Kendall, and Charles L. Hulin, *The Measurement of Satisfaction in Work and Retirement* (Chicago: Rand McNally, 1969). Eugene Litwak and Powhatan Wooldridge first impressed upon this author the importance of comparison by means other than standardization.

4. The importance of the comparative study of organizations for the development of theory is set forth in Peter M. Blau, "The Comparative Study of Organizations," *Industrial and Labor Relations Review*, 18 (April, 1965), 323–338 (esp. p. 323).

5. There are several recent compilations of measures. See, for example, Allen H. Barton, *Organizational Measurement* (New York: College Entrance Examination Board, 1961); Bonjean, *op. cit.*; Delbert C. Miller, *Handbook of Research Design and Social Measurement* (New York: McKay, 1970); John P. Robinson, Jerrold G. Rush, and Kendra B. Head, *Measures of Political Attitudes* (Ann Arbor, Mich.: Survey Research Center, University of Michigan, 1968); John P. Robinson, Robert Athanasiou, and Kendra B. Head, *Measures of Occupational Attitudes and Occupational Characteristics* (Ann Arbor, Mich.: Survey Research Center, University of Michigan, 1969); John P. Robinson and Phillip R. Shaver, *Measures of Social Psychological Attitudes* (Ann Arbor, Mich.: Survey Research Center, University of Michigan, 1969); and Marvin E. Shaw and Jack M. Wright, *Scales for the Measurement of Attitudes* (New York: McGraw-Hill, 1967).

   The pioneering compilation of organizational measures is the research completed by Barton. Barton's compilation, while different in several significant respects from this handbook, indicated the direction that this handbook has attempted to follow.

6. A discussion of indicators and indices is found in Bonjean, *op. cit.*, pp. 2–3.

7. Validity and reliability are discussed in the next section of this introductory chapter.

8. A theory of organizational effectiveness is presented in James L. Price, *Organizational Effectiveness* (Homewood, Ill.: Irwin, 1968). Systematic verification of this theory is urgently needed.

9. An example of a book that is basically concerned with the presentation of factual information is Murray Hausknecht, *The Joiners* (New York: Bedminster, 1962).

10. The best single compendium of theory and facts about organizations is probably *The Handbook of Organizations*, ed. James G. March (Chicago: Rand McNally, 1965).

11. This definition of organization comes from Talcott Parsons, *Structure and Process in Modern Societies* (Glencoe, Ill.: The Free Press, 1960), p. 17. Etzioni's influential work has been partially responsible for the wide usage of the Parsonian definition of organization. See, for example, Amitai Etzioni, *A Comparative Analysis of Complex Organizations* (Glencoe, Ill.: The Free Press, 1961), p. 79 and Amitai Etzioni, *Modern Organizations* (Englewood Cliffs, N.J.: Prentice-Hall, 1964), p. 3. An alternative to the Parsonian definition of organization is provided in the widely used text by Blau and Scott. See Peter M. Blau and W. Richard Scott, *Formal Organizations* (San Francisco: Chandler, 1962), pp. 2–8.

   There are problems involved with the definitions of organization advanced by Parsons–Etzioni and Blau–Scott. Resolution of such problems is beyond the scope of this handbook.

12. The distinction between organizations that are primarily composed of full-time members and those that are not comes from Robert A. Dahl, *Who Governs?* (New Haven, Conn.: Yale, 1961), p. 97. What Dahl refers to as "vocational and avocational associations," this handbook refers to as "administrative organizations and voluntary associations," respectively. The word "primarily" is not

included in Dahl's definition. The terms "administrative organizations" and "voluntary associations" come from Wilbert E. Moore, "Management and Union Organizations: An Analytical Comparison," *Research in Industrial Human Relations*, ed. Conrad M. Arensberg, Solomon Barkin, W. Ellison Chalmers, Harold L. Wilensky, James C. Worthy, and Barbara D. Dennis (New York: Harper, 1957), pp. 119–130. Moore, however, does not define these terms as they are used in this handbook. The most widely used typologies of organizations are formulated by Blau and Scott, *op. cit.*, pp. 40–58 and Etzioni, *A Comparative Analysis of Complex Organizations*, *op. cit.*, pp. 3–67.

This handbook uses the Moore typology (administrative organizations and voluntary associations) because no particular typology of organizations has received wide acceptance by organizational researchers. The use of one typology rather than another is also not basic to the primary purposes of this handbook.

13. This definition of measurement is based on Shaw and Wright, *op. cit.*, p. 15 and Sidney Siegel, *Nonparametric Statistics* (New York: McGraw-Hill, 1956), p. 21.

14. This discussion of these four levels of measurement is based on Siegel, *ibid.*, pp. 21–30.

15. Fred N. Kerlinger, *Foundations of Behavioral Research* (New York: Holt, Rinehart & Winston, 1964), p. 444.

16. *Ibid.*, p. 430.

17. Two sources that have material relevant to this distinction between subjective data and objective data are Kerr Inkson, Roy Payne, and Derek Pugh, "Extending the Occupational Environment; The Measurement of Organizations," *Occupational Psychology*, 41 (January, 1967), 1–15 (esp. pp. 3–4) and Lyman W. Porter and Edward E. Lawler, III, *Managerial Attitudes and Performance* (Homewood. Ill.: Irwin, 1968), pp. 25–28.

There are problems with the distinction between subjective data and objective data. Records, for example, are referred to as objective data. It might be noted, however, that records always contain the results of subjective impressions because they are maintained by individuals. The distinction between subjective data and objective data is helpful if an attempt is not made to defend it rigorously. This handbook will make no such rigorous attempt!

18. These two measures of centralization are discussed in the chapter on centralization.

19. Bonjean *et al.*, *op. cit.*, p. 10.

20. Bonjean *et al.* refer to their work as an "inventory" rather than a "handbook."

21. Smith *et al.*, *op. cit.* The work of Smith and her colleagues and the work of Tannenbaum and his colleagues are discussed, respectively, in the chapters on satisfaction and centralization.

22. The following reviews of the organizational literature were especially helpful: Bernard M. Bass, *Leadership, Psychology, and Organizational Behavior* (New York: Harper, 1960); Peter M. Blau, *Bureaucracy in Modern Society* (New York: Random House, 1956); Blau and Scott, *op. cit.*; Etzioni, *op. cit.*, Ferrel Heady, *Public Administration* (Englewood Cliffs, N. J.: Prentice-Hall, 1966); Daniel Katz and Robert L. Kahn, *The Social Psychology of Organizations* (New York: Wiley, 1966); Rensis Likert, *New Patterns of Management* (New York: McGraw-Hill, 1961); James G. March and Herbert A. Simon, *Organizations* (New York: Wiley, 1958); Edgar H. Schein, *Organizational Psychology* (Englewood Cliffs,

N.J.: Prentice-Hall, 1965); Arnold S. Tannenbaum, *Social Psychology of the Work Organization* (Belmont, Calif.: Wadsworth, 1966); James D. Thompson, *Organizations in Action* (New York: McGraw-Hill, 1967); and Victor H. Vroom, *Work and Motivation* (New York: Wiley, 1964).

23. A complex, objective procedure could, of course, be devised. Such a procedure would, however, require too great an investment of resources for the returns received.

24. This strategy has been influenced by Merton's strategy for constructing middle-range theories. See, for example, Robert K. Merton, *Social Theory and Social Structure* (New York: The Free Press, 1968), pp. 39–72.

25. An example is William M. Evan, "Indices of the Hierarchical Structure of Industrial Organizations," *Management Science*, 9 (April, 1963), 468–477. This article is an early example of an organizational researcher who recognizes the need for the compilation of organizational measures. Barton, *op. cit.*, and Evan were among the first to recognize this need.

26. The fourth and fifth guides are contradictory because indices are more complex than indicators. However, in practice, few problems arise because there is not an abundance of good measures from which to choose. Where there is an abundance of good indices, then the simpler indices are given preference over the complex indices.

27. The concluding chapter of this handbook provides a detailed discussion of one such example.

28. The work of the following researchers and their colleagues have been especially helpful in constructing this handbook's frame of reference: Michael T. Aiken, Peter M. Blau, Jerald T. Hage, David J. Hickson, Derek S. Pugh, W. Richard Scott, and Stanley H. Udy, Jr. The work of these individuals is cited throughout this handbook.

    Special mention must be made of the work of Stanley H. Udy, Jr. All of Udy's work was reviewed for possible inclusion in this handbook. It is solidly grounded in theory and uses acceptable methodological procedures; his comparative perspective is also valuable, especially his focus on nonmodern nations. Udy's work is not cited elsewhere in this handbook because his theoretical work, while stimulating and helpful, departs from the current consensus among most organizational researchers in many respects. His focus on nonmodern nations, while very much needed, does not result in many general measures.

29. D. S. Pugh, D. J. Hickson, C. R. Hinings, K. M. McDonald, C. Turner, and T. Lupton, "A Scheme for Organizational Analysis," *Administrative Science Quarterly*, 8 (December, 1963), 289–315 and D. S. Pugh, D. J. Hickson, C. R. Hinings, and C. Turner, "Dimensions of Organizational Structure," *Administrative Science Quarterly*, 13 (June, 1968), 65–105.

30. Jerald Hage and Michael Aiken, *Social Change in Complex Organizations* (New York: Random House, 1970), p. 28.

ABSENTEEISM

1

Definition. *Absenteeism* is the degree to which the members of a social system fail to report for work at the time they are scheduled to work.[1] In the typical administrative organization,[2] for example, this includes absences due to work injuries or work disease, accidents and illness not caused by employment, and time taken out for the employee's personal reasons, that is, because of death or illness in the family, business matters, transportation difficulties, and so forth. However, time out for authorized regular vacations, involuntary lay-offs, lack of work, and work stoppages are not generally counted as absences.

Absenteeism is generally defined in such a way that its use is limited to administrative organizations. Kossoris, for example, advances the following definition: "For the purpose of this survey, an absence was defined as a failure to report for work at any time when the *employee* was scheduled to work . . . ." (M. Kossoris, *Monthly Labor Review*, 66 (March, 1948) 266.) (Emphasis supplied.) Since voluntary associations typically have few "employees," the type of definition that Kossoris gives is not applicable to voluntary associations. However, in this handbook Kossoris' definition of absenteeism is adapted to apply to administrative organizations and voluntary associations.

It is common in organizational literature to find absenteeism used as a measure of satisfaction (often termed "morale"), as a measure of withdrawal from the work situation, and as a measure of participation.[3] The most common of these practices is the use of absenteeism as a measure of satisfaction. Absenteeism seems to be correlated with satisfaction,[4] but the two should be distinguished. Absenteeism has a behavioral referent (failure "to report for work"), whereas satisfaction has an orientational referent.[5] Concepts with these two types of referents, although they may be correlated, should be analytically distinguished.

Measurement. Frequency and length,[6] two measures of absenteeism, are commonly used. Frequency refers to how often an individual is absent, whereas length refers to the amount of time an individual loses as a result of his absences. An individual may be absent many times and yet lose relatively little total time if his many absences are each of brief duration; conversely, an individual may be absent but a few times and yet lose a sizeable amount of total time if his few absences are each of long duration. The study selected for this handbook (Metzner and Mann) illustrates these two commonly used measures. Researchers at the Survey Research Center of the University of Michigan have long been interested in the study of absenteeism, and Metzner and Mann's much cited study is a good example of their research.[7]

THE MEASURE

METZNER AND MANN

Description. This study examines the relationship between absenteeism and satisfaction. The data for the study were collected from white-collar and blue-collar employees in an electric light and power company. The white-collar sample consists of 163 men and 212 women in the major accounting department. These white-collar employees prepare customers' billings, accounts, financial statements, and tax reports. The blue-collar sample consists of 251 men who work at outside jobs involved in the construction and maintenance of overhead lines. About half of the blue-collar sample work at highly skilled electrical jobs, whereas the remainder work at tree-trimming and other supporting tasks. The time period for the study of the white-collar sample is from December, 1949 through May, 1950; that of the blue-collar sample is from July through December, 1950.

Definition. Absenteeism is not explicitly defined in the study. However, in connection with the computations, mention is made of "a half day out" from work and "prolonged illness" is cited as an example of absence.[8] Therefore, an implicit definition of absenteeism would appear to be the length of time the employees are away from work.

Data Collection. This study does not indicate how the data on absenteeism were collected. However, another publication which refers to the same study indicates that data were obtained from "company records."[9]

Computation. Two measures of absenteeism are used, a "man-days lost" rate and a "frequency of absence" rate. The man-days lost rate refers to the number of days lost per month over a six month period. The frequency of absence rate refers to the average number of absences per month over a six month period. One absence, for the frequency of absence rate, is defined as a minimum of a half day out or any longer period consisting of a series of consecutive working days. The six month period refers to the time just prior to the date the questionnaires were administered to obtain data on satisfaction. Both measures of absenteeism are used for the white-collar sample, whereas only one measure (the frequency of absence rate) is used for the blue-collar sample.

Validity. (1) Previous research led the authors to predict an inverse relationship between absenteeism and satisfaction, that is, the higher the absenteeism, the lower the satisfaction. The findings of the study only partially confirm this prediction. There is an inverse relationship between absenteeism and satisfaction for white-collar men working at low skill level jobs and for blue-collar men; however, the inverse relationship is not found for white-collar women or white-collar men working at higher level jobs. (2) The frequency of absence measure proves to be much more successful than the man-days lost measure in yielding relationships between satisfaction and absenteeism for white-collar men. The frequency of absence measure yields more relationships with satisfaction because it minimizes the effect of absenteeism due to prolonged illness. The authors believe that the frequency of absence measure should be used for further research into the relationship between absenteeism and other concepts.

Reliability. The study contains no data relevant to reliability.

Comments. (1) Metzner and Mann's implicit definition of absenteeism—the length of time for which the employees are away from work—is consistent with the definition of absenteeism used in this handbook: the degree to which the members of a social system fail to report for work at any time when they are scheduled to work. "Employees" are one type of "member" and an electric light and power company is one type of social system (an administrative organization). (2) Metzner and Mann should have used an explicit definition of absenteeism. The reader should not have to reconstruct a definition from a discussion of measurement.[10] (3) The researchers should have indicated their method of data collection. The reader should not have to locate the source of data ("company records") in another publication. The type of company records used to collect the data about absenteeism should also have been specified. There are many types of records and other researchers cannot replicate Metzner and Mann's study unless the relevant parts of the records are specified.

Source. Helen Metzner and Floyd C. Mann, "Employee Attitudes and Absences," *Personnel Psychology*, 6 (Winter, 1953), 467–485.

Further Sources.[11] 1. Howard Baumgartel and Ronald Sobol, "Background and Organizational Factors in Absenteeism," *Personnel Psychology*, 12 (Autumn, 1959), 431–443.
2. Basil S. Georgopoulos and Floyd C. Mann, *The Community General Hospital* (New York: Macmillan, 1962).
3. Floyd C. Mann and Howard Baumgartel, *Absences and Employee Attitudes in an Electric Power Company* (Ann Arbor, Mich.: Survey Research Center, University of Michigan, 1952).
4. Floyd C. Mann and John E. Sparling, "Changing Absence Rates," *Personnel*, 32 (March, 1956), 392–408.
5. Floyd C. Mann and L. Richard Hoffman, *Automation and the Worker* (New York: Holt, 1960).

6. Martin Patchen, "Absence and Employee Feelings About Fair Treatment," *Personnel Psychology*, 13 (Autumn, 1960), 349–360.

ADDITIONAL READINGS[12]

1. Max D. Kossoris, "Illness Absenteeism in Manufacturing Plants in 1947," *Monthly Labor Review*, 66 (March, 1948), 265–267.[13]
2. Max D. Kossoris, "Absenteeism and Injury Experience of Older Workers," *Monthly Labor Review*, 67 (July, 1948), 16–19.
3. Frank S. McElroy and Alexander Moros, "Illness Absenteeism in Manufacturing Plants, 1947," *Monthly Labor Review*, 67 (September, 1948), 235–239.

NOTES

1. This definition is adapted from Max D. Kossoris, "Illness Absenteeism in Manufacturing Plants in 1947," *Monthly Labor Review*, 66 (March, 1948), 265–267 (esp. p. 266). A good general discussion of absenteeism is found in Gordon S. Watkins, Paul A. Dodd, Wayne L. McNaughton, and Paul Prasow, *The Management of Personnel and Labor Relations* (New York: McGraw-Hill, 1950), pp. 375–404.
2. The previous chapter distinguishes administrative organizations and voluntary associations.
3. An example of the use of absenteeism as a measure of satisfaction is The Acton Society Trust, *Size and Morale, Part II* (London: The Acton Society Trust, 1957), p. 1. Absenteeism is used as a measure of withdrawal from the work situation in J. M. M. Hill and E. L. Trist, *Industrial Accidents, Sickness, and Other Absences* (London: Tavistock Institute of Human Relations, 1962). An example of absenteeism to measure participation is Bernard P. Indik, "Organization Size and Member Participation," *Human Relations*, 18 (November, 1965), 339–350.
4. For a recent summary of the evidence of the relationship between absenteeism and satisfaction, see Victor H. Vroom, *Work and Motivation* (New York: Wiley, 1964), pp. 178–180.
5. Satisfaction is discussed in a later chapter.
6. A number of researchers note the use of frequency and length as measures of absenteeism. The following are some examples: Philip Ash, "The SRA Employee Inventory—A Statistical Analysis," *Personnel Psychology*, 7 (Autumn, 1954), 337–364 (esp. p. 351); Robert Cooper and Roy Payne, "Age and Absence: A Longitudinal Study in Three Firms," *Occupational Psychology*, 35 (January, 1965), 30–35; Gwynneth de la Marc and R. Sergean, "Two Methods of Studying Changes in Absence with Age," *Occupational Psychology*, 35 (October, 1961), 245–252; R. Oliver Gibson, "Toward a Conceptualization of Absence Behavior of Personnel in Organizations," *Administrative Science Quarterly*, 11 (June, 1966), 107–133; Hill and Trist, *op. cit.*; and Willard A. Kerr, George J. Koppelmeier, and James J. Sullivan, "Absenteeism, Turnover and Morale in a Metals Fabrication Factory," *Occupational Psychology*, 25 (January, 1951), 50–55 (esp. pp. 50 and 53).

7. Research on absenteeism has also been conducted by a number of researchers at Harvard. The following selections are examples of this research: Bernard J. Covner, "Management Factors Affecting Absenteeism," *Harvard Business Review*, 28 (September, 1950), 42–48; John B. Fox and Jerome F. Scott, *Absenteeism: Management's Problem* (Boston: Graduate School of Business Administration, Harvard, 1943); and Arthur N. Turner and Paul R. Lawrence, *Industrial Jobs and the Worker* (Boston: Graduate School of Business Administration, Harvard, 1965). Researchers at the Tavistock Institute of Human Relations have also conducted a sizeable amount of research on absenteeism. The previous research by Hill and Trist, *op. cit.* is an example of the research conducted at the Tavistock Institute. The research of the Tavistock Institute represents, of course, but one segment of a long-standing concern with absenteeism exhibited by British researchers.

8. Helen Metzner and Floyd C. Mann, "Employee Attitudes and Absences," *Personnel Psychology*, 6 (Winter, 1953), p. 470.

9. Floyd C. Mann and Howard Baumgartel, *Absences and Employee Attitudes in an Electric Power Company* (Ann Arbor, Mich.: Survey Research Center, University of Michigan, 1952), p. 4.

10. Researchers at the Survey Research Center are not generally much concerned with conceptual discussions of absenteeism; instead they assume that the concept is reasonably clear and devote the bulk of their resources to measurement and empirical research. These conceptual issues, from the perspective of this handbook, are problematic and require explicit treatment.

11. These Further Sources, as may be recalled from the introductory chapter, consist of literature relevant to the measures included in the handbook. In this instance, the relevant literature includes selected studies of absenteeism conducted at the Survey Research Center.

12. These Additional Readings, as previously indicated in the introductory chapter, consist of measures examined but not included in this handbook.

13. The Bureau of Labor Statistics of the Department of Labor has long been interested in research on absenteeism. These three additional readings are representative of the research conducted by the Department of Labor. A general discussion of publications by the Federal Government is found in James L. Price, *Annotated Bibliography of Federal Government Publications Presenting Data About Organizations* (Iowa City, Ia.: Center for Labor and Management, University of Iowa, 1967).

ADMINISTRATIVE STAFF

2

Definition. The members of a social system may be classified into those who directly or indirectly contribute to the system's primary output. In a business firm, for example, the blue-collar workers generally perform the activities that directly contribute toward its primary output, whereas the white-collar workers generally perform the activities that indirectly contribute toward its primary output. On the other hand, in a university, the professors and students generally perform the activities that directly contribute toward its primary output, whereas the central administrators and the physical plant managers and operators generally perform the activities that indirectly contribute toward its primary output. The *administrative staff* refers to the full-time career members of a social system who primarily perform the activities that indirectly contribute to its primary output. Most of these indirect activities involve decision-making, coordination, and control. It should be noted, however, that some of these administrative staff activities—such as the maintenance of the physical plant—involve relatively little decision-making, coordination, and control.

Three comments are required about the definition of administrative staff. First, the organization is the unit of analysis for most studies of the administrative staff. However, communities, especially the larger ones, often have sizeable administrative staffs which should be encompassed by the suggested definition. This handbook's definition encompasses the administrative staffs of organizations and communities. Second, the term "administrative staff" has historically been used to refer to the nonpolitical members of an organization. The governing board of a university, for example, is political because its members are either elected by the citizens or appointed by an elected governor. The governing board is thus not generally considered part of the university's administrative staff. To maintain this historical tradition, the definition refers to "full-time, career members." Third, the same member often performs administrative staff and nonadministrative staff activities. The teaching and research activities of university professors are nonadministrative staff activities; however, when these same professors sit on various university committees, they are generally performing administrative activities. Professors are not included as part of the administrative staff of universities because their roles do not "primarily" consist of such indirect activities as decision-making, coordination, and control.

Material relevant to administrative staff is found in discussions of "nonproduction workers," "line-staff employees," "nonoperatives," "administrative apparatus," "supportive component," and "bureaucracy." The terms "supportive component" and "bureaucracy" require brief discussions.

Haas and his colleagues suggest the term "supportive component" for what this handbook terms the "administrative staff."[1] They believe that the activities of the administrative staff (to use this handbook's term) are not exclusively administrative and that the term "supportive component" more accurately indicates the nature of the activities performed by this component of the organization.[2] Their argument is sound and it was taken into account in the preceding discussion of the definition.[3] However, the term "administrative staff" is retained because of its wide usage in organizational literature. This handbook is reluctant to depart from the use of a highly standardized term, such as "administrative staff," especially when a very brief discussion can perhaps clarify its intended meaning.

Organizational literature makes widespread use of the concept of bureaucracy—yet this handbook does not devote a chapter to the measures of bureaucracy. A separate chapter is not devoted to bureaucracy because its different conceptual elements are treated separately in this handbook. Hall's much cited article lists six conceptual elements of bureaucracy commonly cited in the organizational literature: (1) a division of labor based upon functional specialization; (2) a well-defined hierarchy of authority; (3) a system of rules covering the rights and duties of positional incumbents; (4) a system of procedures for dealing with work situations; (5) impersonality of interpersonal relations; and (6) promotion and selection for employment based upon technical competence.[4] This handbook treats the "division of labor" as a component of "complexity"; the "hierarchy of authority" is treated under "centralization"; systems of "rules and procedures" are treated under "formalization"; and "technical competence" is included in the discussion of "distributive justice." No measures of "impersonality" could be located. Although a separate chapter is not devoted to the term "bureaucracy," this handbook provides measures for five of the six conceptual elements of bureaucracy commonly cited in organizational literature.

Measurement. The best measures of the administrative staff involve ratios based on occupational data. The most widely used of these ratios is Melman's "A/P Ratio"—the number of administrative staff employees divided by the number of production workers.[5] (These ratios are typically converted into percentages by multiplying them by 100.) Melman's A/P Ratio has been criticized by Rushing, who proposes to supplement it with a set of administrative ratios.[6] The second measure (Rushing) illustrates Melman's A/P Ratio and the set of proposed administrative ratios. It should also be noted that Melman supplements his A/P Ratio with additional measures.[7] Melman's seminal research bears careful study by researchers interested in the measurement of administrative staff.

A number of researchers measure the administrative staff by a different type of ratio than that used by Melman and Rushing. The first measure (Galambos) illustrates this alternative type of ratio.[8] As indicated in the introductory chapter, the measures are arranged in alphabetical order.

The Galambos and Rushing ratios are used to study organizations *and* societies. This handbook's preference for measures that use the organization as the unit of analysis (a preference indicated in the introductory chapter) does not mean the exclusion of measures that can be used with different units of analysis. To prefer organizational measures is to insist on measures that have been used to study organizations; these ratios meet this standard. (The Galambos and Rushing ratios may also be used to study communities, an important consideration since communities also have administrative staffs.)

THE MEASURES

1. GALAMBOS

Description. The purpose of the study is to analyze the growth of administrative, technical, and clerical employees in British manufacturing industries from 1948 to 1962.[9] There are two parts to the study. Part I examines some characteristic features of the growth of administrative, technical, and clerical employees, and Part II considers some economic factors that may be related to this growth.

Definition. This study contains no definition of administrative, technical, and clerical employees.

Data Collection. Galambos' data come from the *British Census of Production For 1954*, Summary Tables, Part I (London: Her Majesty's Stationery Office). The term "nonoperatives"—an abbreviation for administrative, technical, and clerical employees—refers to a class of occupations. The *Census of Production* does not make any distinctions between the different occupations within this classification. However, in May, 1963, the Ministry of Labor made a study which lists the following four types of occupations within the nonoperative classification: (1) managers, superintendents, and foremen; (2) research, design, and development staff; (3) draftsmen and teachers; and (4) office staff not elsewhere specified. Galambos does not reproduce the instrument used to collect this occupational data.

Computation. The following formula is used for the computations: $P =$ (employment of nonoperatives $\div$ total employment) $\times$ 100. P refers to the number of nonoperatives, expressed as a percentage of the total employment in any given industry, or group of industries. Nonoperatives, as previously indicated, is an abbreviation for administrative, technical, and clerical employees.

Validity. (1) The study finds that there has been a consistent increase in the proportion of nonoperatives in total employment in all British manufacturing industries from 1948 to 1962. This finding is consistent with other research for comparable Western countries.[10] (2) The study indicates that the proportion of nonoperatives in total employment varies by industry. As predicted by Galambos, the proportions are consistently large in the newer, expanding industries—particularly in the chemical group, electrical engineering, aircraft, and vehicles—but relatively small in the older industries of the textile group, clothing, and leather. (3) and (4) As Galambos predicted, there are positive relationships between the proportion of nonoperatives in total employment, on the one hand, and capital expenditure and value added, on the other hand. (5) There is no conclusive evidence for a relationship between the size of the firms and the proportion of nonoperatives in their total employment. There is, in fact, a small positive relationship between size of the firm and the proportion of nonoperatives. This finding is not consistent with other research which typically indicates a negative relationship between size of the firm and the proportion of nonoperatives.[11]

Reliability. The study contains no data relevant to reliability.

Comments. (1) Although Galambos gives no definition of nonoperatives, his implied meaning of the term seems to correspond to the meaning this handbook assigns to administrative staff. The four classes of occupations that constitute nonoperatives appear to be full-time, career members of organizations who primarily perform activities (decision-making, coordination, and control) that indirectly contribute to the primary output of the organization. (2) Galambos should have provided a discussion of his basic concept, nonoperatives. The reader should not be required to ferret out its implied meaning.[12] (3) Since Galambos is making a secondary analysis of data published in the British *Census of Production,* it is understandable that he does not reproduce the instrument used to collect data on nonoperatives. It is unreasonable to expect a secondary analysis to reproduce the instruments used in the original research. However, the researcher who desires to replicate Galambos' study must either write to the Ministry of Labor for a copy of the instrument or devise his own instrument. Such alternatives do not make it easy to conduct the type of replication required in organizational research. The concluding chapter of this handbook discusses the problem of providing instruments of data collection in articles. (4) Galambos has data on both industries and firms. Since his discussion of the relationship between size and the proportion of nonoperatives is based on his data on firms, Galambos is innocent of using industry data to verify propositions concerning firms. In short, Galambos is not guilty of confusing *ecological correlations*—correlations based on industries —with individual correlations—correlations based on firms.[13]

Source. P. Galambos, "On the Growth of the Employment of Non-Manual Workers in the British Manufacturing Industries, 1948–1962," *Bulletin of the*

Oxford University Institute of Economics and Statistics, 26 (November, 1964), 369–383.

2. RUSHING

Description. This study investigates the effects of industry size and the division of labor on the relative number of administrative personnel. Forty-one American industries were investigated.

Definition. Administrative personnel are defined in terms of a primary concern with coordination. However, coordination is not explicitly defined.

Data Collection. Rushing's data come from the U.S. Bureau of the Census, *U.S. Census of Population: 1960. Subject Reports. Occupation by Industry* (Washington, D.C.: U.S. Government Printing Office, 1963). Rushing does not reproduce the instrument the Bureau of the Census used to collect its occupational data, probably because he is doing a secondary analysis.

Computation. Rushing distinguishes six occupational categories: (1) Managers, officials, and proprietors (referred to as managerial personnel); (2) professional personnel; (3) clerical personnel; (4) craftsmen; (5) operatives; and (6) laborers. The first three categories are classified as administrative personnel, whereas the last three are classified as production personnel. Four ratios are computed with these six occupational categories: (1) the ratio between the number of administrative personnel and the number of production personnel; (2) the ratio between the number of managerial personnel and the number of production personnel; (3) the ratio between the number of professional personnel and the number of production personnel; and (4) the ratio between the number of clerical personnel and the number of production personnel. Rushing's first ratio is Melman's A/P Ratio.

Validity. (1) and (2) The division of labor is directly related to the relative number of administrative personnel, whereas size is inversely related to the relative number of administrative personnel. These relationships apply to the four administrative ratios and are consistent with other findings in organizational literature.[14] (3) Rushing uses four ratios because, on the basis of his previous research,[15] he predicted that the different ratios would be differently related to the division of labor. As previously indicated, all of the ratios are directly related to the relative number of administrative personnel. However, as the division of labor increases, the ratio of professional and clerical personnel increases at a faster rate than does the ratio of managerial personnel. This is the type of finding that Rushing predicted when he decided to use the four ratios. Had Rushing used only Melman's A/P Ratio, he would not have located this finding.

Reliability. The study contains no data relevant to reliability.

Comments. (1) Rushing's definition of administrative personnel corresponds very closely to the definition of administrative staff advanced in this handbook. Both definitions emphasize a primary concern with coordination; however, this handbook's definition also refers to decision-making and control activities. It is possible that Rushing intends, as do many other researchers, to encompass decision-making and control activities under the label of coordination. Since coordination is not discussed in the article, this possibility could not be eliminated. (2) This handbook includes what Rushing refers to as the "division of labor" under the term "complexity." The relationship between division of labor and complexity is discussed in a later chapter which focuses on complexity.[16] (3) The findings in Rushing's study are based on data for industries and not organizations. There is an immense documentary literature which contains data relevant to the study of organizations[17] and Rushing is to be commended for making a secondary analysis on a small fragment of this data. However, his findings, as Rushing clearly recognizes, require replication with data collected about organizations. (4) It would have been helpful had Rushing reproduced the instrument used to collect the occupational data he uses in his calculations. However, as indicated in the comments on Galambos' study, it is unreasonable to expect a secondary analysis to reproduce the instruments used in the original study. (5) Galambos and Rushing use occupational data in their calculations. Their assumption is that occupational labels correctly indicate the nature of the activities performed. Rushing, for example, assumes that managerial, professional, and clerical occupations are primarily concerned with coordination. This is probably a reasonable assumption. However, the assumption must ultimately be verified empirically in a series of different organizational settings before it can be accepted.

Source. William A. Rushing, "The Effects of Industry Size and Division of Labor on Administration," *Administrative Science Quarterly*, 12 (September, 1967), 273–295.

Further Source. William A. Rushing, "Organizational Size and Administration: The Problems of Causal Homogeneity and a Heterogeneous Category," *Pacific Sociological Review*, 9 (Fall, 1966), 100–108.

ADDITIONAL READINGS

1. Peter M. Blau, Wolf V. Heydebrand, and Robert E. Stauffer, "The Structure of Small Bureaucracies," *American Sociological Review*, 31 (April, 1966), 179–191.[18]

2. Ernest Dale, *The Great Organizers* (New York: McGraw-Hill, 1960), pp. 217–238.[19]

3. Seymour Melman, "The Rise of Administrative Overhead in the Manufacturing Industries of the United States, 1899–1947," *Oxford Economic Papers* (*New Series*), 3 (January, 1951), 62–112.

4. Seymour Melman, "Production and Administration Cost in Relation to Size of Firm," *Applied Statistics*, 3 (March, 1954), 1–11.

5. Paul D. Montagna, "Professionalization and Bureaucratization in Large Professional Organizations," *American Journal of Sociology*, 74 (September, 1968), 138–145.

NOTES

1. Eugene Haas, Richard H. Hall, and Norman J. Johnson, "The Size of the Supportive Component in Organizations: A Multi-Organizational Analysis," *Social Forces*, 42 (October, 1963), 9–17. This handbook has benefited from this valuable article by Haas and his colleagues. The term "supportive component" is also used by other researchers. See, for example, D. S. Pugh, D. J. Hickson, C. R. Hinings, and C. Turner, "Dimensions of Organizational Structure," *Administrative Science Quarterly*, 13 (June, 1968), 65–105.

2. Haas *et al., op. cit.*, p. 12.

3. The distinction between direct and indirect contribution to primary output in the definition of administrative staff is a result of the article by Haas and his colleagues.

4. Richard H. Hall, "The Concept of Bureaucracy: An Empirical Assessment," *American Journal of Sociology*, 69 (July, 1963), 32–40 (esp. p. 33). The two classic pieces on bureaucracy are Max Weber, *The Theory of Social and Economic Organization* (New York: Oxford, 1947), pp. 329–341, and Max Weber, *From Max Weber: Essays in Sociology* (New York: Oxford, 1946), pp. 196–244. Unfortunately, many discussions of Weber's work on bureaucracy make no reference to his work on political sociology. Weber's work on bureaucracy is discussed in the context of his work on political sociology by Bendix. See Reinhard Bendix, *Max Weber* (Garden City, N.Y.: Doubleday, 1960), pp. 289–459.

5. The A/P Ratio is used by Melman in the following sources: Ernest Dale, *The Great Organizers* (New York: McGraw-Hill, 1960), pp. 217–238; Seymour Melman, "The Rise of Administrative Overhead in the Manufacturing Industries of the United States, 1899–1947," *Oxford Economic Papers (New Series)*, 3 (January, 1951), 62–112; Seymour Melman, *Dynamic Factors in Industrial Productivity* (Oxford, Eng.: Basil Blackwell, 1956); and Seymour Melman, *Decision-Making and Productivity* (Oxford, Eng.: Basil Blackwell, 1958). Melman contributes one of the appendices for Dale's *The Great Organizers*.

6. Bendix and Delehanty also use a set of ratios to measure the relative size of the administrative staff. See Reinhard Bendix, *Work and Authority in Industry* (New York: Wiley, 1956), pp. 211–226, and G. E. Delehanty, *Nonproduction Workers in U.S. Manufacturing* (Amsterdam, Holland: North-Holland Publishing Company, 1968), pp. 116–209. Delehanty's study also contains a valuable critique of Melman's A/P Ratio.

7. The sources for Melman's additional measures are cited under "Additional Readings" at the end of the chapter.

8. The type of ratio that Galambos uses is also used by the following studies: Bendix, *op. cit.*, pp. 211–226 (esp. p. 211); T. E. Chester, *A Study of Post-War Growth in Management Organizations* (Paris, France: European Productivity

Agency of the Organization for European Cooperation, 1961), esp. pp. 40–46, 70, and 81–83; D. G. Holland, "Costs, Productivities and the Employment of Salaried Staff," *Bulletin of the Oxford University Institute of Economics and Statistics*, 25 (August, 1963), 127–164; S. R. Klatzky, "Relationship of Organizational Size to Complexity and Coordination," *Administrative Science Quarterly*, 15 (December, 1970), 428–438; and Arthur L. Stinchcombe, "Bureaucratic and Craft Administration of Production: A Comparative Study," *Administrative Science Quarterly*, 4 (September, 1959), 168–187.

9. The terms "administrative, technical, and clerical" employees are used in the British census. For a discussion of these terms, see Melman, *Dynamic Factors in Industrial Productivity, op. cit.*, pp. 217–218.

10. Bendix, *op. cit.*, pp. 211–244.

11. See, for example, William A. Rushing, "The Effects of Industry Size and Division of Labor on Administration," *Administrative Science Quarterly*, 12 (September, 1967), 273–295 (esp. p. 274).

12. It is likely that Galambos does not discuss nonoperatives because its wide usage in the British census has clearly established its meaning among British researchers who specialize in the study of organizations.

13. William S. Robinson, "Ecological Correlations and the Behavior of Individuals," *American Sociological Review*, 15 (June, 1950), 351–357.

14. Rushing summarizes these findings in his article.

15. William A. Rushing, "Organizational Size and Administration: The Problems of Causal Homogeneity and a Heterogeneous Category," *Pacific Sociological Review*, 9 (Fall, 1966), 100–108.

16. Rushing also uses the term "complexity." He equates complexity and the division of labor.

17. Some of this immense documentary literature is cited in James L. Price, *Annotated Bibliography of Federal Government Publications Presenting Data About Organizations* (Iowa City, Ia.: Center for Labor and Management, University of Iowa, 1967).

18. The fifth selection under Additional Readings uses the same measure as the first selection.

19. Melman contributes one of the appendices in Dale's book.

ALIENATION

3 _____

Definition. *Alienation* is the degree to which the members of a social system believe that their behavior can determine the outcomes they seek. If workers in a factory or students in a university, for example, seek to modify the rules of their respective organizations, but believe that their behavior can effect little if any changes in these rules, then the workers and the students are highly alienated. In his classic article, Seeman refers to this usage of alienation as "powerlessness" and indicates that it is the most frequent usage in the literature.[1] He also indicates that the powerlessness usage of alienation originated in the Marxian view of the worker's condition in a capitalistic society.

Another fairly widespread usage of alienation is termed "self-estrangement" by Seeman.[2] This usage is defined in the following manner: ". . . the degree of dependence of the given behavior upon anticipated future rewards, that is, upon rewards that lie outside the activity itself . . . ."[3] The first usage is used by this handbook because of its widespread acceptance.

This handbook distinguishes alienation from satisfaction, motivation, and centralization. These latter three terms are discussed later. Here it is sufficient to note that satisfaction and motivation, though social psychological concepts like alienation, refer to different social psychological dimensions than alienation.[4] Centralization, though often measured social psychologically, is a structural term, that is, it refers to patterns of social interaction.

Literature relevant to alienation is found in discussions of "organizational climate." Litwin and Stringer's widely cited study distinguishes nine dimensions of organizational climate: (1) structure, the feeling employees have about the constraints in the group; (2) responsibility, the feeling of being one's own boss; (3) reward, the feeling of being rewarded for a job well done; (4) risk, the sense of challenge in the job and in the organization; (5) warmth, the feeling of general good fellowship that prevails in the work group atmosphere; (6) support, the perceived helpfulness of the managers and other employees in the group; (7) standards, the perceived importance of implicit and explicit goals and performance standards; (8) conflict, the feeling that managers and other workers want to hear different opinions; and (9) identity, the feeling that one belongs to a company and is a valuable member of the team.[5] Litwin and Stringer's dimension of "responsibility" corresponds to this handbook's concept of alienation. Individuals who feel they are their own boss—Litwin and Stringer's definition of responsibility—are probably individuals who believe that their behavior can determine the outcomes they seek—this handbook's definition of alienation.

Since there is no chapter devoted to organizational climate in this handbook, despite the existence of a sizeable amount of research devoted to the topic, it may be relevant to note briefly how the other dimensions of organizational climate are treated. The chapter on "distributive justice" contains material relevant to "reward"; the chapter on "motivation" is pertinent to "standards"; and the chapter on "satisfaction" has data related to "warmth," "support," and "identity." In short, this handbook treats, although under different labels, six of Litwin and Stringer's nine dimensions of organizational climate. The remaining three dimensions ("structure," "risk," and "conflict") are not commonly used, as social psychological concepts, in organizational literature.[6]

Measurement. The two measures of alienation selected represent, respectively, the "powerlessness" (Pearlin) and "self-estrangement" (Miller) usages of the term, the two most common usages.

Most of the measurement research with respect to alienation uses society rather than the organization as its unit of analysis. The excellent measurement research of a series of researchers who have, at one time or another, been faculty or students at Ohio State University illustrates measures of alienation that use society as their unit of analysis.[7] It is acceptable to define alienation generally; all of the definitions in this handbook are defined so that they are applicable to all types of social systems. However, since this is a handbook of organizational measurement, the measures selected must be usable in the study of organizations. The research of the Ohio State group is cited at the end of the chapter under Additional Readings, but none of their measures is included in this handbook because they cannot be used to study organizations.

There is also some research with respect to alienation that measures what this handbook terms "satisfaction."[8] As previously indicated, this handbook considers alienation and satisfaction to be analytically different concepts. Therefore, if organizational measures focus on satisfaction—from the perspective of this handbook—but label their referent alienation, then these measures are considered in connection with satisfaction and not alienation.

THE MEASURES

1. PEARLIN

Description. This study examines structural conditions that produce alienation from work. The organization is a large Federal mental hospital which draws its patients mainly from the District of Columbia. Alienation from work is examined among the nursing personnel. Three ranks of nurses are studied. First, there is the group of nursing assistants who have the lowest rank and who comprise 70 percent of the nursing personnel. Second, there is the group of charge attendants who have been given charge of wards in the absence of a professional nurse; the charge attendants represent 16 percent of the nursing personnel. Third, there is the group of registered nurses who direct the nursing personnel and who make up the remaining 14 percent of the nursing personnel. Of the 1315 nursing personnel who received questionnaires, 1138, or 86 percent, returned completed and usable questionnaires.

Definition. Alienation is defined as "subjectively experienced powerlessness to control one's own work activities."[9]

Data Collection. The data for the measurement of alienation were collected by a self-administered questionnaire given to all the nursing personnel. The four questionnaire items are presented below. The alienative responses are italicized; the original questionnaire, of course, does not distinguish between the different responses.

1. How often do you do things in your work that you wouldn't otherwise do if it were up to you?

    ____Never

    ____Once in a while

    ____Fairly often

    ____*Very often*

2. Around here, it's not important how much you know; it's who you know that really counts.

    ____*Agree*

    ____Disagree

3. How much say or influence do people like you have on the way the hospital is run?

    ____A lot

    ____Some

    ____*Very little*

    ____*None*

4. How often do you tell [your superior][10] your own ideas about things you might do in your work?

    ____*Never*

    ____*Once in a while*

    ____Fairly often

    ____Very often

Computation. The responses to the four questionnaire items are scored "0" and "1." A nonalienative response is scored "0," whereas an alienative response is scored "1." The scores are totaled for each respondent; the scores range from "0" to "4." The lower the score, the lower the alienation.

Validity. Pearlin indicates three structural conditions that produce alienation from work. (1) Alienation is highest where authority relations are such as to limit the reciprocal influence of subordinates. (2) Limited career achievement and dissatisfaction with extrinsic work rewards produce alienation. (3) Personnel working in isolation and without outside social ties to fellow workers are subject to a higher degree of alienation. These three findings appear to be consistent with other research which has investigated the structural conditions that produce alienation from work.[11]

Reliability. The four-item Guttman scale that Pearlin uses has a coefficient of reproducibility of .91.

Comments. (1) Pearlin's definition of alienation ("powerlessness") is the definition this handbook uses. Therefore, his measure is appropriate to this handbook's definition of alienation. (2) The third question will naturally have to be modified slightly when used outside the hospital setting. The term "hospital" may simply be replaced by the type of organizational unit being studied ("business firm," "government agency," and so forth). (3) The brackets around "your superior" in the fourth question should be removed. On Pearlin's original questionnaire, the "[your superior]" refers to the individual on the ward who has the most say or influence on what the respondent did in her daily work. Since the individual with the most say or influence in a subordinate's daily work is generally the subordinate's superior, it seems appropriate to remove the brackets.

Source. Leonard I. Pearlin, "Alienation From Work: A Study of Nursing Personnel," *American Sociological Review*, 27 (June, 1962), 314–326.

Further Source. Louis A. Zurcher, Jr., Arnold Meadow, and Sue Lee Zurcher, "Value Orientation, Role Conflict, and Alienation from Work," *American Sociological Review*, 30 (August, 1965), 539–548.

2. MILLER

Description. This study investigates the relationship between the type of organizational structure in which professionals perform their work and their experienced feelings of alienation from work. Data were gathered during the summer of 1965 from scientific and engineering personnel employed in two divisions of one of the largest aerospace companies in the United States. One of the divisions is more concerned with basic scientific research, the other with traditional research and development work. All of the scientists and engineers are nonsupervisors and hold the degree of M.A., M.S., or Ph.D. in science, engineering, or mathematics. The sample consists of 419 scientists and engineers.

Definition. Miller defines alienation in terms of Seeman's self-estrangement usage,[12] that is, ". . . the degree of dependence of the given behavior upon . . . rewards that lie outside the activity itself . . . ."[13] Miller clearly believes that self-estrangement from work is not the same as dissatisfaction with work.

Data Collection. Data were collected by means of a mailback questionnaire sent to the home of the study participants. The following questions were used:

1. I really don't feel a sense of pride or accomplishment as a result of the type of work that I do.

    ___Strongly agree

    ___Agree

    ___Disagree

    ___Strongly disagree[14]

2. My work gives me a feeling of pride in having done the job well.

3. I very much like the type of work that I am doing.

4. My job gives me a chance to do the things that I do best.

5. My work is my most rewarding experience.

Computation. Each response category is dichotomized into "Agree" and "Disagree." "Strongly agree" and "Agree" become "Agree," whereas "Disagree" and "Strongly disagree" become "Disagree." An "Agree" response is scored as "0," whereas a "Disagree" response is scored as "1." (The first question is stated negatively, whereas the other four are stated positively. Therefore, the scoring is reversed for the first question.) The scores ranged from a low of "0" to a high of "5." The higher the score, the higher the alienation from work.

Validity. Miller made three sets of predictions based on his survey of the literature. First, the degree of alienation from work should be positively related to the degree of organizational control and negatively related to the number of professional incentives for all professional personnel. Second, the above relationships should be stronger for those professionals with the Ph.D. and those professionals trained as scientists than for professionals with either the M.A. or M.S. degree and professionals trained as engineers. Third, there should be less organizational control and more professional incentives in the laboratory that is more concerned with basic research than in the laboratory that is more concerned with traditional research and development work. Therefore, less alienation from work should be experienced by professionals employed in the basic research laboratory than in the traditional research and development laboratory. The first and third sets of predictions came out as anticipated, whereas the second set of predictions is only partially supported. Scientists and engineers differ less in their experience of alienation than previous research would indicate.

Reliability. Miller's measures yielded a Guttman scale with the following characteristics: Coefficient of Reproducibility (Goodenough technique) = .91; Minimum Marginal Reproducibility = .70; Coefficient of Scability = .69; and Coefficient of Sharpness = .69.[15]

Comments. (1) Miller's self-estrangement usage for alienation is different from the powerlessness usage adopted by this handbook. However, alienation, defined in terms of self-estrangement, is a common usage and is probably second in frequency to alienation defined in terms of powerlessness. (2) Despite the fact that Miller does not intend to measure satisfaction, he notes explicitly that his questions refer to "intrinsic pride or meaning of work," which is a commonly used dimension of satisfaction. Two of Miller's questions even come from Morse's widely cited study of satisfaction.[16] Miller's measures seem clearly to refer to satisfaction, as defined by this handbook. (3) Miller's first question is stated negatively, whereas the remaining four questions are stated positively. This format is confusing with respect to the computations. It would be simpler to state all the questions either positively or negatively.

Source. George A. Miller, "Professionals in Bureaucracy: Alienation Among Industrial Scientists and Engineers," *American Sociological Review*, 32 (October, 1967), 755–768.

ADDITIONAL READINGS

1. John P. Clark, "Measuring Alienation Within a Social System," *American Sociological Review*, 24 (December, 1959), 849–852.[17]
2. Dwight G. Dean, "Alienation and Political Apathy," *Social Forces*, 38 (March, 1960), 185–189.[18]
3. Dwight G. Dean, "Meaning and Measurement of Alienation," *American Sociological Review*, 26 (October, 1961), 753–758.
4. John W. Evans, *Stratification, Alienation, and the Hospital Setting* (Columbus, Ohio: Engineering Experiment Station, The Ohio State University, 1960).
5. Arthur G. Neal and Salomon Rettig, "Dimensions of Alienation Among Manual and Non-Manual Workers," *American Sociological Review*, 28 (August, 1963), 599–608.

6. Arthur G. Neal and Melvin Seeman, "Organizations and Powerlessness: A Test of the Mediation Hypothesis," *American Sociological Review*, 29 (April, 1964), 216–226.

7. Gwynn Nettler, "A Measure of Alienation," *American Sociological Review*, 22 (December, 1957), 670–677.[19]

8. Gwynn Nettler, "Antisocial Sentiment and Criminality," *American Sociological Review*, 24 (April, 1959), 202–208.

9. Julian B. Rotter, Melvin Seeman, and Shephard Liverant, "Internal versus External Control of Reinforcements: A Major Variable in Behavior Theory," in Norman F. Washburne *Decisions, Values and Groups*, ed. Norman F. Washburne (New York: Macmillan, 1962), pp. 473–516.

10. Melvin Seeman, "On The Meaning of Alienation," *American Sociological Review*, 24 (December, 1959), 783–791.

11. Melvin Seeman and John W. Evans, "Alienation and Learning in a Hospital Setting," *American Sociological Review*, 27 (December, 1962), 772–782.

12. Melvin Seeman, "Alienation and Social Learning in a Reformatory," *American Journal of Sociology*, 69 (November, 1963), 270–284.

13. Melvin Seeman, "On The Personal Consequences of Alienation in Work," *American Sociological Review*, 32 (April, 1967), 273–285.

14. Harold L. Wilensky, "Varieties of Work Experience," in *Man in a World of Work*, ed. Henry Borow (Boston: Houghton Mifflin, 1964), pp. 125–153.[20]

15. Harold L. Wilensky, "Work as a Social Problem," in *Social Problems: A Modern Approach*, ed. Howard S. Becker (New York: Wiley, 1966), pp. 138–142.

NOTES

1. This definition is adapted from Melvin Seeman, "On the Meaning of Alienation," *American Sociological Review*, 24 (December, 1959), 783–791 (esp. pp. 784–785). The following three selections are critical of Seeman's article: Charles J. Browning, Malcolm F. Farmer, H. David Kirk, and G. Duncan Mitchell, "On the Meaning of Alienation," *American Sociological Review*, 26 (October, 1961), 780–781 (Seeman also has a reply to Browning *et al.*, in the same issue of the *American Sociological Review*); Lewis Feuer, "What is Alienation?" *New Politics*, 1 (Spring, 1962), 116–134; and Harold Mizruchi, *Success and Opportunity* (New York: The Free Press of Glencoe, 1964), pp. 25–60. Blauner slightly modifies Seeman's concept of alienation in his excellent study. See Robert Blauner, *Alienation and Freedom* (Chicago: University of Chicago Press, 1964), pp. 15–34.

2. Seeman, *op. cit.* pp. 789–790. Seeman cites three additional usages of alienation in his article: "meaninglessness," "normlessness," and "isolation." These usages of alienation are seldom found in organizational literature.

3. *Ibid.*, p. 790.

4. Bell views alienation, defined as self-estrangement, in structural rather than social psychological terms. See Daniel Bell, "Two Roads from Marx: The Themes of Alienation and Exploitation and Workers' Control in Socialist Thought," in *The End of Ideology*, Daniel Bell (New York: Collier Books, 1961), pp. 355–392.

5. This list of dimensions comes from George H. Litwin and Robert A. Stringer, Jr., *Motivation and Organizational Climate* (Boston: Graduate School of Business Administration, Harvard, 1968), pp. 81–82. This handbook, to simplify the presentation, excludes several elements of Litwin and Stringer's dimensions. The reader should consult the measurement chapter (pp. 66–92) and the two conceptual chapters (pp. 28–65). A good general introduction to the concept of organizational climate is contained in *Organizational Climate*, ed. Renato Tagiuri and George H. Litwin (Boston: Graduate School of Business Administration, Harvard 1968).

6. These social psychological concepts have structural counterparts in organizational literature. "Formalization," "routinization," and "coordination" are, respectively, the structural counterparts to "structure," "risk," and "conflict." (Coordination may only partially be the structural counterpart to conflict.) This handbook has chapters devoted to formalization, routinization, and coordination.

7. A study of alienation by Clark is an exception to this pattern. Clark uses the organization rather than the society as his unit of analysis. See John P. Clark, "Measuring Alienation Within a Social System," *American Sociological Review*, 24 (December, 1959), 849–852. Clark's study helped make it clear to the author of this handbook that studies of alienation use different units of analysis.

8. An example of alienation defined as satisfaction is Michael Aiken and Jerald Hage, "Organizational Alienation: A Comparative Analysis," *American Sociological Review*, 31 (August, 1966), 497–507. Aiken and Hage's work is based on Neal Gross, Ward S. Mason, and Alexander W. McEachern, *Explorations in Role Analysis* (New York: Wiley, 1958), pp. 349–365.

9. Leonard I. Pearlin, "Alienation From Work: A Study of Nursing Personnel," *American Sociological Review*, 27 (June, 1962), p. 314.

10. The "[your superior]" comes from Pearlin's article in the *American Sociological Review*. The original version of the questionnaire refers to "this person" rather than to "[your superior]". However, "this person" and "[your superior]" appear to be very similar in meaning.

11. See, for example, Blauner, *op. cit.*

12. George A. Miller, "Professionals in Bureaucracy: Alienation Among Industrial Scientists and Engineers," *American Sociological Review*, 32 (October, 1967), p. 759.

13. Seeman, *op. cit.*, p. 790.

14. The same response pattern is also used for the other four questions; therefore, it is not necessary to include the response pattern for the other four questions. Since Miller does not reproduce the original format of his questionnaire, this handbook's format may not be the actual one Miller used in his research. However, the format used in this handbook is common for this type of question.

15. The following comments by Miller are relevant to the reliability of his measures:

The best description of the Goodenough technique is Allen L. Edwards, *Techniques of Attitude Scale Construction* (New York: Appleton-Century-Crofts, 1957), pp. 184 ff. Edwards states that, unlike the C.R. [Coefficient of Reproducibility] produced by the Cornell technique, the C.R. produced by the Goodenough technique *accurately* represents the extent to which individual responses can be reproduced from scale scores.

The Coefficient of Scalability is described in Herbert Menzel, "A New Coefficient for Scalogram Analysis," *Public Opinion Quarterly*, 17 (Summer, 1953), 268–280. The Coefficient of Sharpness is described by James A. Davis, "On Criteria for Scale Relationships," *American Journal of Sociology*, 63 (January, 1958), 371–380." Miller, *op. cit.*, pp. 759–760.

16. Nancy Morse, *Satisfactions in the White Collar Job* (Ann Arbor, Mich.: University of Michigan Press, 1953).

17. The Ohio State studies of alienation are numbered 1–6 and 9–12. As previously indicated, Clark's study is the only Ohio State study that uses the organization rather than the society as the unit of analysis.

18. Dean's research has been criticized by Angell and Bell. See Robert C. Angell, "On Nettler's 'Antisocial Sentiment,' " *American Sociological Review*, 24 (August, 1959), p. 543 and Daniel Bell, "Sociodicy: A Guide to Modern Usage," *The American Scholar*, 35 (Autumn, 1966), 696–714 (esp. pp. 698–702). Note also the Dean and Bell correspondence in the Summer, 1967, issue of *The American Scholar*, 461–463.

19. Nettler's research has been criticized by Angell and Wilensky. See Angell, *op. cit.* and Harold L. Wilensky, "Varieties of Work Experience," in *Man in a World of Work*, ed. Henry Borow (Boston: Houghton Mifflin, 1964), pp. 125–153. Nettler also replies to Angell in the August, 1959, issue of the *American Sociological Review*.

20. The comments on Miller's study suggest that his usage of self-estrangement measures satisfaction, as defined by this handbook, rather than self-estrangement, as defined by Seeman. The research by Wilensky, when it is completely published, will probably provide a measure of self-estrangement that is closer to Seeman's meaning than Miller's measure. Complete publication of Wilensky's research is eagerly awaited because self-estrangement represents a widespread usage of alienation.

AUTONOMY

4

Definition. Since autonomy is defined in terms of power, the concept of power must first be discussed.

Power refers to the degree to which an individual has the capacity to obtain performance from other individuals.[1] The foreman who determines the work performance of his crew, the policeman who physically removes demonstrators from a building, the secretary who directs the work performance of the office manager, the criminal who obtains protection money from a small businessman as a result of a bombing of the business—all are examples of power.

Legitimate and illegitimate power are commonly distinguished. The first two examples—those of the foreman and the policeman—illustrate legitimate power (commonly termed "authority"), whereas the examples of the secretary and the criminal illustrate illegitimate power (which may be termed "influence").

Authority and influence may, or may not, be accompanied by the exercise of force (or "coercion"). The example of the foreman illustrates authority that is exercised without the use of force, whereas the example of the policeman illustrates authority exercised by means of force. The third example—that of the secretary—illustrates influence without the exercise of force, whereas the fourth example—that of the criminal—illustrates influence exercised by means of force. It is important to distinguish authority and influence, on the one hand, from the exercise of force, on the other hand. Material relevant to power is commonly found in discussions of "control," "leadership," and "decision-making."

Autonomy is the degree to which a social system has power with respect to its environment.[2] For example, the typical government agency and business firm differ greatly in their degrees of autonomy. The government agency is subject to external power with respect to determination of its budget, personnel policies, and purchasing procedures; in a business firm, none of these issues is decided by groups outside the firm. Consequently, business firms generally have a higher degree of autonomy than government agencies.

Autonomy should be distinguished from centralization. The distribution of power between a social system and its environment is the referent for autonomy; the referent for centralization is the distribution of power within the social system. Autonomy and power should be distinguished because they can vary independently. An organization, for example, that exercises little power over its internal affairs vis-à-vis its environment will be unable to distribute much power among its membership. However, an organization may exercise immense power over its internal affairs vis-à-vis its environment, but decide to distribute little of this power among its membership. Information relevant to autonomy, however, is sometimes found in discussions of "centralization."

Measurement. The best measure of autonomy that could be located is contained in a study by Inkson, Pugh, and Hickson and is the one selected for this handbook. It is one of a series of first-class organizational studies performed by the Industrial Administration Research Unit of the University of Aston in Birmingham, England.

THE MEASURE

INKSON, PUGH, AND HICKSON

Description. The aim of this study is methodological, specifically, to develop a short form of an interview schedule to represent accurately the concepts of "context" and "structure" used in previous research by Inkson, Pugh, and Hickson. A long form of the interview schedule was used in previous research on 52 organizations in the English Midlands. To develop the short form, the researchers studied 40 organizations which, like the previous 52, are located in the English Midlands. Twenty-four of these organizations are manufacturing firms, whereas 16 are service organizations. Most of the service organizations are government agencies. Table 4–1 contains the size distribution of these 40 organizations.

TABLE 4–1 Manufacturing and Service Organizations, by Size

Size	Manufacturing	Service
250–499	8	2
500–999	3	3
1,000–1,999	6	4
2,000–4,999	5	3
Over 5,000 employees	2	4

Definition. The study investigates two aspects of "context" and two aspects of "structure." "Workflow integration and dependence" are the two aspects of context and "structuring of activities and concentration of authority" are the two aspects of structure. Concentration of authority, the aspect of structure which is relevant to autonomy, "describes the level at which formal authority rests."[3] The concentration of authority encompasses autonomy, centralization, percentage of workflow superordinates, and standardization of procedures for selection and advancement.[4] Autonomy is thus one component of the concentration of authority and the concentration of authority is one aspect of structure. Inkson, Pugh, and Hickson do not explicitly define autonomy as a distinct analytical concept.

Data Collection. The information was collected from the chief executive of the organizations by means of an interview. In some cases, an "appropriate substitute," rather than the chief executive, supplied the information. The following part of the schedule was used to collect information about that component of the "concentration of authority" that is relevant to autonomy:[5]

AUTHORITY

WHO HAS AUTHORITY TO DECIDE:
(Authority = action can be taken on the decision without waiting for confirmation from above, even if the decision is later ratified at a higher level.
Above the chief executive = at the level of the controlling board of parent company, committee of local council, board of company if a majority of its members are not executive subordinates of the chief executive, head office department, etc.
Inside the organization = chief executive level or below.)

AUTHORITY TO DECIDE	IS AUTHORITY INSIDE THE ORGANIZATION? Circle:	
SUPERVISORY ESTABLISHMENT	YES	NO
APPOINTMENT OF SUPERVISORY STAFF FROM OUTSIDE THE ORGANIZATION (external recruitment)	YES	NO
PROMOTION OF SUPERVISORY STAFF	YES	NO
SALARIES OF SUPERVISORY STAFF	YES	NO
TO DISMISS A SUPERVISOR	YES	NO
TO DETERMINE A NEW PRODUCT OR SERVICE	YES	NO
TO DETERMINE MARKETING TERRITORIES COVERED (where new or existing outputs are to be marketed)	YES	NO
THE EXTENT AND TYPE OF MARKET TO BE AIMED FOR	YES	NO
THE PRICE OF THE OUTPUT	YES	NO
WHAT TYPE, OR WHAT BRAND, NEW EQUIPMENT IS TO BE	YES	NO
WHAT SHALL BE COSTED (to what the costing system, if any, shall be applied)	YES	NO

WHAT SHALL BE INSPECTED (i.e. to what the inspection system, if any, shall be applied)	YES	NO
WHAT OPERATIONS SHALL BE WORK STUDIED	YES	NO
WHICH SUPPLIERS OF MATERIALS ARE TO BE USED	YES	NO
BUYING PROCEDURES (what procedure is to be followed when buying materials, etc.)	YES	NO
TRAINING METHODS TO BE USED (how training shall be done)	YES	NO
WHAT AND HOW MANY WELFARE FACILITIES ARE TO BE PROVIDED	YES	NO
TO SPEND UNBUDGETED OR UNALLOCATED MONEY ON CAPITAL ITEMS (using money not previously ear-marked for a particular purpose for what would be classed as capital expenditure)	YES	NO
TO SPEND UNBUDGETED OR UNALLOCATED MONEY ON REVENUE ITEMS (using money not previously ear-marked, for what would be classed as current expenditure)	YES	NO
TO ALTER RESPONSIBILITIES/AREAS OF WORK OF SPECIALIST DEPARTMENTS	YES	NO
TO ALTER RESPONSIBILITIES/AREAS OF WORK OF LINE DEPARTMENTS	YES	NO
TO CREATE A NEW DEPARTMENT (functional specialist or line)	YES	NO
TO CREATE A NEW JOB (functional specialist or line, of any status, probably signified by a new job title)	YES	NO

Computation. Each of 23 questions used to collect information about the "concentration of authority" is scored as either "1" or "0."[6] If a decision is made inside the organization (a YES response on the interview schedule), the score is "1." If a decision is made outside the organization (a NO response on the interview schedule), the score is "0." The higher the score, when the 23 scores are summed, the more decisions made inside the organization. No range is presented for the entire sample of 40 organizations. However, the scores for 14 of the 40 organizations are presented; the range of these scores is from 0 to 13, with a mean of 5.21.[7]

Validity. (1) The short form of the interview schedule was applied to the 52 organizations previously studied by means of the long form of the interview schedule. The correlation for concentration of authority for the two forms on the same sample is .93. (2) The previous study finds a positive relationship between concentration of authority and dependence; the present study of 40 organizations finds a similar relationship. (3) Fourteen of the 40 organizations of the present study were also included in the previous study of 52 organizations. Two sets of scores were thus obtained by two different instruments for the same set of 14 organizations. The product-moment correlations between the two sets of scores is .70 for concentration of authority. (4) A typology of organizations was developed on the basis of the previous study. The present study finds the same range of types as the previous study. The same typology is thus established by the two studies. (5) The researchers, based on their previous study, formulated a development sequence that predicted a decrease in the concentration of authority. This decrease is confirmed for 37 of the 40 organizations.

Reliability. An item analysis is reported for the two aspects of context and the two aspects of structure. The general biserial correlation coefficient, originally developed by Brogden,[8] is used for the item analysis. The coefficient for concentration of authority is .83; a coefficient of this size indicates that the measures are unidimensional.

Comments. (1) Inkson, Pugh, and Hickson's definition of concentration of authority, as previously indicated, encompasses autonomy, centralization, percentage of workflow superordinates, and standardization of procedures for selection and advancement. Concentration of authority is thus more general than this handbook's definition of autonomy. Although the researchers do not explicitly define autonomy, an examination of their instrument indicates an implied concept similar to this handbook's. To collect information about whether or not "authority" to take specific types of action is "inside the organization," as do the researchers, is to collect information about the degree to which a social system has power with respect to its environment, this handbook's definition of autonomy. (2) There is a boundary problem which must ultimately be faced. Inkson, Pugh, and Hickson operationally define "inside the organization" as the "chief executive level or below." This operational definition means that the governing board (termed "controlling board" by the researchers), for example, is not included within the boundary of the organization. Whether or not the governing board is included depends on how boundary is defined, and the researchers do not discuss the boundary problem.[9] However it is resolved, the format of the instrument of data collection is flexible enough to continue to be used. Researchers, for example, could very easily operationally define "inside the organization" to be the "governing board level or below." (3) The researchers have large samples, 40 organizations in the present study and 52 in the previous one. Samples of this size greatly increase one's confidence in the validity and reliability of the findings. (4) The researchers should be applauded for their development of a short form of their original interview schedule. The average interview lasted about one hour with the short form. The goal of researchers must be the collection of the maximum amount of valid and reliable data with the least expenditure of resources; the present type of study makes possible the realization of this type of goal. (5) The researchers collect information about "authority to decide" with respect to 23 different types of actions. It would seem that this list could be shortened somewhat. The researchers might even further shorten their short form. (6) The validity and reliability of the measures are adequate; the information about validity is very adequate. More organizational researchers should exercise such care with respect to the validity and reliability of their measures. The only problem is that the researchers' discussion of validity and reliability pertains to the concentration of authority as a unit rather than to the component of autonomy. From the perspective of this handbook, it would have been best to have data about the validity and reliability of the autonomy component of concentration of authority. Perhaps separate data about the measure of autonomy will be provided in future publications.

Source. J. H. K. Inkson, D. S. Pugh, and D. J. Hickson, "Organization Context and Structure: An Abbreviated Replication," *Administrative Science Quarterly*, 15 (September, 1970), 318–329.

Further Sources. The Industrial Administration Research Unit of the University of Aston has published a large number of articles reporting the results of its research. Unfortunately, the published work of this Research Unit is not yet available in monograph form. However, the references at the end of the present article contain the major publications of the Research Unit.

NOTES

1. This definition is adapted from Talcott Parsons, "On the Concept of Influence," *Public Opinion Quarterly*, 27 (Spring, 1963), 37–62 (esp. p. 45). Also relevant is Talcott Parsons, "On the Concept of Political Power," *Proceedings of the American Philosophical Society*, 107 (June, 1963), 232–262.
2. This definition of autonomy is based on Philip Selznick, *TVA and the Grass Roots* (Berkeley, Calif.: University of California Press, 1953), pp. 29–37. Major studies of autonomy have been made by Selznick and his students.
3. J. H. K. Inkson, D. S. Pugh, and D. J. Hickson, "Organization Context and Structure: An Abbreviated Replication," *Administrative Science Quarterly*, 15 (September, 1970), p. 320.
4. These components of the concentration of authority are found in D. S. Pugh, D. J. Hickson, C. R. Hinings, and C. Turner, "Dimensions of Organizational Structure," *Administrative Science Quarterly*, 13 (June, 1968), 65–105 (esp. p. 89).
5. The interview schedule is supplied through the courtesy of D. J. Hickson, a senior member of the Industrial Administration Research Unit of the University of Aston, Birmingham, England. That part of the interview schedule that is relevant to autonomy is slightly simplified for the sake of clarity. Nothing essential is removed from the interview schedule. Even the lines used in the original schedule are reproduced.

6. This information about the computations was supplied through the courtesy of D. J. Hickson.

7. The reader, to obtain more data about the range of this measure of autonomy, should also examine the scores obtained in the previous research on 52 organizations in the English Midlands. See Pugh *et al.*, *op. cit.*, especially p. 104, Table D.1, Scale 54.10.

8. H. E. Brogden, "A New Coefficient: Applications to Biserial Correlation and to Estimation of Serial Efficiency," *Psychometrika*, 14 (September, 1949), 169–182.

9. Discussions of the boundary problem are contained in Robert K. Merton, *Social Theory and Social Structure* (Glencoe, Ill.: Free Press, 1968), pp. 338–342 and Amitai Etzioni, *A Comparative Analysis of Complex Organizations* (New York: Free Press of Glencoe, 1961), pp. 16–21.

CENTRALIZATION

5

Definition. *Centralization* is the degree to which power is concentrated in a social system.[1] In an organization, for example, the maximum degree of centralization would exist if all the power was exercised by a single individual; conversely, the minimum degree of centralization would exist if all the power was exercised equally by all the members of the organization. Most organizations, of course, fall somewhere between the maximum and minimum degrees. Discussions of the following topics contain information pertinent to centralization: "power stratification," "hierarchy of authority," "participative management," "close-general supervision," monocratic-democratic authority," "executive-colleague authority," "unilateral-bilateral decision-making," and "devolution."

Centralization is sometimes used to designate the "dispersion" of a social system.[2] Dispersion is defined and illustrated later; it is sufficient to note at this point that the spatial distribution of the membership of a social system is not generally encompassed under centralization.

Centralization is distinguished from alienation. The degree to which power is distributed in a social system—this handbook's definition of centralization —refers to a particular type of patterned social interaction. In short, centralization refers to an objective situation. The degree to which the members of a social system believe that their behavior can determine the outcomes they seek—this handbook's definition of alienation—refers to the manner in which the members of a social system perceive a particular type of patterned social interaction. In short, alienation refers to a subjective variable. Despite the fact that centralization is commonly measured by subjective reports, the concept should be analytically distinguished from alienation. An individual may perceive himself to be relatively powerless when, objectively, he may exericse considerable power; conversely, an individual may perceive himself to exercise considerable power when, objectively, he may be almost powerless.

Measurement. Two types of measures of centralization are used. First, there are specific questions designed to collect information about power with respect to the making of definite types of commonly made decisions. Second, there are global questions designed to collect information about power in general. Both measures rely on the subjective reports of respondents. The first measure (Aiken and Hage) uses specific questions, whereas the third measure (Williams,

Hoffman, and Mann) uses global questions. The third measure is commonly referred to as the "control graph" and is probably the most widely used measure of centralization. Tannenbaum and his colleagues at the Survey Research Center of the University of Michigan have devised and widely used the control graph.

The measurement of centralization is sometimes based on objective data, such as official records and observations. The second measure (Whisler) is an example of this. If centralization is going to be distinguished from alienation—and this seems to be customary—and if attempts are going to be made to relate the two concepts—this is the objective in theory construction —then centralization will ultimately have to be measured by some type of objective measure.

Three commonly used measures of centralization, all of which are based primarily on objective data (mostly official records), are not included in this handbook: the "span of control," "number of levels of authority," and "time-span of discretion."[3] This handbook distinguishes span of control and number of levels of authority from centralization. Span of control is a separate concept and number of levels of authority is conceptualized as a dimension of complexity; these concepts are discussed later. The time-span of discretion is not used as a measure because the written descriptions are too complex to permit widespread replication and the unit of analysis is the superordinate-subordinate relationship rather than the organization. The second objection is not as critical as the first. It is possible to convert the time-span of discretion into an organizational measure by an examination of all the superordinate-subordinate relationships in the organization. However, as now reported, the measure is too complex to permit widespread replication. The relevant literature for the time-span of discretion is cited under Additional Readings at the end of the chapter.

THE MEASURES

1. AIKEN AND HAGE

Description. This study investigates the relationship between organizational interdependence and internal organizational behavior. The number of joint programs with other organizations is the aspect of interdependence that is investigated. The following five concepts are used to describe internal organizational behavior: complexity, innovation, communication, centralization, and formalization. The data were collected from 16 social welfare and health organizations located in a large midwestern metropolis in 1967. Ten organizations are private; 6 are either public or branches of public agencies. The 16 organizations are all the larger welfare organizations that provide rehabilitation, psychiatric services, and assistance for the mentally retarded. The organizations vary in size from 24 to over 600 persons. Interviews were conducted with 520 staff members. Respondents within each organization were selected by the following three criteria: (1) all executive directors and department heads; (2) in departments of less than ten members, one-half of the staff was selected randomly; and (3) in departments of more than ten members, one-third of the staff was selected randomly. Nonsupervisory administrative and maintenance personnel are not included in the study.

Definition. Centralization is not explicitly defined; however, the implicit definition is "the degree of participation in decision-making."[4] Two kinds of decisions are distinguished, organizational and work. The first type of decision concerns the organization as a unit, whereas the second concerns the respondent's degree of control over his immediate work environment.

Data Collection. The data were collected by interviews. Four questions are used to collect information about organizational decisions; the result is an "index of actual participation." Five questions are used to collect information about work decisions; the result is a scale of "the hierarchy of authority." The questions for the index of actual participation are as follows:

1. How frequently do you usually participate in the decision to hire new staff?

    ____Never

    ____Seldom

    ____Sometimes

    ____Often

    ____Always[5]

2. How frequently do you usually participate in the decisions on the promotion of any of the professional staff?

3. How frequently do you participate in decisions on the adoptions of new policies?

4. How frequently do you participate in the decisions on the adoptions of new programs?

The questions for the scale of the hierarchy of authority are as follows:

1. There can be little action taken here until a supervisor approves a decision.

    ____Definitely false

    ____False

    ____True

    ____Definitely true[6]

2. A person who wants to make his own decisions would be quickly discouraged here.

3. Even small matters have to be referred to someone higher up for a final decision.

4. I have to ask my boss before I do almost anything.

5. Any decision I make has to have my boss' approval.

Computation. The computations differ for the two types of decisions. For the index of actual participation, the five responses are assigned numbers from "1" (low participation) to "5" (high participation). A "Never" response receives a "1"; at the other extreme, an "Always" response receives a "5." An average score on these five questions is computed for each respondent. Each respondent is then classified by "social position" and a second mean computed for each social position in the organization. "A social position," according to Aiken and Hage, "is defined by the level or stratum in the organization and the department or type of professional activity. For example, if an agency's professional staff consists of psychiatrists and social workers, each divided into two hierarchical levels, the agency has four social positions: supervisory psychiatrists, psychiatrists, supervisory social workers, and social workers . . . ."[7] The organizational score is determined by computing the average of all social position means in the organization.

Computations for the hierarchy of authority scale are similar to those for the index of actual participation. The responses are assigned numbers from "1" (definitely false) to "4" (definitely true). As with the index of actual participation, the organizational score for the hierarchy of authority scale is based on social position means which, in turn, are based on the means for each respondent.

Validity. Aiken and Hage predicted that the number of joint programs—the type of organizational interdependence which they investigated—would be inversely related to centralization. The predictions are confirmed for the index of actual participation, but not for the hierarchy of authority scale. The results for the hierarchy of authority scale actually come out in the opposite direction from the predictions.

Reliability. The article contains no data relevant to reliability.

Comments. (1) Aiken and Hage's definition of centralization corresponds to this handbook's definition. "Participation in decision-making"—Aiken and Hage's definition of centralization—is typically equated with the exercise of power. (2) Centralization is commonly discussed as if there were no differences among decisions. There are actually significant differences among decisions and Aiken and Hage's distinction between organizational and work decisions is a much-needed refinement with respect to the conceptualization of centralization. (3) Aiken and Hage's computations are confusing. A high degree of centralization on the index of actual participation is indicated by a "1," whereas a high degree of centralization on the hierarchy of authority scale is indicated by a "4." The computations would be less confusing if the same number had the same meaning throughout the article.

Source. Michael Aiken and Jerald Hage, "Organizational Interdependence and Intra-Organizational Structure," *American Sociological Review*, 33 (December, 1968), 912–930.

Further Sources. 1. Michael Aiken and Jerald Hage, "Organizational Alienation," *American Sociological Review*, 31 (August, 1966), 497–507.
2. Jerald Hage and Michael Aiken, "Program Change and Organizational Properties," *American Journal of Sociology*, 72 (March, 1967), 503–519.
3. Jerald Hage and Michael Aiken, "Relationship of Centralization to Other Structural Properties," *Administrative Science Quarterly*, 12 (June, 1967), 72–92.
4. Jerald Hage and Michael Aiken, *Social Change in Complex Organization* (New York: Random House, 1970).
5. Richard H. Hall, "An Empirical Study of Bureaucratic Dimensions and Their Relation to Other Organizational Characteristics." (unpublished Ph.D. dissertation, Columbus, The Ohio State University, 1961).[8]
6. Richard H. Hall, "The Concept of Bureaucracy: An Empirical Assessment," *American Journal of Sociology*, 69 (July, 1963), 32–40.

2. WHISLER

Description. This study focuses on the measurement of the centralization of control. Three sets of data about business organizations are presented. First, there is K Company, which is about 100 years old and which shifted from a functional form of structure to a product-division form in 1955. Second, there are two small units of a nationwide corporation. These units are hundreds of miles apart, but perform identical functions. Third, there are data about 48 firms compiled from a survey conducted by a professional association in the field of business management. All of the employees were studied in K Company and the two small units of the nationwide corporation; however, for K Company, more detailed information was collected about salaried employees than about wage employees. The professional association only collected information from the top executives in the 48 firms it surveyed.

Definition. Control is defined as "... effective influence upon everything affecting goal achievement of the group ...."[9] Examples of control are the allocation of human and nonhuman resources, choice of production techniques, selection and analysis of information, and choice of level of personal energy expenditure.

Data Collection. Data were collected about monetary compensation and perceived influence. The instrument of data collection for monetary compensation is not reproduced; however, this information probably comes from payroll records. The control graph is used as the measure of perceived influence and is described as the third measure of this chapter. However, it should be noted that Whisler does not construct the control graph with exactly the same questions that are used in the third measure. Whisler states that his questions are similar, but he does not reproduce them in his article.

Computation. The basic computation is a ratio between the amount of monetary compensation received by a certain fraction of the members of the organization and the total monetary compensation paid by the organization. An example of the computations for the K Company is contained in Table 5–1.

TABLE 5–1   Percent of Total Wages and Salaries Paid to Stipulated Fractions of Those on the Payroll in K Corporation: 1955, 1958, and 1960

	1955 ($N = 8,800$)	1958 ($N = 7,300$)	1960 ($N = 7,150$)
Top 1 percent	4.11	4.02	3.93
Top 2 percent	6.38	6.35	6.22
Top 25 percent	34.23	34.83	36.77

The ratio, as is customary, is converted into a percentage in the table. *A change in the percentage indicates a change in the distribution of control. A downward change in the percentages indicates a decrease in control, whereas an upward change indicates an increase in control.* The computations in Table 5–1 indicate a decrease in control among the top 1 and 2 percent of the membership which, of course, means an increase in control among the top 25 percent of the membership. There has, in brief, been some decrease in centralization of control in the K Company between 1955 and 1960. Table 5–1 presents the percentages for three fractions of the membership (the top 1, 2, and 25 percents). The number of fractions computed will vary with the detail required by the research and the amount of data collected.

Validity. The data relevant to validity vary with the set of data analyzed. With respect to K Company, for example, there was an attempt made by the president and vice-president for organization to reduce the degree of centralization of control. Whisler provides documentary evidence which indicates that an attempt was made to reduce the degree of centralization. As previously indicated, Table 5–1 does indicate that this attempt was successful. The

distribution of control in the two small units of the nationwide corporation—
the second set of data—is measured in two ways, the distribution of monetary
compensation and the control graph. The two measures should rank order
the two small units of the nationwide corporation in the same manner. The
results of the two measures, which are too complex to be briefly summarized,
are inconclusive. Whisler doubts whether the two measures are describing
the same phenomenon. The data collected on the 48 firms by the professional
association—the third set of data—are used to test a prediction derived from
the economic theory of the firm. The prediction is that size and centralization
are inversely related, that is, as size increases, centralization decreases. The
prediction is not disproved by the data.

Reliability. The study contains no data relevant to reliability.

Comments. (1) Whisler provides little information about the business organizations he studied. The reader cannot generalize the findings of a study
unless he has adequate information about the sample. Therefore, Whisler
should have provided more information about the organizations. (2) Whisler
only collected data about business organizations; furthermore, he believes
that his measure applies most readily to business organizations because they
operate in a market environment. His measures should be applied to nonbusiness organizations to verify his beliefs. The measures may be applicable
to a wide range of nonbusiness organizations. (3) Whisler's concept of "control" is more general than this handbook's concept of "power." Power is
defined in social terms, that is, it involves interaction among people. Control
includes interaction among people plus influences on goal achievement that
do not involve influences on other people. This handbook's conceptualization
of power, plus the term "power" rather than the term "control," are preferred
because of their widespread usage in the study of organizations. (4) There are
almost no measures of centralization based on objective data in the literature;
therefore, Whisler's use of monetary compensation to measure centralization
is a welcome addition to the literature. Measures based on objective data are
critically needed in the study of organizations. (5) Information about monetary
compensations can be obtained by different procedures; therefore, Whisler
should have reproduced his instrument for collecting data about monetary
compensation. Replication cannot be performed unless researchers reproduce
their instruments. The concluding chapter of this handbook discusses the
problem of including instruments in articles. (6) Whisler was able to collect
information about monetary compensation for all personnel in two out of
three of his sets of data. Somewhat more detailed information was collected
about the salaried personnel than about the wage personnel. If monetary
compensation is to be used as a measure of centralization, then detailed data
must be collected about all the personnel of the organization. (7) Whisler
indicates that the major disadvantage of his measure is that it applies only to
organizations that use monetary compensation. This is not too serious a

disadvantage because most administrative organizations, Western and Eastern, use monetary compensation. Most voluntary associations,[10] however, do not rely primarily on monetary compensation to motivate the performance of their members. Additional objective measures will ultimately have to be developed for voluntary associations. (8) Whisler is aware of the fact that monetary compensation, as he uses the measure, excludes such "fringe benefits" as deferred compensation and stock options. These fringe benefits, especially for the major executives, are substantial.[11] Ultimately, it will be desirable to construct "current income equivalents" for these fringe benefits to measure more accurately the distribution of monetary compensation in the organization.[12]

Source. Thomas L. Whisler, "Measuring Centralization of Control in Business Organizations," in *New Perspectives in Organization Research*, ed. W. N. Cooper, H. J. Leavitt, and M. W. Skelly, II (New York: Wiley, 1964, pp. 314–333.

Further Source. Thomas L. Whisler, Harold Meyer, Bernard H. Baum, and Peter F. Sorensen, Jr., "Centralization of Organizational Control: An Empirical Study of Its Meaning and Measurement," in *Control in Organizations*, ed. Arnold S. Tannenbaum (New York: McGraw-Hill, 1968).

3. WILLIAMS, HOFFMAN, AND MANN

Description. This study investigates the utility of the control graph method of measuring influence. The study was conducted in the Personnel Division of a large midwestern electrical power company. Of the 125 members of the division, representing all but the clerical employees, 75 completed a questionnaire to measure influence. Eight levels are used as reference points to describe the influence structure: top executives and corporate officers, managers, the personnel manager, assistant personnel managers, department heads, supervisors, nonsupervisory professional staff, and clerical-secretarial employees. The top executive and corporate officers are the uppermost members of the company management. The managers direct various divisions of the company, such as Sales, Construction, and Purchasing. The personnel manager heads one of the divisions; however, because of his direct concern with the activities of the Personnel Division, his position is described separately. The manager, assistant managers, department heads, and supervisors are the managerial staff of the Personnel Division. The nonsupervisory staff are specialists in employee relations; they are professionals engaged in activities that involve considerable responsibility and initiative. Of the respondents in the study, 53 are from this nonsupervisory group.

Definition. Influence is not defined in the study. The authors comment upon the lack of a stringent definition of influence in the literature. "Influence" is equated with "power" and "control" at several points in the study.

Data Collection. The data for the measurement of influence were collected by means of a questionnaire. Data were collected for group and individual measures. The question format is as follows when "Managers" as a group are used as the reference point:

> In general, how much influence do the *Managers*[13] have on what the following individuals or groups do in the company?

	Little or no Influence	Some Influence	Quite a bit of Influence	A great deal of Influence	A very great deal of Influence[14]
Top Executive and Corporate Officers	___	___	___	___	___
Personnel Manager	___	___	___	___	___
Your Assistant Personnel Manager	___	___	___	___	___
Your Director or Department Head	___	___	___	___	___
Supervisors (other than your Director)	___	___	___	___	___
Nonsupervisory Professional Staff People	___	___	___	___	___
Clerical and Secretarial People in Personnel	___	___	___	___	___
On what you do	___	___	___	___	___

The question is successively repeated with each level in the left column (the levels of the company hierarchy) appearing in turn as the reference point. The group used as a reference point is not included in the left column when it is used as a reference point. "Managers," for example, on the preceding question, is not included in the left column.

There are also three questions about the individual's perception of his own influence relationship as distinct from those of particular levels. The following questions are used with the previously described format to collect information about the influence exercised, received, and desired by the respondent himself:

> How much influence do *you have* over what the following levels do in the company?
> How much influence do the following levels have over what *you do* in the company?
> How much influence do you think *you* personally *should have* over what the following levels do in the company?[15]

In addition to the questionnaire survey, two investigators spent three months interviewing a sample of the respondents. The materials from the interviews supplemented the questionnaire data to support the interpretations of the control graphs.

Computation. Numbers from "1" to "5" are assigned to the five response categories. A "1" represents "little or no influence," whereas a "5" represents "a very great deal of influence." Consider the computation for "Managers" in the previous example. The influence exercised by the Managers on the Top Executives is the mean of the responses for the Top Executive row. The mean of the means for all rows, with the Managers used as the reference point, is the total amount of influence exercised by the Managers. Again using the Managers as the reference point, the mean of the Top Executive row also measures the amount of influence received by the Top Executives from the Managers. The mean of the means for the Top Executive rows for all reference points is the total amount of influence received by the Top Executives.

The computations are plotted on a graph; the result is the well-known "control graph." The horizontal axis of the graph represents the level in the organization, whereas the vertical axis represents the amount of influence. Figure 5–1 presents a control graph of the influence structure of the company

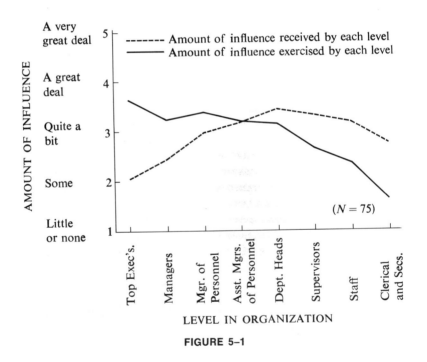

LEVEL IN ORGANIZATION

FIGURE 5–1

with respect to the activities of the Personnel Division. A smoothly descending line for the amount of influence exercised indicates a highly centralized organization, whereas a smoothly ascending line for the amount of influence exercised indicates a lowly centralized organization. (The meaning of descend and ascend is, of course, reversed for the amount of influence received.) It is the slope of the line along the horizontal axis which measures centralization;

the height of the line with respect to the vertical axis represents the amount of control exercised by the organization. The slope of the line along the horizontal axis with respect to the amount of influence exercised is generally used as the measure of centralization by researchers who use the control graph. The Personnel Division whose activities are represented in Figure 5-1, because it has a smoothly descending line for the amount of influence exercised, is a highly centralized system.

Validity. (1) Williams, Hoffman, and Mann's findings indicate that the range for the amount of influence *exercised* across levels within the power plant is greater than the range for the amount of influence *received*. The receipt of influence is thus more widely perceived than the exercise of influence. This finding agrees with a similar finding reported by Tannenbaum and Georgopoulos in their study of a nationally organized delivery company.[16] The correspondence of these findings was anticipated in two business organizations. (2) Williams, Hoffman, and Mann compare the control graphs of the Personnel Division for two groups of differentially ranked employees. Only the influence-exercised lines are compared. The control graphs for the two groups are very similar. (3) The researchers compare the control graphs of the Personnel Division for two groups of employees contrasted, not by hierarchical level, but by different subgroups at the same organizational level. Based on their interview data,[17] the authors anticipated that one of the groups would be characterized by greater influence exercised. The control graphs generally confirm this prediction. (4) The researchers relate influence to satisfaction. Their findings indicate that the smaller the proportion of influence desired, the higher the satisfaction. In other words, the greater the unrealized desire for influence, the less satisfied the group is with the amount of influence they have. This finding is in accord with other studies that relate influence and satisfaction.[18]

There is a large amount of research that uses the control graph. Many of these studies are included in the Tannenbaum book cited under Further Sources. Tannenbaum sums up the case for the validity of the control graph very well in the following statement:

> Perhaps the strongest support for the measures comes from what we believe are meaningful relationships between patterns of control as measured and other aspects of organizational structure and functioning independently measured. Ultimately our case for the validity of the measure hinges on the extent to which the meaning that we claim for them fits meaningfully the predictions that we have made and the substantiation for these predictions that we find . . . .[19]

Reliability. The study summarized in this handbook contains no data relevant to reliability. However, one study that uses the control graph reports split-half reliability correlations, corrected by the Spearman-Brown formula, of .67 and .87.[20]

Comments. (1) Since Williams, Hoffman, and Mann do not define influence, it is not possible to compare their definition of influence with this handbook's definition of power. However, these authors are from the Survey Research Center of the University of Michigan, and the researchers of this Center have elsewhere defined influence. Tannenbaum, for example, equates influence, power, authority, and control and then defines control in the following manner: " . . . any process in which a person or group of persons or organization of persons determines, that is, intentionally affects, the behavior of another person, group, or organization."[21] To determine personally the behavior of other persons—the essential element of Tannenbaum's definition of control— is basically the same as an individual who has the capacity to obtain performance from other individuals—the essential elements of this handbook's definition of power.[22] Tannenbaum's concept of control, and probably that of the Survey Research Center, is thus very similar to this handbook's concept of power. (2) The horizontal axis of the control graph, it may be recalled, refers to the hierarchical level in the organization, whereas the vertical axis refers to the amount of power. The control graph thus distinguishes the distribution of power, the horizontal axis, from the amount of power, the vertical axis. Centralization refers to the distribution of power, the horizontal axis. There has been little organizational research that deals with the amount of power, with the exception of that done by the Survey Research Center; therefore, this concept is not included in this handbook. (3) The exact instrument of data collection used in this study is not used in all of the Further Sources. The researchers at the Survey Research Center have not completely standardized their measurement of centralization. The question formats, however, are quite similar. Most of the existing standardization of measures in organizational research is found in centers like the Survey Research Center and among the students of major researchers. However, as this example of centralization indicates, even within such centers, standardization is not complete. (4) The control graph for this study has two lines, one for the amount of influence received and the other for the amount of influence exercised. Most of the research—to emphasize a point previously made— which uses the control graph uses a single line. The most commonly used line corresponds to the amount of influence exercised, although the questions used to collect the information for the line, as previously indicated, are slightly different. (5) The control graph has been in the literature for almost a decade and a half. During this time data relevant to reliability are reported in but a single study. More data should be collected about the reliability of the control graph.

Source. Lawrence K. Williams, L. Richard Hoffman, and Floyd Mann, "An Investigation of the Control Graph: Influence in a Staff Organization," *Social Forces*, 37 (March, 1959), 189–195.

Further Sources. 1. Martin Patchen, "Alternative Questionnaire Approaches to the Measurement of Influence in Organizations," *American Journal of Sociology*, 69 (July, 1963), 41–52.

2. Arnold S. Tannenbaum, ed., *Control in Organizations* (New York: McGraw-Hill, 1968).[23]

ADDITIONAL READINGS

1. Edwin F. Beal, "In Praise of Job Evaluation," *California Management Review*, 5 (Summer, 1963), 9–16.[24]
2. J. M. M. Hill, "The Time-Span of Discretion in Job Analysis," *Human Relations*, 9 (1956), 295–323.
3. J. M. M. Hill, "A Note on Time-Span and Economic Theory," *Human Relations*, 11 (1958), 373–379.
4. Elliott Jacques, *Measurement of Responsibility* (London: Tavistock, 1956).
5. Elliott Jacques, *Equitable Payment* (New York: Wiley, 1961).
6. Elliott Jacques, "Objective Measures for Pay Differentials," *Harvard Business Review*, 40 (January/February, 1962), 133–138.
7. Elliott Jacques, *Time-Span Handbook* (London: Heineman, 1964).
8. D. S. Pugh, D. J. Hickson, C. R. Hinings, K. M. Mcdonald, C. Turner, and T. Lupton, "A Scheme for Organizational Analysis," *Administrative Science Quarterly*, 8 (December, 1963), 289–315.
9. D. S. Pugh, D. J. Hickson, C. R. Hinings, and C. Turner, "Dimensions of Organizational Structure," *Administrative Science Quarterly*, 13 (June, 1968), 65–105.[25]
10. Ralph M. Stogdill and Carroll L. Shartle, *Methods in the Study of Administrative Leadership* (Columbus, Ohio: Bureau of Business Research, The Ohio State University, 1955).[26]
11. Ralph M. Stogdill, Ellis L. Scott, and William E. Jaynes, *Leadership and Role Expectations* (Columbus, Ohio: Bureau of Business Research, The Ohio State University, 1956).
12. Ralph M. Stogdill, *Leadership and Structures of Personal Interaction* (Columbus, Ohio: Bureau of Business Research, The Ohio State University, 1957).

NOTES

1. This is a common way to define centralization in the organizational literature. Power is defined and illustrated in Chapter 4, which is concerned with autonomy.
2. An example of centralization used as dispersion is John M. Blair, "Does Large-Scale Enterprise Result in Lower Costs?" *American Economic Review*, 38 (May, 1948 Supplement), 121–152. The articles in *Fortune* magazine often use centralization, as defined by this handbook, as dispersion. Most of the literature refers to "ecology" rather than "dispersion."

3. These measures, plus the relative size of the administrative staff as a measure of centralization, are described in William M. Evan, "Indices of the Hierarchical Structure of Industrial Organizations," *Management Science*, 9 (April, 1963), 468–477.

4. Aiken and Hage have, of course, explicitly defined centralization elsewhere. See, for example, Jerald Hage and Michael Aiken, "Relationship of Centralization to Other Structural Properties," *Administrative Science Quarterly*, 12 (June, 1967), 72–92 (esp. p. 77).

5. The other three questions of the index of actual participation use these same five responses. Therefore, it is not necessary to reproduce the responses for the other three questions.

6. The other four questions of the scale of the hierarchy of authority use these same four responses.

7. Michael Aiken and Jerald Hage, "Organizational Interdependence and Intra-Organizational Structure," *American Sociological Review*, 33 (December, 1968), p. 918.

8. The questions for Aiken and Hage's hierarchy of authority scale were obtained by a factor analysis from two scales developed by Hall, "hierarchy of authority" and "rules." Hall refers to these two scales in his much cited article on bureaucracy (Further Source No. 6). He describes these scales in his dissertation: chapter two describes the construction of the scales, while the instruments of data collection are found in Appendix V.

9. Thomas L. Whisler, "Measuring Centralization of Control in Business Organizations," in *New Perspectives in Organization Research*, ed. W. W. Cooper, H. J. Leavitt, and M. W. Skelly, II (New York: Wiley, 1964), p. 315.

10. The introductory chapter discusses the distinction between administrative organizations and voluntary associations.

11. An excellent study of these fringe benefits is Wilbur G. Lewellen, *Executive Compensation in Large Industrial Corporations* (New York: Columbia, 1968).

12. Lewellen in *ibid.* constructs these "current income equivalents" to measure fringe benefits.

13. The italics are in the original article.

14. The format of this question comes, not from the article by Williams, Hoffman, and Mann, but from Arnold S. Tannenbaum, ed., *Control in Organizations* (New York: McGraw-Hill, 1968), p. 75.

15. The italics for these three questions are in the original article.

16. Arnold S. Tannenbaum and Basil S. Georgopoulos, "The Distribution of Control in Formal Organizations," *Social Forces*, 36 (October, 1957), 44–50.

17. The reliance on interview data at this point is implicit in the study.

18. See, for example, Robert Blauner, *Alienation and Freedom* (Chicago: University of Chicago Press, 1964).

19. Tannenbaum, *op. cit.*, p. 25. A somewhat less optimistic view of the validity of the control graph is provided in Martin Patchen, "Alternative Questionnaire Approaches to the Measurement of Influence in Organizations," *American Journal of Sociology*, 69 (July, 1963), 41–52. The type of research which Patchen reports in this article is, unfortunately, rare in organizational literature.

20. Tannenbaum, *op. cit.*, p. 150.

21. *Ibid.*, p. 5.

22. Power is defined and illustrated in chapter five dealing with autonomy.

23. This book contains a number of studies which use the control graph. Some studies which use this measure, but which are not included in this compilation, are cited on pp. 74–75.

24. The first seven readings pertain to the "time-span of discretion."

25. The measure of centralization reported in this article by Pugh and his colleagues is an alternative which is more than the previously discussed measure of autonomy. The University of Aston researchers include autonomy as part of their measure of centralization.

26. The last three readings pertain to the "RAD scales" developed by researchers located at the Ohio State University, Columbus, Ohio.

COMMUNICATION

Definition. *Communication* is the degree to which information is transmitted among the members of a social system.[1] This transmission of information assumes many forms in organizations: formal discussions between superordinates and subordinates; informal conferences among subordinates; publication of various types of newsletters (often referred to as "house organs"); production of radio and television programs; posting of announcements on bulletin boards; the use of public address systems; and so forth. "Socialization," "feedback," "ambiguity," "acculturation," "assimilation," "diffusion," "indoctrination," "education"—these are some of the many labels under which communication is discussed.

Four types of communication are distinguished. The first, and probably the most common distinction, is between *formal* and *informal communication*. The basis of this distinction is whether or not the information is officially or unofficially transmitted. Formal communication refers to officially transmitted information. The sanctions at the disposal of the organization—its wealth and prestige, for example—are used to support the system of formal communication, whereas the system of informal communication receives no such support. Second, *vertical* and *horizontal communication* are also commonly distinguished. Vertical communication refers to the transmission of information in the superordinate-subordinate relationships, whether from superordinate to subordinate or from subordinate to superordinate, whereas horizontal communication refers to the transmission of information among peer relationships. Third, *personal* and *impersonal communication*, while not explicitly indicated in organizational literature as often as the two previous distinctions, is implicit in much of the literature. The basis of this distinction is whether or not the information is transmitted in situations where mutual influence is possible during the transmission event. Personal conversations and telephone calls are examples of personal communication, whereas the mass media are examples of impersonal communication. Fourth, *instrumental* and *expressive communication* may be distinguished. The transmission of cognitive information is the distinguishing characteristic of instrumental communication, whereas the transmission of normative and affective information is the distinguishing characteristic of expressive communication. The scientific and technological information necessary to perform a job is an example of cognitive information. The "rules and regulations" of the organization constitute an example of normative information, whereas the information about "dislikes and likes," whether directed toward people, objects, or the organization as a unit, constitute an example of affective information. Like personal and impersonal communication, the meaning of instrumental and expressive communication is usually implicit in the literature; however, both terms indicate significant components of communication and should be explicitly distinguished.[2]

Measurement. Communication is one of the most commonly treated topics in organizational literature. All of the textbooks allocate a sizeable amount of space to its discussion, and it is ignored by few empirical studies. Popular literature is enamored with the possibilities of communication as a panacea for whatever ails the organization. If one is to judge by the amount of space allocated, then communication is indeed one of the most significant topics in the organizational literature.

The measurement of communication is a neglected topic, however. There is no measure for communication that even remotely resembles the control graph for centralization. The first measure selected (Georgopoulos and Mann) represents the commonly used questionnaire approach to data collection. The Georgopoulos and Mann study is probably the most impressive study of communication, both theoretically and methodologically, in the organizational literature. The second measure selected (Lawler, Porter, and Tennenbaum) represents a little-used method of data collection, a self-reporting form. Both procedures deserve to be applied widely, and additional measures of communication urgently need to be developed.

THE MEASURES

1. GEORGOPOULOS AND MANN

Description. This is a study of the determinants of organizational effectiveness. The setting for the study is ten voluntary, nonprofit, nongovernmental, nondenominational, short-stay, community general hospitals. Data were collected from the hospital administrator, nonmedical department heads, trustees, medical staff with and without administrative responsibilities, supervisory and nonsupervisory registered nurses, and x-ray and laboratory technicians. The nonsupervisory registered nurses, because of their critical role in the hospital, were the subjects of a special study on the impact of communication on their performance. The data for the measurement of communication come from this special study of nonsupervisory registered nurses. In the ten hospitals, out of a total of 213 nurses initially selected to participate in the study and still working for the hospital during data collection, 196 finally completed appropriate questionnaires. The overall questionnaire rate is 92 percent. The number of nurses who were selected and who completed questionnaires in each hospital range across hospitals from a low of 14 persons in one hospital to a high of 27 in another; the average is 20 per hospital.

Definition. The researchers implicitly define communication as the transmission of information. Six aspects of communication are distinguished: adequacy, amount, frequency, quality, informality, and direction.

Data Collection. The data were collected by questionnaires. Seven questions are used to collect information about each aspect of communication. The following question is used to collect information about the adequacy of communication:

> In general, how do you feel about the kind of communication which you receive from your *immediate superior?*[3] (Check one.)
>
> > ____The kind of communication I receive from my immediate superior is completely adequate
> >
> > ____Very adequate
> >
> > ____Fairly adequate
> >
> > ____Rather inadequate
> >
> > ____The kind of communication I receive from my immediate superior is inadequate.[4]

The following question is used to collect information about the amount of communication between nurses and their superiors:

> On the whole, what is the average amount of time per week you talk with your *immediate superior* in the hospital? (Check one.)
>
> > ____I usually talk with my immediate superior less than ¼ hour per week
> >
> > ____Between ¼ and ½ hour per week
> >
> > ____Between ½ and 1 hour per week
> >
> > ____Between 1 and 2 hours per week
> >
> > ____Between 2 and 4 hours per week
> >
> > ____I usually talk with my immediate superior more than 4 hours per week.

The following question is used to collect information about the frequency with which the nurses communicate with their immediate superior and the amount of time they spend communicating about certain topics related to their jobs:

> How often do you usually talk with your immediate superior about each of the following things? (Check one for each item.)

	Once a month or less often	Two or three times a month	About once a week	Several times a week	Once a day or more often[5]
( )[6] About ways in which patient care could be improved	____	____	____	____	____ [7]
( ) About ways in which nursing supervision could be improved	____	____	____	____	____
( ) About work	____	____	____	____	____
( ) About employee wages, hours, or benefits	____	____	____	____	____
( ) About ways in which working relations between departments could be improved	____	____	____	____	____
( ) About ways in which satisfaction or morale among nursing personnel could be improved	____	____	____	____	____
( ) About things, people, or happenings outside the hospital	____	____	____	____	____

The following two questions are asked to collect information about the qualitative aspects of communication between the nurses and their immediate superiors:

1.[8] How often does your immediate superior express appreciation for your work? (Check one.)

____Always or nearly always expresses appreciation for my work

____Very often

____Often

____Sometimes

____Seldom or never expresses appreciation for my work.

2. Check in the appropriate column below how often your *immediate superior* talks to you in the following ways: (Check one for each item.)

	Always or nearly always	Most of the time	Some- times	A few times	Seldom or never
( ) Shows appreciation for your work, shows confidence in you	____	____	____	____	____

( ) Gives you directions or
    orders   _____   _____   _____   _____   _____

( ) Explains things or gives
    information and suggestions _____   _____   _____   _____   _____

( ) Asks for your suggestions
    or opinions   _____   _____   _____   _____   _____

( ) Asks you for information,
    explanation, or clarification   _____   _____   _____   _____   _____

( ) Criticizes you, refuses
    to help, or is
    unnecessarily formal   _____   _____   _____   _____   _____

( ) Gives excess, unnecessary
    information or comments   _____   _____   _____   _____   _____

The preceding five questions collect data about communication between nurses and their immediate superiors; therefore, these data represent formal communication. The following three questions are used to collect information about informal communication:

1. When people work together they talk about work, their personal interests, and other things which may or may not be related to the job. And, usually people talk more with certain persons than with others. Think of that person in this hospital *with whom you talk the most.* Then check the average amount of time *per week* you talk with this person while at the hospital. (Check one.)

    ___I usually talk with this person less than ½ hour per week

    ___Between ½ and 1 hour per week

    ___Between 1 and 2 hours per week

    ___Between 2 and 4 hours per week

    ___Between 4 and 6 hours per week

    ___I usually talk with this person more than 6 hours per week

2. How often do you usually talk with this person about each of the following things? (Check one for each item.)

	Once a month or less often	*Two or three times a month*	*About once a week*	*Several times a week*	*Once a day or more often*
( ) About ways in which patient care could be improved	_____	_____	_____	_____	_____
( ) About ways in which nursing supervision could be improved	_____	_____	_____	_____	_____

( ) About work   _____ _____ _____ _____ _____
( ) About employee wages,
    hours or benefits   _____ _____ _____ _____ _____
( ) About ways in which
    working relations between
    departments could be
    improved   _____ _____ _____ _____ _____
( ) About ways in which
    satisfaction or morale
    among nursing personnel
    could be improved   _____ _____ _____ _____ _____
( ) About things, people, or
    happenings outside the
    hospital   _____ _____ _____ _____ _____

3. What position in the hospital does this person with whom you talk most frequently have? (Check one.)

    ____This person has a position lower than mine

    ____This person has a position at the same level as mine

    ____This person is my immediate superior

    ____This person has a position higher than mine (but is not my immediate superior)

This third question also collects information about the direction of communication.

Computation. The unit of analysis for all computations is the group of respondents in each hospital, that is, all nonsupervisory registered nurses in each hospital separately rather than the individual group members across hospitals. In short, the number of cases is ten, the number of hospitals in the study. The computational information is presented separately for each of the six aspects of communication.

(1) The five responses to the question about the adequacy of communication are scored from "1" to "5." The "completely adequate" response is scored as "1," whereas, at the other extreme, the "inadequate" response is scored as "5." Arithmetic means are computed for the responses, by hospital. The range of the means is from 1.69—the hospital where communication is most adequate—to 2.36—the hospital where such communication is least adequate.

(2) The six responses to the question about the amount of communication are scored from "1" to "6." "Less than ¼ hour per week" is scored as "1," whereas, at the other extreme, "more than 4 hours per week" is scored as "6." The range of the means is from 3.73—the hospital where the nurses talk most with their immediate superiors—to 2.79—where the nurses talk least with their immediate supervisors.

(3) The five responses to the question about frequency of communication

with respect to the seven items of communication are scored from "1" to "5." "Once a month or less often" is scored as "1," whereas "once a day or more often"—the other extreme—is scored as "5." The hospital means for the seven items range as follows: from 2.00 to 2.86 concerning communication about patient care; 1.25 to 2.06 concerning nursing supervision; 2.83 to 3.71 concerning work; 1.07 to 1.81 concerning employee wages and hours; 1.31 to 1.87 concerning relations between departments; 1.57 to 2.18 concerning satisfaction and morale; and from 2.47 to 3.58 concerning things outside the organization.

(4) Two questions relate to the qualitative aspects of communication. The five responses to the first question are scored from "1" ("Always or nearly always . . .") to "5" ("Seldom or never . . ."). The hospital means range from 2.50 to 3.65. The five responses to the second question are scored from "1" ("Always or nearly always") to "5" ("Seldom or never"). The hospital means for the items on the second question range across hospitals as follows: from 2.06 to 2.86 for the item about explaining things; 2.46 to 3.35 for the item about asking for suggestions; 2.29 to 3.45 for the item asking for information; 4.50 to 4.89 for the item about criticism; and 4.39 to 4.95 for the item about unnecessary information or comments. The researchers do not present the ranges for the first two items, "shows appreciation" and "gives direction."

(5) The second question about informal communication is used to calculate the extent to which communication is concentrated in formal channels. There seem to be four steps involved in this computation. First, hospital means are computed for each of the seven items of the questions. No ranges are presented for these computations. Second, hospital means for each of the seven items are then subtracted from the hospital means for each of the seven items collected with respect to the frequency of communication. These subtractions are possible because the questions have identical formats; the only difference is that the question about frequency is concerned with formal communication rather than informal communication. Third, the larger the difference between the means for an item for a hospital, the greater the concentration of communication in formal channels. Fourth, the ten hospitals are ranked by the extent to which communication is concentrated in the formal channels; these rankings are then used to verify the predicted propositions. Similar computations are not performed for the first question, which collects information about informal communication; nor are any ranges presented for the first question. The third question cited in connection with informal communication is used in connection with the direction of communication, the sixth aspect of communication investigated.

(6) The response alternatives to the question about the direction of communication do not form a scale like the previous questions; therefore, percentages instead of means are used to indicate direction of communication in the various hospitals. The data obtained from this question show that, of all nurses in all hospitals combined, 51 percent say that the person with whom they talk most is at the same level as they are; 20 percent say that this person is at a lower level; 22 percent say that this person is their immediate

superior; and the remaining seven percent say that this person is at a higher level but that the person is not their immediate superior. The corresponding percentage figures for the individual hospitals range, respectively, as follows: from 24 percent to 70 percent; from zero percent to 36 percent; from four percent to 48 percent; and from zero percent to 21 percent.

Validity. Georgopoulos and Mann made ten predictions with respect to the relationship between communication and role performance. Eight of these ten predictions are confirmed.

Reliability. The study contains no data relevant to reliability.

Comments. (1) Georgopoulos and Mann's definition of communication—the transmission of information—is the same as this handbook's. (2) Georgopoulos and Mann distinguish six aspects of communication: adequacy, amount, frequency, qualitative, informality, and direction. This handbook has no distinctions that correspond to the researchers' "adequacy" and "amount." "Frequency," as used by the researchers, refers to task-relevant communication (communication about ways to improve patient care) and thus corresponds very closely to this handbook's instrumental communication. The first question Georgopoulos and Mann use to collect information about the "qualitative" aspect of communication—the frequency with which the immediate superior expresses appreciation—corresponds very closely to this handbook's expressive communication, especially its normative component. The second question about qualitative communication refers both to instrumental and expressive communication. Georgopoulos and Mann, like this handbook, distinguish "formal-informal" and "vertical-horizontal" communication. However, the researchers focus exclusively on personal communication and ignore impersonal communication. Most organizational research refers only to communication and does not distinguish types of communication; therefore, Georgopoulos and Mann are to be applauded for the distinctions they make. Personal communication is probably more important for organizational effectiveness than impersonal communication; however, impersonal communication, like the mass media in the larger society, is significant and should not be totally ignored. (3) Three of the researchers' questions contain hospital references—amount, frequency, and informality (the second question). These questions will have to be modified slightly to be of general use in organizational research. (4) It is generally easy to understand the researchers' computations. However, their usual clarity is absent when they present the computations with respect to the extent to which communication is concentrated in formal channels. These computations will have to be simplified if Georgopoulos and Mann's instruments are to be widely used by organizational researchers.

Source. Basil S. Georgopoulos and Floyd C. Mann, *The Community General Hospital* (New York: Macmillan, 1962), pp. 1–88 and 500–543.

2. Lawler, Porter, and Tennenbaum

Description. The purpose of this study is to explore the possibility of gathering data to link certain kinds of managerial attitudes to specific behavioral episodes. Specifically, the study investigates managerial feelings toward communication-type interaction episodes. The study was conducted in five organizations. One is a large manufacturing plant with over 3,000 employees. The other four are local social service agencies—a YMCA, a visiting nurse service, a girl scout council, and a city department of health. The sample includes 105 middle-level and lower-level managers. Thirty-four of the managers are middle-level and 71 are lower-level. The lower-level managers are on the lowest level of management and are generally the first line of supervision. The middle-level managers are in positions above the first level of supervision, but below the vice-presidential, company officer, or major departmental head level. Fifty of the managers are from the manufacturing plant; the other 55 managers are employed by the four local social service agencies. The 105 managers represent about 40 percent of the lower-level and middle-level managers employed by the manufacturing plant and all of the managers employed by the social service organization.

Definition. The term "behavioral episode" is defined as "any situation that has an integrity of its own" (e.g., a meeting, a telephone conversation, etc.).[9]

Data Collection. Each respondent is asked to complete a number of self-recording forms. Figure 6–1 is a reproduction of the self-recording form. Each respondent is given a copy of instructions for completing the form. The instructions are not reproduced in the article. The researchers held a meeting with the respondents to describe the methods of data collection.

Computation. The behavioral episodes are measured by the three following percentages: types of contacts reported; within-organization contacts that involve superiors, peers, and subordinates; and self-, other-, and both-initiated contacts. Table 6–1 is an example of one of the sets of percentages.

TABLE 6–1   Percentage of Types of Contacts Reported

Type of Contact	% Manufacturing Company	% Social Service
Groups	33	14
Individual	40	41
Telephone	14	28
Letter	6	8
Records	5	10

Validity. (1) The researchers predicted that the managers would evaluate

TIME   OTHERS INVOLVED_____

FROM_____TO_____

1. TYPE OF CONTACT   2. POSITION OF OTHERS INVOLVED

_____ Letter or Memo   _____ Superiors
_____ Discussion in Group   _____ Subordinates
_____ Discussion with <u>one</u>   _____ Peers
        individual   _____ Outsiders in Upper Management
_____ Telephone   _____ Outsiders in Middle Management
_____ Records or Reports   _____ Outsiders in Lower Management
_____ Other   _____ Other Outsiders
                                     _____ None

3. TYPE OF ACTIVITY   4. CONTACT INITIATED BY

_____ Production/Operations   _____ Self
_____ Sales/Distribution   _____ Other
_____ Personnel/Industrial
        Relations
_____ Public Relations/
        Advertising
_____ General Administration
_____ Research and Development
_____ Engineering
_____ Finance/Accounting
_____ Other

5. PURPOSE OF EPISODE

	Information or Advice	Instructions or Decisions
Giving		
Receiving		
Creating		

6. ATTITUDE TOWARD EPISODE

Valuable	:_:_:_:_:_:_:	Worthless
Dissatisfying	:_:_:_:_:_:_:	Satisfying
Boring	:_:_:_:_:_:_:	Interesting
Precise	:_:_:_:_:_:_:	Vague
Challenging	:_:_:_:_:_:_:	Not Challenging

FIGURE 6-1   Copy of the Self-Recording Form.

episodes they initiated more highly than episodes initiated for them. This prediction is confirmed by the data. (2) The researchers find that managers evaluate contacts with their superiors more highly than contacts with their subordinates. This finding, while not predicted, corresponds with the results of other research.

Reliability. The study contains no data relevant to reliability.

Comments. (1) The referent of Lawler, Porter, and Tennenbaum's "behavioral episode" seems to approximate closely the referent of this handbook's "communication." The fifth question of the self-recording form refers to "information or advice" and "instructions or decisions." These terms would seem to be encompassed by the handbook's "information." (2) The researchers do not explicitly distinguish types of communication. However, three implicit distinctions are contained on the self-reporting form. The first question on the self-recording form implicitly distinguishes personal and impersonal communication; the second question on the form implicitly distinguishes vertical and horizontal communication; and the fifth question implicitly distinguishes cognitive information ("information or advice") from normative information ("instructions or decisions"). The self-recording form has no questions that provide a means to distinguish formal and informal communication. (3) The researchers should have provided a copy of the instructions for completing the self-recording form. Replication of a study cannot proceed without the instruments of data collection. The concluding chapter of this handbook discusses the problem of including instruments in articles. (4) The sample of the study consists of middle-level and lower-level managers. Further research will have to be performed before it can be determined whether or not the self-recording form can be used as a method of data collection for top-level managers, nonmanagerial white-collar employees, and blue-collar employees. The form may only have limited utility for many types of blue-collar employees.

Source. Edward E. Lawler, III, Lyman W. Porter, and Allen Tennenbaum, "Managers' Attitudes Toward Interaction Episodes," *Journal of Applied Psychology*, 52 (December, 1968), 432–439.

Further Sources. 1. T. Burns, "The Directions of Activity and Communication in a Department Executive Group: A Quantitative Study in a British Engineering Factory with a Self-Recording Technique," *Human Relations*, 7 (1954), 73–97.[10]

2. Lyman W. Porter, "A Study of Perceived Need Satisfaction in Bottom and Middle Management Jobs," *Journal of Applied Psychology*, 45 (February, 1961), 1–10.

3. Lyman W. Porter, "Job Attitudes in Management: I. Perceived Deficiencies in Need Fulfillment as a Function of Job Level," *Journal of Applied Psychology*, 46 (December, 1962), 375–384.

NOTES

1. This definition of communication is based on *Control in Organizations*, ed. Arnold S. Tannenbaum (New York: McGraw-Hill, 1968), p. 129.
2. A slightly-modified version of this typology of communication is used in prop-

ositions in James L. Price, *Organizational Effectiveness* (Homewood, Ill.: Irwin, 1968), pp. 163–183.

3. The italics are in the original version of the questionnaire. All of the italics that appear in the instrument are in the original version of the questionnaire.

4. In the original questionnaire, the scoring for each response immediately follows the dash. The scoring is included in this manner in every section of the instrument for this type of question.

5. In the original questionnaire, the scoring for each response is located immediately beneath the response. The scoring is included in this manner in every section of the instrument for this type of question.

6. In the original questionnaire, numbers are included within each of these parentheses. Numbers are found in the original questionnaire within all parentheses in this type of question.

7. Rather than dashes to be checked, the original questionnaire contained boxes. Each question of this type in the instrument uses boxes rather than dashes. Dashes are simpler to construct than boxes—thus the dashes in this handbook.

8. This number is not included in the original questionnaire. Numbers of this type that appear in the instrument as presented in this handbook are not found in the original questionnaire.

9. Edward E. Lawler, III, Lyman W. Porter, and Allen Tennenbaum, "Managers' Attitudes Toward Interaction Episodes," *Journal of Applied Psychology*, 52 (December, 1968), p. 433.

10. Lawler, Porter, and Tennenbaum's self-reporting form is an adaptation of an earlier self-reporting form used by Burns.

COMPLEXITY

7

Definition. *Complexity* is the degree of structural differentiation within a social system. A highly complex organization, for example, is characterized by many levels of authority, a large number of occupational roles, and many subunits (divisions and departments). *Vertical* and *horizontal complexity* may be distinguished. The number of levels of authority illustrates vertical complexity, whereas the number of occupational roles and the number of subunits illustrates horizontal complexity.[1] Material relevant to vertical complexity is found in discussions of "flatness-tallness," "configuration," and "social stratification." Discussions of "division of labor," "specialization," "role differentiation," "fragmentation," "segmentation," "fractionalization," "job enlargement," "work simplification," "functional differentiation," "social differentiation," and "departmentalization" contain information pertinent to horizontal complexity.

The different dimensions of complexity are often treated as separate concepts. This is especially true of the number of levels of authority (most commonly treated as "flatness-tallness") and the number of occupational roles (most commonly treated as "division of labor"). There is little agreement among organizational researchers on conceptualizing complexity either as a single concept with a series of dimensions—such as proposed by this handbook —or as a series of separate concepts—as a number of researchers favor. This handbook favors a single concept with a series of dimensions because it logically relates hitherto disparate elements. The levels of authority and the division of labor, quite disparate concepts in the study of organizations, are logically related as types of complexity.[2]

The term "complexity" is sometimes used to designate the "importance of skills" in a social system.[3] When defined in this manner, complexity is measured by such indicators as the number of occupational specialties, the length of training required for each, and the degree of professional activity associated with it. This handbook treats the importance of skills under a different concept, routinization. Routinization is discussed in a later chapter.

Organizational researchers are much concerned with horizontal complexity, especially the number of occupational roles ("division of labor"). Some researchers, however, define the division of labor differently than this handbook. Two alternate definitions are used. First, Rushing defines the division of labor in terms of the distribution of individuals among the different occupations.[4] The more equal the distribution, the greater the division of labor. Consider two organizations, each with ten occupational roles. One organization has 90 percent of its members in a single occupation, whereas the second organization has its members equally distributed throughout the ten occupations. Rushing would classify the division of labor as greater in the second organization. This handbook, because it defines the division of labor as the number of occupational roles rather than the distribution of individuals among these roles, would classify the two organizations as having the same division of labor. Second, Pugh and his colleagues define the division of labor (which they term "specialization") as " . . . the distribution of official duties among a number of positions . . . ."[5] The conceptualization, however, excludes the "workflow activities of the organization," and thus limits the division of labor to what this handbook terms the administrative staff. These two definitions are advanced by reputable researchers and are viable alternatives to the conceptualization advanced by this handbook. However, this handbook's conceptualization seems to represent the majority position with respect to the division of labor. Where there is agreement with respect to a concept, this handbook generally follows this agreement in the hope of standardizing concepts.

Some organizational researchers include a dispersion dimension ("ecology" is the common label) in their conceptualization of complexity.[6] This practice does not seem to be widespread and is thus not followed by this handbook. Dispersion is treated as a separate concept later.

Measurement. The first selection (Hall, Haas, and Johnson) provides some indicators for the number of subunits (this is one dimension of horizontal complexity) and the number of levels of authority (vertical complexity). The Hall, Haas, and Johnson measures, however, provide no indicators for the division of labor, another dimension of horizontal complexity. The second selection (Indik) provides a measure for the division of labor.

THE MEASURES

1. HALL, HAAS, AND JOHNSON

Description. This study investigates the relationship between size, complexity, and formalization. Seventy-five organizations were studied. The organizations range in size from six members to over 9,000 members. They represent a wide range of types, such as educational, commercial, military, governmental, manufacturing, religious, and penal organizations. The researchers collected their information from "top management."[7]

Definition. Complexity is defined as " . . . the degree of internal segmentation —the number of separate 'parts' of the organization as reflected by the division of labor, number of hierarchical levels, and the spatial dispersion of the organization . . . ."[8]

Data Collection. The data for the study were collected by tape-recorded interviews and the study of documents ("printed matter"). The exact questions asked in the interviews and the specific documents used are not included in the study.

Computation. Four sets of computations are provided. First, there is the general division of labor. Two subcategories are provided within the general division of labor, the number of goals (1, 2, and 3 or more) and the presence of a second major activity ("No second activity" and "Second activity present"). Second, there is the specific division of labor. Three subcategories are provided within the specific division of labor: number of major divisions (1–4, 5–6, and 7 or more), divisions within most specialized single department (1–3 subdivisions, 4–6 subdivisions, and 7 or more subdivisions), and mean number of subdivisions per department (1 or 2 subdivisions, 3 subdivisions, and 4 or more subdivisions). Third, there is hierarchical differentiation. Two subcategories are provided within hierarchical differentiation, the number of levels in deepest single division (two or three levels, four levels, and five or more levels) and the mean number of levels for the organization as a whole (two or three and four or more). Four, there is spatial dispersion. Four subcategories are provided within spatial dispersion: dispersion of physical facilities (All in one location, Mostly in one location, some in field, and Mostly in field—dispersed[9]), location of physical facilities (1 location, within city or county, and state-national-international), degree of dispersion of personnel (All in one location, Mostly at one location, some in field, and Mostly in field—dispersed[10]), and location of personnel (1 location, within city or county, and state-national-international).

The four sets of computations (general division of labor, specific division of labor, hierarchical differentiation, and spatial dispersion) are treated separately. Table 7–1 indicates how the general division of labor is related to size.

TABLE 7–1   General Division of Labor, By Organizational Size

General Division of Labor	Size		
	Less than 100 ($N = 20$)	100–999 ($N = 35$)	1,000 or more ($N = 20$)
1. Number of Goals		Percentage	
1	30	29	20
2	45	46	45
3 or more	25	25	35
2. Presence of Second Major Activity			
No Second Activity	65	69	70
Second Activity Present	35	31	30

Kendall's Tau C is used as a measure of association. For the relationship between the number of goals and size, Kendall's Tau C is .08. A Kendall's Tau C of .04 is obtained for the relationship between the presence of a second major activity and size.

Validity. The study indicates that there is a slight tendency for larger organizations to be more complex. The strongest relationships are found between size and hierarchical differentiation. The researchers view their findings as similar to those of previous research.

Reliability. The study contains no data relevant to reliability.

Comments. (1) The referent for Hall, Haas, and Johnson's "degree of internal segmentation" is similar to and different from the referent for this handbook's "degree of structural differentiation." Hall, Haas, and Johnson's "specific division of labor" and "hierarchical differentiation" correspond, respectively, to this handbook's "number of subunits" and "vertical complexity." The researchers view the "general division of labor" in terms of the number of goals, whereas the handbook views the division of labor in terms of the "number of occupations." The researchers also include "spatial dispersion" as part of their degree of internal segmentation, whereas this handbook does not include this idea in its degree of structural differentiation. (2) It is unfortunate that the researchers never reproduce their instruments of data collection, because replication is impossible without these. The concluding chapter of this handbook discusses the problem of including instruments in articles. (3) The researchers are to be commended for the care they have exercised in the collection of data with respect to the number of levels of authority (what they term "hierarchical differentiation"). Most organizational research which deals with this concept simply states that the number of levels must be counted. This injunction ignores the fact that the number of levels varies at different places in the organization. The researchers have thoughtfully anticipated this difficulty and have created two subcategories of the "number of levels in deepest single division" and the "mean number of levels for organization as a whole." (4) Additional information concerning "assistants" and "secretaries" should have been provided in order to make clear the number of levels of authority.[11] The researchers, for example, should indicate how assistants and secretaries enter into their computations. (Assistants and secretaries do not generally count as different levels of authority.) (5) The data with respect to validity may be stronger than the researchers indicate. If "general division of labor" and "spatial dispersion" are ignored (and this is reasonable because most researchers do not define complexity by these dimensions), then "specific division of labor" and "hierarchical differentiation" are the remaining dimensions. These remaining dimensions are where the evidence is strongest about a relationship between size and complexity.

Source. Richard H. Hall, J. Eugene Haas, and Norman J. Johnson, "Organizational Size, Complexity, and Formalization," *American Sociological Review*, 32 (December, 1967), 903–912.

2. INDIK

Description. This study investigates the relationship between organizational size and membership participation. Three sets of data are used. First, there is a set of 32 delivery organizations varying in size from 15 to 61 members. All members of these organizations are male. Second, there is a set of 36 automobile sales dealership organizations varying in size from 25 to 132 members. The various dealerships, while independently owned, operate within certain common policies of the supplying firm concerning the basic objective of profitable sales and the servicing of cars and trucks. Virtually all members of these organizations are male; there are a few females in clerical positions, however. Third, there is a set of 28 units of a voluntary association; these units vary in size from 101 to 2,989 members. Each unit operates within the policies of the parent national association toward the goal of increasing citizen participation in political activities. All members of this association are female.

Definition. Specialization is defined in terms of "varied job content." The less varied the job content, the greater the specialization.

Data Collection. The data for this study were taken from the research archives of the Survey Research Center of the University of Michigan. The study is thus a secondary analysis. Both organizational records and questionnaires were used to collect the data in the original research. However, Indik reproduces neither the records nor the questionnaires.

Computation. Specialization is measured by the number of different job titles. The more job titles, the greater the specialization.

Validity. Indik predicted that a high degree of specialization would produce a low degree of satisfaction that would, in turn, produce a low degree of membership participation. The prediction is confirmed for the delivery organization and the automobile dealerships, but not for the voluntary associations. However, the results for the voluntary associations are in the right direction, but are not significant.

Reliability. The study contains no data relevant to reliability.

Comments. (1) Indik's "specialization" corresponds partially to this handbook's "horizontal complexity." An organization with a great many different job titles will be characterized by a great many occupational roles. Horizontal complexity, as conceptualized in this handbook, refers to the number of occupational roles and the number of subunits. (2) It is unreasonable to expect a secondary analysis to reproduce the instruments of data collection used in the original research. This deficiency of secondary analysis not only prevents replication, but it leaves the reader uncertain about the direction in which to proceed. Indik, for example, measured specialization by counting the number of different job titles. However, what is a "different job title?" Would "Personnel Technician I" and "Personnel Technician II" be counted as one or two job titles?[12] This uncertainty would have been removed if Indik could have reproduced his instruments of data collection.

Source. Bernard P. Indik, "Organization Size and Member Participation," *Human Relations*, 18 (1965), 339–349.

Further Source. Bernard P. Indik, "Organization Size and Member Participation" (unpublished Ph.D. dissertation, Ann Arbor, Michigan, University of Michigan, 1961).[13]

ADDITIONAL READINGS

1. Peter M. Blau, Wolf V. Heydebrand, and Robert E. Stauffer, "The Structure of Small Bureaucracies," *American Sociological Review*, 31 (April, 1966), 179–191.[14]
2. Peter M. Blau, "The Hierarchy of Authority in Organizations," *American Journal of Sociology*, 73 (January, 1968), 453–467.
3. David J. Hickson, D. S. Pugh, and Diana C. Pheysey, "Operations Technology and Organization Structure: An Empirical Appraisal," *Administrative Science Quarterly*, 14 (September, 1969), 378–397.[15]
4. Marshall W. Meyer, "Two Authority Structures of Bureaucratic Organization," *Administrative Science Quarterly*, 13 (September, 1968), 211–228.
5. Marshall W. Meyer, "Automation and Bureaucratic Structure," *American Journal of Sociology*, 74 (November, 1968), 256–264.
6. D. S. Pugh, D. J. Hickson, C. R. Hinings, and C. Turner, "Dimensions of Organizational Structure," *Administrative Science Quarterly*, 13 (June, 1968), 65–105.
7. Richard A. Schoenherr and Judith Fritz, "Some New Techniques in Organization Research," *Public Personnel Review*, 28 (July, 1967), 156–161.
8. Richard E. Stauffer, Peter M. Blau, and Wolf V. Heydebrand, "Organizational Complexities of Public Personnel Agencies," *Public Personnel Review*, 27 (April, 1966), 83–87.

NOTES

1. This conceptualization of complexity has been very much influenced by the work of Blau and his colleagues. The Additional Readings at the end of the chapter cite the relevant research.

2. This handbook typically separates such concepts as "bureaucracy," "organizational climate," and "primary-secondary" social relationships into a series of separate concepts. (These concepts are discussed, respectively, in the chapters on administrative staff, alienation, and formalization.) This pattern is not violated in the treatment of complexity. The different conceptual elements of bureaucracy, for example, are not logically related to a more general concept as types of bureaucracy; the assumption is merely that the different conceptual elements cohere as a unit and this unit is labeled "bureaucracy." The levels of authority and the division of labor, on the other hand, are types of a' more general concept, complexity. The number of subunits is also a type of complexity. Parallels for this handbook's treatment of complexity are found in the chapters on communication, satisfaction, and succession.

3. See, for example, Jerald Hage and Michael Aiken, *Social Change in Complex Organizations* (New York: Random House, 1970), pp. 15–18. The following articles are also relevant: Jerald Hage and Michael Aiken, "Program Change and Organizational Properties: A Comparative Analysis," *American Journal of Sociology*, 72 (March, 1967), 503–519; Jerald Hage and Michael Aiken, "Relationship of Centralization to Other Structural Properties," *Administrative Science Quarterly*, 12 (June, 1967), 72–92; and Michael Aiken and Jerald Hage, "Organizational Interdependence and Intra-Organizational Structure," *American Sociological Review*, 33 (December, 1968), 912–930.

4. See, for example, William A. Rushing, "The Effects of Industry Size and Division of Labor on Administration," *Administrative Science Quarterly*, 12 (September, 1967), 273–295 and William A. Rushing, "Hardness of Material as Related to Division of Labor in Manufacturing Industries," *Administrative Science Quarterly*, 13 (September, 1968), 229–245.

5. D. S. Pugh, D. J. Hickson, C. R. Hinings, and C. Turner, "Dimensions of Organizational Structure," *Administrative Science Quarterly*, 13 (June, 1968), 65–105 (esp. pp. 72–73).

6. An example of complexity that includes a dispersion dimension is Richard H. Hall, J. Eugene Haas, and Norman J. Johnson, "Organizational Size, Complexity, and Formalization," *American Sociological Review*, 32 (December, 1967), 903–912 (esp. pp. 905–906).

7. The source of this information is not contained in the article, but in a private communication by Hall to this handbook.

8. Hall *et al.*, *op. cit.*, p. 906.

9. The word "dispersed" is within parentheses in the article.

10. The word "dispersed" is within parentheses in the article.

11. This type of data is provided by Pugh and his associates. See Pugh *et al.*, *op. cit.*, p. 104. The data are found in the "height" component of "configuration."

12. This example comes from Peter M. Blau, Wolf V. Heydebrand, and Robert E. Stauffer, "The Structure of Small Bureaucracies," *American Sociological Review*, 31 (April, 1966), 179–191 (esp. p. 181).

13. Indik's article is based on the data contained in his dissertation.

14. The following readings should be viewed as a unit because they all refer to research performed by Blau and his colleagues at the University of Chicago: Nos. 1, 2, 4, 5, 7 and 8. Not cited because it appeared too late to be included in

this handbook is Peter M. Blau and Richard A. Schoenherr, *The Structure of Organizations* (New York: Basic Books, 1971).

15. Readings 3 and 6 should be viewed as a unit because all of the researchers were, at one time or another, members of the Industrial Administration Research Unit, University of Aston, Birmingham, England.

CONSENSUS

8 _____

Definition. *Consensus* is the degree of agreement on values among the members of a social system.[1] There would be a high degree of consensus in a university, for example, if all its members—faculty, students, and administrators—were highly committed to the value of teaching and research in the learned disciplines. Material relevant to consensus is found in discussions of "integration," "moral integration," "moral diversity," and "normative consensus."

Consensus is often used to refer, not to agreement on values, but to agreement on culture.[2] Culture in this context refers to values, beliefs, and sentiments. The more restrictive meaning is adopted by this handbook because attempts to measure consensus generally define the concept in terms of agreement on values.

Measurement. The Allport-Vernon-Lindzey questionnaire is perhaps the instrument most often used to measure values in organizational research. The measurement selection for this chapter (Tagiuri) uses the Allport-Vernon-Lindzey questionnaire.

Tagiuri's study is different from the previous selections in this handbook in two ways. First, it is based on an instrument whose wide usage has made possible the compilation of a manual describing the instrument. The description of Tagiuri's study uses the manual and its accompanying test booklet. Tagiuri does not, of course, reproduce the instrument in his article. Second, Tagiuri's study is different because it is based on an instrument which is not limited to organizations. Up to this point, all of the measures selected have been designed primarily for use in organizations. The Allport-Vernon-Lindzey questionnaire is used because organizational researchers have designed no measures for use in organizations.

THE MEASURE

TAGIURI

Description. This study investigates the amount of difference in value orientations among executives, research managers, and scientists. The executives are 555 American businessmen who attended the Advanced Management Program at Harvard University between 1960 and 1964. These executives achieved their positions through traditional routes (manufacturing, sales, finance, and so forth). The research managers are 236 members of the Industrial Research Institute who attended research and development management seminars at Harvard in 1961, 1962, or 1963. These managers, who were in charge of research personnel and units, began their careers as scientists or engineers. The scientists are 204 men who have been in industry for at least seven years with no management responsibilities except the supervision of research assistants.

Definition. Kluckhohn's definition of values is used by Tagiuri, that is, a value is a conception of the desirable.[3] However, Tagiuri does not have a term, such as "consensus," for his concern with differences in value orientations.

Data Collection. The Allport-Vernon-Lindzey questionnaire was used to collect data about the value orientations of the executives, research managers, and scientists. This questionnaire can be purchased as a "test booklet" for respondents to use; the booklet is twelve pages long and is entitled *Study of Values.* Unfortunately, permission to reproduce the questionnaire items in the booklet could not be obtained.

Computations. Instructions for the computations are included at the end of the test booklet to allow the respondent to score himself. They are as follows:

1. First make sure that every question has been answered. *Note:* If you have found it impossible to answer all the questions, you may give equal scores to the alternative answers under each question that has been omitted; thus, Part I. 1½ for each alternative. The sum of the scores for (a) and (b) must always equal 3.
   Part II. 2½ for each alternative. The sum of the scores for the four alternatives under each question must always equal 10.
2. Add the vertical columns of scores on each page and enter the total in the boxes at the bottom of the page.
3. Transcribe totals from each of the foregoing pages to the columns on p. 80. For each page enter the total for each column (R, S, T, etc.) in the space that is labeled with the same letter. Note that the order in which the letters are inserted in the columns on following page differs for the various pages.
4. Add the totals for the six columns. Add or subtract the correction figures as indicated.
5. Check your work by making sure that the total score for all six columns equals 240. (Use the margins for your additions, if you wish.)
6. Plot the scores by marking points on the *vertical lines* in the graph on the next page.[4] Draw lines to connect these six points.

The scoring system is designed so that the total for the six values (theoretical, economic, aesthetic, social, political, and religious) is always 240 points. It is the distribution of these points over the six values that is important. What

Page Totals	Theo-retical	Eco-nomic	Aes-thetic	Social	Po-litical	Re-ligious	The sum of the scores for each row must equal the figure given below.
Part I Page 3	(R)	(S)	(T)	(X)	(Y)	(Z)	24
Page 4	(Z)	(Y)	(X)	(T)	(S)	(R)	24
Page 5	(X)	(R)	(Z)	(S)	(T)	(Y)	21
Page 6	(S)	(X)	(Y)	(R)	(Z)	(T)	21
Part II Page 8	(Y)	(T)	(S)	(Z)	(R)	(X)	60
Page 9	(T)	(Z)	(R)	(Y	(X)	(S)	50
Page 10	(R)	(S)	(T)	(X)	(Y)	(Z)	40
Total							240
Correction Figures	+2	−1	+4	−2	+2	−5	
Final Total							240

the questionnaire shows is the relative strength the six values have within a particular individual's value system.

Tagiuri computes means and standard deviations for each of the six values for the executives, research managers, and scientists. The distribution of the means makes it possible to discover the relative strengths of each of the six values for the executives, research managers, and scientists. The closer the agreement of the means for each of the six values, the greater the similarity in values between the three groups of respondents.

Validity. Tagiuri finds that while the value profiles of these three groups (executives, research managers, and scientists) vary in the differentiation of their value systems, the relative order of their values is very similar. Evidence from the literature would predict the differences, but not the essential similarity, between these three groups.

More adequate data about validity are contained in the manual which accompanies the text booklet. The questionnaire has been standardized on a college population and the manual presents collegiate averages (referred to as "norms"). "... Common experience leads us to expect," according to the manual, "that women will on the average be more *religious, social,* and *aesthetic* than men. We likewise expect students of engineering by and large to stand relatively high in *theoretical* and *economic* values ...."[5] In nearly all cases, according to the collegiate averages contained in the manual, the high and low scores correspond well to prior expectations.[6]

Reliability. Tagiuri's study contains no data which are relevant to reliability. However, the manual presents three sets of relevant data. First, it reports a set of split-half reliability coefficients. The items measuring each value are divided into two subscales. Table 8–1, for a sample group, contains the product-moment correlations (Spearman-Brown).

TABLE 8–1 Split-Half Reliability Coefficients

	$(N = 100)$
Theoretical	.84
Economic	.93
Aesthetic	.89
Social	.90
Political	.87
Religious	.95

The mean reliability coefficient, using a z transformation, is .90. Second, the manual reports an item analysis. The manual makes the following comments about this analysis:

> Successive revisions of the test have shown that each *theoretical* item is positively associated with the total score derived from all the *theoretical* items, and that the items for each of the other values likewise hang together consistently. The final item analysis—carried out on a group of 780 subjects of both sexes from six different colleges—shows a positive correlation for each item with the total score for its value, significant at the .01 level of confidence.[7] (Emphasis not supplied.)

Third, the manual reports some repeat reliability coefficients. These measures are determined for two populations, one after an interval of one month, the other after an interval of two months. The coefficients for the two populations are contained in Table 8–2.

TABLE 8–2 Repeat Reliability Coefficients

	One Month 1951 $(N = 34)$	Two Months 1957 $(N = 53)$
Theoretical	.87	.85
Economic	.92	.84
Aesthetic	.90	.87
Social	.77	.88
Political	.90	.88
Religious	.91	.93

The mean repeat reliability coefficient, using the z transformation, is .89 for the one-month study and .88 for the two-month interval.

Comments. (1) Tagiuri's concern, differences in values, corresponds to this handbook's conceptualization of consensus. The only difference is that Tagiuri never assigns a label to the object of his concern. (2) Standard deviations should be used as measures of consensus. The smaller the standard deviations for each of the six values on the Allport-Vernon-Lindzey questionnaire, the greater the consensus of the organization. Tagiuri computes standard deviations; however, his focus on value differences among executives, research managers, and scientists prompted him to use means for purposes of comparison.

Sources. 1. G. W. Allport, P. E. Vernon, and G. Lindzey, *Manual for the Study of Values* (Boston: Houghton Mifflin, 1960).
2. G. W. Allport, P. E. Vernon, and G. Lindzey, *Study of Values* (Boston: Houghton Mifflin, 1960).
3. Renato Tagiuri, "Value Orientations and the Relationship of Managers and Scientists," *Administrative Science Quarterly*, 10 (June, 1965), 39–51.

Further Sources. 1. Ralph M. Hower and Charles D. Orth, 3rd, *Managers and Scientists* (Boston: Division of Research, Graduate School of Business Administration, Harvard, 1963).
2. Anne Roe, *The Psychology of Occupations* (New York: Wiley, 1956).
3. Renato Tagiuri, "Value Orientations of Managers and Scientists," in *Administering Research and Development*, ed. Charles D. Orth, 3rd, Joseph C. Bailey, and Francis W. Wolek (Homewood, Ill.: Irwin and Dorsey, 1964).

ADDITIONAL READINGS

1. Edwin A. Fleishman and David R. Peters, "Interpersonal Values, Leadership Attitudes, and Managerial 'Success,'" *Personnel Psychology*, 15 (Summer, 1962), 127–143.
2. L. V. Gordon, *Manual for Administering the Survey of Interpersonal Values* (Chicago: Science Research Associates, 1960).[8]
3. William D. Litzinger, "Interpersonal Values and Leadership Attitudes of Branch Bank Managers," *Personnel Psychology*, 18 (Summer, 1965), 193–198.
4. Charles Morris, *Varieties of Human Values* (Chicago: University of Chicago Press, 1956).

NOTES

1. The concept of consensus is very important in sociological research. See, for

example, Talcott Parsons, *The Structure of Social Action* (Glencoe, Ill.: The Free Press, 1949).

2. See, for example, Edward Gross, "Symbiosis and Consensus in Small Groups," *American Sociological Review*, 21 (April, 1956), 174–179.

3. Clyde Kluckhohn, "Values and Value-Orientations in the Theory of Action: An Exploration in Definition and Classification," in *Toward a General Theory of Action*, ed. Talcott Parsons and Edward A. Shils (Cambridge: Harvard, 1954), pp. 388–433 (esp. p. 395).

4. The graph referred to in this sentence is not included in this handbook. The graph is a "profile of values" and is found in the test booklet.

5. G. W. Allport, P. E. Vernon, and G. Lindzey, *Manual for the Study of Values* (Boston: Houghton Mifflin, 1960), p. 13.

6. An older form of the questionnaire was extensively validated. The sources for this extensive validation are cited in the manual.

7. Allport *et al.*, *op. cit.*, p. 9.

8. Gordon's instrument is used in readings 1 and 3.

COORDINATION

Definition. *Coordination* is the degree to which each of the various interdependent parts of a social system operates according to the requirements of the other parts and of the total system.[1] "Integration," "conflict," and "cooperation" are terms commonly used to designate the subject matter of this chapter.[2]

Measurement. Few organizational studies contain measures of coordination. Like communication, the importance of coordination is much emphasized, but seldom measured. A notable exception is Georgopoulos and Mann's study of community general hospitals which is, by all odds, the most theoretically and methodologically sophisticated treatment of coordination in the literature. The Georgopoulos and Mann study is also used for its measurement of communication.

THE MEASURE

GEORGOPOULOS AND MANN

Description. This study investigates the determinants of organizational effectiveness by studying ten community general hospitals. The following sample of respondents was used to collect information about coordination: nonmedical department heads, the hospital administrator, supervisory and nonsupervisory registered nurses, medical staff members with and without administrative responsibilities, and x-ray and laboratory technicians. Two units of analysis are used, the hospitals and the departments of nursing. Only the data that use the hospital as the unit of analysis are used for the measurement of coordination.

Definition. This handbook uses Georgopoulos and Mann's definition of coordination. The researchers also distinguish four major types of coordination: corrective, preventive, regulatory, and promotive. Two general classes are also used, programmed coordination and general coordination.

Data Collection. The data for the measurement of coordination were collected by questionnaires. Two sets of questions are used. First, a set of seven questions are used to collect data about the four major types and two general classes of coordination. Second, a set of two questions are used to collect specific data about the reliability of the first set of seven questions. The first set of seven questions are as follows:

1. How well do the different jobs and work activities around the patient fit together, or how well are all things geared in the direction of giving good patient care? (Check one.)

   ___Perfectly

   ___Very well

   ___Fairly well

   ___Not so well

   ___Not at all well[3]

2. To what extent do the people from the various interrelated departments make an effort to avoid creating problems or interference with each other's duties and responsibilities? (Check one.)

   ___To a very great extent

   ___To a great extent

   ___To a fair extent

   ___To a small extent

   ___To a very small extent

3. To what extent do people from different departments who have to work together do their job properly and efficiently without getting in each other's way? (Check one.)[4]

4. In general, how do the patients feel about how smoothly the various personnel around them work together? (Check one.)

   ___The patients feel that the personnel work together completely smoothly

   ___The patients feel that the personnel work together very smoothly

   ___The patients feel that the personnel work together fairly smoothly

   ___The patients feel that the personnel do not work together smoothly

   ___The patients feel that the personnel do not work together smoothly at all

5. To what extent are all related things and activities well timed in the everyday routine of the hospital? (Check one.)

    ____All related things and activities in the everyday routine are perfectly timed

    ____They are very well timed

    ____They are fairly well timed

    ____They are not so well timed

    ____They are rather poorly timed

6. How well planned are the work assignments of the people from the different departments who work together? (Check one.)

    ____Extremely well planned

    ____Very well planned

    ____Fairly well planned

    ____Not so well planned

    ____Not well planned at all

7. In general, how well established are the routines of the different departments that have to work with one another? (Check one.)

    ____Their routines are extremely well established

    ____Very well established

    ____Fairly well established

    ____Not too well established

    ____Their routines are not well established

The two questions used only as reliability measures are as follows:

1. In your opinion, to what extent has this hospital been able to achieve *singleness of direction* in the efforts of its many groups, departments, and individuals?[5] (Check one.)

    ____To a very great extent

    ____To a considerable extent

    ____To a fair extent

    ____To a small extent

    ____To a very small extent

2. How well do the different jobs and work activities around the

patient fit together, or how well are all things geared in the direction of giving good patient care? (Check one.)

____Perfectly

____Very well

____Fairly well

____Not so well

____Not at all well

Computation. Three general sets of computations, each with different steps, are involved. Consider the computations with respect to the first set of seven questions.

(1) For each of the seven questions and for each hospital in the study, the following steps are taken: (a) The responses are scored from "1" to "5." The lower the score, the more favorable the coordination. No ranges are presented for these questions. (b) Means for individual hospitals are then computed for each of the seven questions. (c) Finally, each hospital is rank-ordered according to its score on each of the seven questions. Seven rank orderings are thus obtained.

(2) Four overall measures of coordination are obtained from the previously described measures. (a) Each of the ten hospitals has a rank for each of the seven questions. A mean of these seven ranks is computed to obtain the first overall measure of coordination. (b) Each of the ten hospitals has a mean for each of the seven questions. A mean of these seven means is computed to yield the second overall measure of coordination. (c) The third overall measure is also based on a mean of the means. However, only the means for the first four questions are used. (d) The fourth overall measure is a mean of the means, but involves only those for the last three questions.

(3) Two questions are included in the questionnaire to obtain data regarding reliability; the third set of computations relates to these two questions. These two questions are scored like the first seven. The means for the first of these two questions range from 2.06 to 2.68; the means for the second question range from 1.60 to 2.68.

Validity. Georgopoulos and Mann use coordination as a dependent and independent variable. The information summarized below relates only to the use of coordination as a dependent variable. Six sets of determinants of coordination are considered. The researchers offer the following summary of their predictions concerning these six sets of determinants: ". . . nearly all of our initial hypotheses as to the . . . determinants of organizational coordination received strong empirical support from the data. . . ."[6]

Reliability. Georgopoulos and Mann present four sets of data about the reliability of their measures. (1) Rank-order intercorrelations among the seven questions are presented. The seven questions intercorrelate positively. Moreover, 15 of the 21 possible correlations are statistically significant. (2) The hospitals are rank-ordered according to their score on each of the four overall measures of coordination. The four measures intercorrelate highly. The rank-order correlation between any two of the four measures is .90 or higher, which is statistically significant beyond the .01 level. (3) Rank-order correlations between the four overall measures of coordination and their component items are presented. Each of the four overall measures correlates positively and significantly with all of its components. (4) The seven specific measures and the four overall measures are intercorrelated with the two questions designed exclusively for the measurement of reliability. The results show empirically that singleness of direction—the first of the two reliability questions—is positively and significantly related to the seven specific measures and the four overall measures; all 11 possible correlations are statistically significant at the .05 level or better. The results for the second reliability question are similar to those obtained for the first question. The four overall measures of coordination correlate .72, .75, .81, and .62, respectively, with how well the efforts of hospital members and groups are tied together toward providing the best possible patient care, the second reliability question. These relationships are statistically significant at better than the .05 level. The seven specific measures of coordination also correlate positively with the second reliability question; the particular coefficients range from .43 to .70. Five of these seven correlations are significant beyond the .05 level.

Comments. (1) There are no conceptual problems involved because this handbook has adopted Georgopoulos and Mann's definition of coordination. Georgopoulos and Mann's measures of coordination are thus appropriate to this handbook's concept of coordination. (2) Georgopoulos and Mann's work on the types of coordination is especially valuable. Their typology is not used by this handbook because it is not used widely in organizational literature. In this instance, the literature lags behind Georgopoulos and Mann. The researchers also distinguish four major types and two general classes of coordination. It will probably be advisable, in the long run, to have a single typology of coordination rather than two different typologies. (3) Three of Georgopoulos and Mann's seven specific questions (1, 4, and 5) refer either to patients or to hospitals and will have to be modified slightly to be used in other types of organizations. (4) Georgopoulos and Mann only partially presented the second question used to collect information about reliability. This handbook searched for the complete question in the questionnaire included in the Appendix. The question found there is similar to the one included in the text. However, there is some question as to whether or not the question is exactly the one that Georgopoulos and Mann used. This problem would have been avoided had the researchers reproduced completely, in the text, all of their questions. (5) Georgopoulos and Mann weight the responses to the seven specific questions about coordination according to "sampling ratio intervals."[7] This handbook could not determine how this weighting is performed; therefore, it is not included among the computations. (6) The measures appears to have adequate validity and reliability. The researchers are to be especially applauded for their detailed findings about reliability. Most of the measures in this handbook contain no data relevant to reliability. It is thus especially gratifying to find a study that treats the topic in such an exemplary fashion.

Source. Basil S. Georgopoulos and Floyd C. Mann, *The Community General Hospital* (New York: Macmillan, 1962), pp. 1–88 and 265–364.

ADDITIONAL READINGS

1. Paul R. Lawrence and Jay W. Lorsch, *Organization and Environment* (Boston: Graduate School of Business Administration, Harvard, 1967).[8]
2. Paul R. Lawrence and Jay W. Lorsch, "Differentiation and Integration in Complex Organizations," *Administrative Science Quarterly*, 12 (June, 1967), 1–47.
3. Jay W. Lorsch, *Product Innovation and Organization* (New York: Macmillan, 1965).
4. Jay W. Lorsch and Paul R. Lawrence, "Organizing for Product Innovation," *Harvard Business Review*, 43 (January/February, 1965), 109–122.

NOTES

1. This definition of coordination comes basically from Basil S. Georgopoulos and Floyd C. Mann, *The Community General Hospital* (New York: Macmillan, 1962), p. 273.
2. Georgopoulos and Mann, however, distinguish coordination and cooperation. See *Ibid.*, pp. 272–273.
3. The original version of the questionnaire has numbers, included within parentheses, immediately following each of the dashes. The numbers indicate the weights assigned to the different responses. Each of the questions used to collect information about coordination includes these numbers.
4. The response alternatives for this question are the same as the response alternatives for the preceding question.
5. The italics are in the original version of the questionnaire.
6. Georgopoulos and Mann, *op. cit.*, p. 342.
7. *Ibid.*, p. 283.
8. These four readings constitute a single measure of coordination.

DISPERSION

10

Definition. *Dispersion* is the degree to which the membership of a social system is spatially distributed.[1] If all the members of an organization, for example, work at a single location, then spatial distribution is at the minimum; on the other hand, if each member of an organization works at a separate location, then spatial distribution is at the maximum. The dispersion of most organizations, of course, falls somewhere between these two extremes. The concept of dispersion is sometimes discussed under the headings of "geographic contiguity," "location," and "ecology."

"Ecology" is the label most commonly used in organizational literature to discuss what this handbook terms "dispersion." It is, however, awkward to state that organization X has more ecology than organization Y. Therefore, despite the more commonly used ecology label, the subject matter of this chapter is referred to as dispersion. It is interesting to note that the awkward formulation (more or less ecology) implied in the ecology label does not seem to appear in organizational literature. It is simpler to state that organization X is more dispersed than organization Y.

Organizational literature focuses, not on the distribution of the membership, but on the distribution of the operating sites.[2] This customary focus seems to be misplaced. It is probably the distribution of the membership, rather than the distribution of the operating sites, that most significantly influences the social structure of the organization. An organization can have many operating sites, but if almost all of its membership is concentrated at a single site, then this organization will probably be no different in terms of its basic social structure than an organization with only a single operating site. Therefore, organizational research should focus on the spatial distribution of the members rather than on the spatial distribution of the operating sites.

Dispersion should be distinguished from centralization and complexity. The distribution of power (centralization) within an organization can vary independently of the distribution of the membership. A widely distributed membership probably creates a situation favorable to a low degree of centralization; however, there is nothing inevitable about such a relationship, especially with modern communication mechanisms (the telephone, for example) at the disposal of organizations.[3] The distribution of the membership—dispersion—must thus be distinguished from the distribution of power—centralization.

The chapter on complexity indicates that some organizational researchers include a dispersion dimension to complexity.[4] There is, of course, no reason why complexity should not have a dispersion dimension. However, the custom in organizational literature is to distinguish the degree of structural differentiation—complexity—from the degree of spatial distribution of the membership—dispersion. In this instance, unlike the situation with respect to the conceptualization of dispersion, there seems to be no compelling reason to depart from the customary focus of the literature.

Measurement. There are a number of measures of dispersion in organizational literature. However, most of these measures focus on the distribution of the operating sites, as could be anticipated from the customary conceptualization of dispersion. Some of the "measures" are not even measures since, instead of assigning numbers to observations, they merely classify the observations.[5] In short, the measurement situation with respect to dispersion is not very promising. A study by Haas, Hall, and Johnson contains a measure rather than a classification, and a measure that might be used for further research on the measurement of dispersion.

THE MEASURE

HAAS, HALL, AND JOHNSON

Description. This study investigates the relative size of the supportive component ("administrative staff" from the perspective of this handbook) and its relation to size, age, number of operating sites, diversification of activities performed, and type of organizational function. The data for the study come from 30 organizations, selected so as to obtain an extensive range of organizational types. Executives from the 30 organizations supplied the data for the study.

Definition. The number of operating sites is defined as ". . . the number of physical locations apart from the central office which were staffed and maintained by the organization . . ."[6] Persons, such as salesmen, who reported to the central office are counted as part of the central office.

Data Collection. The data were collected by means of interviews. The study does not reproduce the questions asked in the interviews to obtain the information about the number of operating sites.

Computation. Numbers are assigned to each operating site. The range is from 1 to 98.

Validity. Haas, Hall, and Johnson predicted a positive relationship between the number of operating sites and the relative size of the supportive component. The predicted relationship is not confirmed by the data.

Reliability. The study contains no data relevant to reliability.

Comments. (1) The number of operating sites—Haas, Hall, and Johnson's concept—does not correspond to the distribution of the membership—this handbook's concept. Nor do Haas, Hall, and Johnson use the term dispersion to refer to their concept, the operating sites. Therefore, this handbook's concept and term does not correspond to Haas, Hall, and Johnson's concept and term. (2) The researchers are to be congratulated on the fact that they have carefully defined operating sites. Much research with respect to this topic falsely assumes that the meaning of operating sites is self-evident. (3) The number of operating sites could be used as a measure of the distribution of the membership: the greater the number of sites, the greater the distribution of the membership. With this measure, there is still the possibility that an organization could have many sites, but still have nearly all its members located at a single site. This concentration at a single site would be very different from an organization with the same number of sites, but which evenly distributes its members among these sites. If the number of operating sites is used as a measure of membership distribution, then care must be taken to consider the evenness of the distribution among the sites. The more even the distribution, the more dispersed the membership. (4) The researchers should have reproduced the instrument they used to collect information about the number of operating sites. Much organizational research, however, fails to reproduce the instrument of data collection. The problem of including instruments in articles is discussed in the concluding chapter of this handbook. (5) The validity and reliability of the measure of number of operating sites is not adequate. The researchers, however, provide one of the few studies that can be used to build an adequate measure of dispersion.

Source. J. Eugene Haas, Richard H. Hall, and Norman J. Johnson, "The Size of the Supportive Component in Organizations: A Multi-Organizational Analysis," *Social Forces*, 42 (October, 1963), 9–17.

ADDITIONAL READINGS

1. Isabel Blain, *Structure in Management* (London: National Institute of Industrial Psychology, 1964).
2. Richard H. Hall, J. Eugene Haas, and Norman J. Johnson, "Organizational Size, Complexity, and Formalization," *American Sociological Review*, 32 (December, 1967), 903–912.
3. Harold Stieglitz, "Optimizing the Span of Control," *Management Records*, 24 (September, 1962), 25–29.[7]
4. John G. Udell, "An Empirical Test of Hypotheses Relating to Span of Control," *Administrative Science Quarterly*, 12 (December, 1967), 420–439.

NOTES

1. This definition comes from Robert K. Merton, *Social Theory and Social Structure* (Glencoe, Ill.: The Free Press, 1968), p. 376. Merton's term, however, is "ecology" rather than "dispersion."

2. One notable exception is Richard H. Hall, J. Eugene Haas, and Norman J. Johnson, "Organizational Size, Complexity, and Formalization," *American Sociological Review*, 32 (December, 1967), 903–916.

3. The Forest Service has a membership that is widely dispersed but that is fairly highly centralized. See Herbert Kaufman, *The Forest Ranger* (Baltimore, Md.: Johns Hopkins, 1960). Note that Kaufman does not view the Forest Service as fairly highly centralized. Unfortunately, measures do not exist which could resolve this difference in interpretation.

4. An example is Hall *et al., op. cit.*

5. Some definitions of measurement would include these classifications. See, for example, Allen H. Barton, *Organizational Measurement* (New York: College Entrance Examination Board, 1961), p. 1. This handbook's definition of measurement is set forth in the first chapter.

6. J. Eugene Haas, Richard H. Hall, and Norman J. Johnson, "The Size of the Supportive Component in Organizations: A Multi-Organizational Analysis," *Social Forces*, 42 (October, 1963), p. 14.

7. The third and fourth readings should be viewed as a single unit because Udell uses a measure of "geographical contiguity" that is similar to the measure used by Stieglitz.

DISTRIBUTIVE JUSTICE

11

Definition. Distributive justice is defined in terms of sanctions. Therefore, sanctions must first be defined.

Sanctions are the social resources used by a social system to obtain conformity to its norms from its members.[1] Examples of sanctions are the use of coercion (force), the distribution of economic goods, and the bestowal of praise or blame. Organizational literature discusses sanctions under such headings as "incentives," "compensation," "rewards," "punishment," "social stratification," and "organizational climate."[2]

Sanctions are often defined in terms of gratification-deprivation.[3] Whatever gratifies an individual is a positive sanction and whatever deprives an individual is a negative sanction. This type of subjective conceptualization of sanctions is very similar to the concept of "satisfaction" (see chapter 19). It is sufficient to note at this point that this handbook defines sanctions in objective terms.

Three aspects of sanctions may be distinguished. 1) the amount of sanctions at the disposal of a social system; 2) the degree to which the sanctions are evenly distributed among the members of a social system (this aspect of sanctions is most often discussed under the heading of "social stratification"); and 3) the structure of the sanctions in a social system. Distributive justice refers to the third aspect of sanctions.

Distributive justice is the degree to which conformity to the norms of a social system is followed by the receipt of positive sanctions from the social system. A high degree of distributive justice exists when a high degree of conformity is followed by the receipt of a high amount of positive sanctions; similarly, a high degree of distributive justice also exists when a low degree of conformity is followed by the receipt of a low amount of positive sanctions. Conversely, a low degree of distributive justice exists when conformity is not followed by the receipt of positive sanctions or when deviance is followed by the receipt of positive sanctions. It is the ratio of conformity to positive sanctions that is basic to distributive justice; the absolute amounts of conformity and positive sanctions must be viewed in a relational perspective. Material relevant to distributive justice is found in discussions of the following topics: "equity theory," "balance theory," "cognitive dissonance," "congruence," "status equilibration," "status crystallization," "merit," and "ascription-achievement" (sometimes referred to as "quality-performance").

The concept of distributive justice is an ancient one. The term "distributive justice" comes from the work of Homans and is adopted by this handbook because of its wide usage.[4] Homans, however, discusses distributive justice with economic terminology;[5] this handbook, on the other hand, discusses distributive justice with sociological terminology, especially from the work of Merton.[6] The sociological terminology is probably more widely used in organizational literature than the economic terminology.

Distributive justice, as defined, does not refer to perceptions of the members; it refers to an objective situation.[7] There is, of course, a difference between a situation of distributive justice and the perception of that situation. An organizational member may, for example, conform to the norms of the system and receive positive sanctions—yet he may not perceive of himself as being positively sanctioned. Conversely, an organizational member may not conform and receive negative sanctions—yet he may perceive of himself as being positively sanctioned.

Two concepts may ultimately be required, one for the objective situation and the other for the perceptions of the membership. This would be similar to the situation with respect to "centralization" and "alienation" discussed earlier. Centralization refers to the objective distribution of power, whereas alienation refers to the perception of this distribution. Until these two concepts are commonly distinguished in the literature, this handbook will follow Homans' and Merton's objective conceptualization of distributive justice.[8]

Measurement. A number of researchers provide measures appropriate to distributive justice. However, many of these measures are used in experiments and cannot be adapted readily to an organizational setting.[9] A study by Porter and Lawler provides the best organizational measure of distributive justice and is the study selected for this handbook.

THE MEASURE

PORTER AND LAWLER

Description. This study investigates the relationship between attitudes and behavior. The specific focus is upon job attitudes and job behavior. The study was carried out in seven organizations, three of which are divisions of state governments and are subject to civil service procedures. The other four are privately owned manufacturing and utility companies. The sample from these seven organizations consists of 563 middle-level and lower-level managers.

Definition. One of the important attitudes studied by Porter and Lawler is the "perceived probability that pay depends upon job performance factors." Pay is defined as the total income received from the organization; pay thus includes basic salary, fringe benefits, and special incentive income. With respect to job performance, the focus is upon the quality and the amount of effort expended.

Data Collection. The attitude data for the study were obtained by questionnaire. The following instructions[10] are used to collect information about the "perceived probability that pay depends upon job performance factors:"

In the section below, you will see several characteristics or qualities that are often used to determine individuals' pay. Please indicate how important your organization considers these for determining *your* present pay. This can be done by using the seven-point scale below each characteristic, which looks like this:

(unimportant) 1   2   3   4   5   6   7 (important)

You are to circle the number on the scale that represents the importance of the characteristic being rated. Low numbers represent low or unimportant characteristics. If you think your organization considers a given characteristic as unimportant in determining the pay for your management position, you would circle numeral 1. If you think it is "just a little" important, you would circle numeral 2, and so on. For each scale circle only one number.

Please do not omit any scales.

1. Quality of your job performance.
   (unimportant)   1   2   3   4   5   6   7   (important)
2. Your productivity on the job.
   (unimportant)   1   2   3   4   5   6   7   (important)
3. Amount of effort you expend on the job.
   (unimportant)   1   2   3   4   5   6   7   (important)

Computation. The three questions are used to construct an index. Each manager's response to the three questions is summed. The higher a manager scores on the index, the higher the perceived probability that for him pay depends upon job performance. No index scores, such as averages and standard deviations, are presented; the information presented refers merely to "high probability" and "low probability." In the computations, the three state government organizations are combined and treated as a single unit; the four business firms are also combined and treated as a unit. There is thus a "government sample" and a "private sample."

Validity. The study develops a model that contains a series of seven predictions concerning the relationship between job attitudes and job performance. Six of the seven predicted relationships are supported by the data.

Reliability. Porter and Lawler compute a series of correlation coefficients among the three questions designed to collect information concerning the managers' perception of the importance of job performance factors in determining their pay. These coefficients are contained in Table 11–1. The intercorrelations among the items in both samples are high.

TABLE 11–1   Correlation among Questions Designed to Collect Information about Managers' Perceptions of the Importance of Job Performance Factors in Determining Their Pay

	Government Sample		Private Sample	
	Q. 2	Q. 3	Q. 2	Q. 3
Question 1 Quality of Job Performance	.80*	.66*	.71*	.50*
Question 2 Productivity on the Job		.67*		.61*
Question 3 Amount of Effort Expended on the Job				

*$p < .01$

Comments. (1) Porter and Lawler's research may be viewed as the use of subjective data to investigate an objective situation. Their focus is on the "perceived probability that pay depends upon job performance." "Perceived probability" refers, of course, to subjective data. However, "pay and job performance" have situational referents. Pay (total income received from the organization) is an important type of positive sanction, whereas job performance (quality of job performance and the amount of effort expended) is an important type of conformity. Positive sanctions and conformity are thus more general concepts than pay and job performance and the data collected by Porter and Lawler can be viewed as subjective data to measure an objective situation of distributive justice. (2) One of the outstanding features of this investigation by Porter and Lawler is that they study distributive justice—to use the term adopted by this handbook—as a part of an explicit theory indicating relationships between attitudes and behavior. Their theory enables them to make a series of seven predictions concerning the relationships between job attitudes and job behavior. The reader is thus spared the torture of abstracting an implied theory from a mass of empirical data. (3) The measures advanced by the researchers appear to have adequate validity and reliability. Since most organizational research includes no data relevant to reliability, it is pleasing to note the researchers' treatment of this topic.

Source. Lyman W. Porter and Edward E. Lawler, III, *Managerial Attitudes and Performance* (Homewood, Ill.: Irwin, 1968), 1–97.

Further Sources. The bibliography at the end of Porter and Lawler's book contains additional studies that are relevant to the one included in this handbook. The following article, however, is relevant, but is not cited there: Edward E. Lawler, III, "Managers' Attitudes Toward How Their Pay Is and Should Be Determined," *Journal of Applied Psychology*, 50 (August, 1966), 273–279.

ADDITIONAL READINGS

1. J. Stacy Adams and William B. Rosenbaum, "The Relationship of Worker Productivity to Cognitive Dissonance About Wage Inequities," *Journal of Applied Psychology*, 46 (June, 1962), 161–164.[11]

2. J. Stacy Adams, "Wage Inequities, Productivity and Work Quality," *Industrial Relations*, 3 (October, 1963), 9–16.

3. J. Stacy Adams, "Toward an Understanding of Inequity," *Journal of Abnormal and Social Psychology*, 67 (November, 1963), 422–436.

4. J. Stacy Adams and Patricia R. Jacobsen, "Effects of Wage Inequities on Work Quality," *Journal of Abnormal and Social Psychology*, 69 (July, 1964), 19–25.

5. J. Stacy Adams, "Inequity in Social Exchange," in *Advances in Experimental Social Psychology*, ed. Leonard Berkowitz (New York: Academic Press, 1965), pp. 267–299.

6. J. Stacy Adams, *A Study of the Exempt Salary Program* (Crotonville, N.Y.: Management Development and Employee Relations Services, General Electric, no date).

7. C. Norman Alexander, Jr. and Richard L. Simpson, "Balance Theory and Distributive Justice," *Sociological Inquiry*, 34 (Spring, 1964), 182–192.[12]

8. Bo Anderson, J. Berger, B. P. Cohen, and M. Zelditch, Jr., "Status Classes in Organization," *Administrative Science Quarterly*, 2 (September, 1966), 264–283.

9. Bo Anderson, Joseph Berger, Morris Zelditch, Jr., and Bernard P. Cohen, "Reactions to Inequity," *Acta Sociologica*, 12 (1969), 1–21.

10. Bo Anderson and Robert R. Shelly, "Reactions to Inequity, II: A Replication of the Adams Experiment and a Theoretical Reformulation," (East Lansing, Michigan: Department of Sociology, College of Social Science, Michigan State University, 1969).

11. Joseph Berger, Morris Zelditch, Jr., and Bo Anderson, *Sociological Theories in Progress* (Boston: Houghton Mifflin, 1966), pp. 244–294.

12. Peter M. Blau, "Justice in Social Exchange," *Sociological Inquiry*, 34 (Spring, 1964), 193–206.

13. A. Friedman and P. Goodman, "Wage Inequity, Self-Qualifications, and Productivity," *Organizational Behavior and Human Performance*, 2 (November, 1967), 406–417.

14. P. Goodman and A. Friedman, "An Examination of the Effect of Wage Inequity in the Hourly Condition," *Organizational Behavior and Human Performance*, 3 (August, 1968), 340–352.

15. George C. Homans, "Status Among Clerical Workers," *Human Organization*, 12 (Spring, 1953), 5–10.

16. George C. Homans, "Social Behavior as Exchange," *American Journal of Sociology*, 63 (May, 1958), 597–606.

17. George C. Homans, *Social Behavior* (New York: Harcourt, Brace World, & 1961).

18. Martin Patchen, *Study of Work and Life Satisfaction* (Ann Arbor, Mich.: Survey Research Center, University of Michigan, 1959).

19. Robert D. Pritchard, "Equity Theory: A Review and Critique," *Organizational Behavior and Human Performance*, 4 (May, 1969), 176–211.

20. Karl E. Weick, "The Concept of Equity in the Perception of Pay," *Administrative Science Quarterly*, 2 (December, 1966), 414–439.

21. A. Zaleznik, C. R. Christensen, and F. J. Roethlisberger, *The Motivation, Productivity, and Satisfaction of Workers* (Boston: Graduate School of Business Administration, Harvard, 1958).

22. Morris Zelditch, Jr., Joseph Berger, Bo Anderson, and Bernard P. Cohen, "Equitable Comparisons," *Pacific Sociological Review*, 13 (Winter, 1970), 19–26.

NOTES

1. This is a slightly modified version of Smelser's definition of sanctions. See Neil J. Smelser, *Essays in Sociological Explanation* (Englewood Cliffs, N.J.: Prentice-Hall, 1968), pp. 10 and 149–150.

2. A discussion of "organizational climate" is contained in the chapter on alienation.

3. An example of this definition of sanctions is found in Neal Gross, Ward S. Mason, and Alexander W. McEachern, *Explorations in Role Analysis* (New York: Wiley, 1958), p. 65.

4. George C. Homans, *Social Behavior* (New York: Harcourt, Brace & World, 1961), pp. 232–264.

5. J. Stacy Adams, whose work is cited at the end of the chapter under Additional Readings, also defines distributive justice (he terms it "equity") with economic terminology.

6. Robert K. Merton, *Social Theory and Social Structure* (Glencoe, Ill.: The Free Press, 1968), pp. 244–246. Merton's concept and terminology is also used in Elinor G. Barber, *The Bourgeoisie in 18th Century France* (Princeton, N.J.: Princeton, 1955).

7. J. Stacy Adams defines "equity" in subjective terms. See especially J. Stacy Adams, "Toward an Understanding of Inequity," *Journal of Abnormal and Social Psychology*, 67 (November, 1963), 422–436.

8. Litwin and Stringer's term "reward"—the feeling of being rewarded for a job well done—is a subjective counterpart to this handbook's concept of distributive justice. See George H. Litwin and Robert A. Stringer, *Motivation and Organizational Climate* (Boston: Graduate School of Business Administration, Harvard, 1968), p. 82. The concept of "organizational climate" is discussed in the chapter on alienation.

9. This comment is especially applicable to the work of J. Stacy Adams.

10. The original version of the questionnaire has six additional "characteristics or

qualities." The three "characteristics or qualities" selected for this handbook are those that are relevant to distributive justice.

11. The following readings relate to the work of J. Stacy Adams and should thus be viewed as a single unit: Numbers 1–6, 8–11, 13–14, 19–20, and 22. Pritchard's article (No. 19) provides a good review of equity theory. The articles by Pritchard and Weick (No. 20) provide a critical analysis of equity theory.

12. Readings that relate to the work of George C. Homans and should thus be viewed as a single unit are: Nos. 7, 12, 15, 16, 17, and 21. The article by Alexander and Simpson (7) relates distributive justice and balance theory. The article by Blau (12) criticizes Homans' concept of distributive justice.

EFFECTIVENESS

12

Definition. *Effectiveness* is the degree to which a social system achieves its goals.[1] For example, a prison, which has a custodial goal, and which has a low escape rate among its inmates, would be considered an effective prison. Or again, a mental hospital, which has a therapeutic goal, and which successfully releases a high proportion of its inmates into the community, would be considered an effective mental hospital. The subject matter of this chapter is also commonly discussed in organizational literature under the headings of "performance" and "organizational success."

Effectiveness must be distinguished from efficiency.[2] A business firm, whose goal is profits as measured by the rate of return on investments, may attain a high degree of efficiency ("productivity"), but, due to a declining market, experience a low degree of effectiveness, that is, a low rate of return on its investments. Effectiveness and efficiency are probably positively related; however, the two concepts are different and can vary independently.

The definition of "goals" is crucial in the definition of effectiveness. Etzioni's definition is widely accepted: "An organizational goal is a desired state of affairs which the organization attempts to realize. . . ."[3] Those who define effectiveness in terms of the degree of goal-achievement typically equate "goal," "objective," "purpose," "mission," "aim," and "task." This handbook's approach to effectiveness, sometimes referred to as the "goal approach," is the customary one.[4]

This approach has been criticized by those who use the "system resource approach."[5] The system resource approach defines effectiveness, not with respect to the degree of goal-achievement, but in terms of the ability of the organization to exploit its environment in the acquisition of scarce and valued resources. According to this approach, the greater the ability of the organization to exploit its environment, the greater its effectiveness.

The most serious criticism made of the goal approach by those who use the system resource approach pertains to goal-identification. If the goals of an organization cannot be distinguished, as suggested by those who use the system resource approach, then effectiveness cannot be measured because, as previously indicated, the goal approach defines effectiveness in terms of the degree of goal-achievement. Those who use the system resource approach are certainly correct to emphasize the difficulty that the goal approach has with goal-identification. However, this problem is reduced to manageable proportions if the focus of research is on the organizational goal that the major decision-makers actually pursue, and if data are collected about the intentions and activities of the major decision-makers.

Measurement. The users of the goal approach do not have general measures of effectiveness.[6] Many measures exist, but they are applicable only to limited types of organizations. For example, some measure of profitability, such as profits as a percentage of net worth, is commonly used to study the effectiveness of business organizations. This measure of profitability is applicable to other business organizations, provided that accounting procedures are well standardized. However, profits as a percentage of net worth are of no assistance in the study of effectiveness in other types of organizations, such as hospitals, schools, and government agencies. On the other hand, studies of hospitals, schools, and government agencies use measures of organizational effectiveness which are limited, respectively, to hospitals, schools, and government agencies. General measures of effectiveness are urgently needed.

Georgopoulos and Mann's study of community general hospitals, whose measures of communication and coordination are used elsewhere in this handbook, contains a measure of effectiveness that might be adapted for general use. The measure is included in the hope that such an adaptation will be made.

THE MEASURE

GEORGOPOULOS AND MANN

Description. This study investigates the determinants of organizational effectiveness. The setting for the study is ten voluntary, nonprofit, nongovernmental, nondenominational, short-stay, community general hospitals. A total of 880 respondents supplied information for the measure of effectiveness. There are four classes of respondents: medical staff, registered nursing staff, technicians (laboratory and x-ray), and the administrative group (hospital administrators, nonmedical department heads, and the members of the executive committees of the boards of trustees of the hospitals).

Definition. "Organizational effectiveness," to Georgopoulos and Mann, "says something about how well an organization is doing in achieving its objectives. . . ."[7]

Data Collection. Georgopoulos and Mann collected information for four measures of effectiveness: nursing care, medical care, noncomparative overall patient care, and comparative overall patient care. This handbook focuses on the third measure—noncomparative overall patient care—because this measure seems to have the greatest potential for adaptation as a general measure.

The bulk of the data for overall patient care (the "noncomparative" is dropped to simplify the presentation) were collected by means of a question-naire. Some data were collected by means of interviews to check the validity of the questionnaire data; however, the focus here is on the main instrument, the questionnaire. The following question is used to collect information regarding overall patient care:

> On the basis of your experience and information, how would you rate the quality of *overall care* that the patients generally receive from this hospital?[8] (Check one.)
>
> ____Overall patient care in this hospital is outstanding
>
> ____Excellent
>
> ____Very good
>
> ____Good
>
> ____Fair
>
> ____Rather poor
>
> ____Overall patient care in this hospital is poor[9]

Computation. Scores of "1" to "7" are assigned to each of the seven responses. The lower the score, the better the overall patient care. These scores are then used to compute arithmetic means, by hospital, for each of the four categories of respondents (medical staff, registered nursing staff, technicians, and ad-ministrators) separately and combined. The combined hospital scores range from 1.99 to 2.94. The study does not present separate ranges, by hospital, for each of the four categories of respondents.

Validity. (1) The ten hospitals differ in the quality of the overall care they provide their patients. As indicated in the preceding paragraph, the scores range from 1.99 to 2.94. (2) The relative standing of the ten hospitals on overall care, as evaluated by a given category of respondent, correlates positively (though not always significantly) with the standing of the hospitals on overall care as evaluated by the other categories of respondents. The correlations for these respondents are not presented in the study. (3) The obtained inter-hospital differences on overall patient care cannot be attributed to response differences due to the particular characteristics of the medical staff and the registered nursing staff. Such control factors as shift of work, hospital division where working, full-time as against part-time work, and medical specialty do not affect differentially the evaluation of overall care by the medical staff and the registered nursing staff. (4) The volunteered remarks of respondents from each hospital, collected by interviews, are quite consistent with the ranking of the ten hospitals on the overall care measure. (5) "Customer satisfaction," as assessed by hospital personnel, is higher in those hospitals that rank better on the measure of overall patient care. (6) A positive relationship exists between the kind of reputation each hospital enjoys in the community, as assessed by hospital personnel, and the quality of overall patient care each hospital provides.

Reliability. Table 12–1 presents the intercorrelations among the four measures of hospital care used by Georgopoulos and Mann.

TABLE 12–1   Rank-Order Intercorrelations Among Four Measures of Patient Care

Patient Care Measures	1	2	3	4
1. Measure of the quality of nursing care	—	.60	.91	.82
2. Measure of the quality of medical care		—	.67	.78
3. Measure of the quality of overall care			—	.96
4. Comparative measure of the quality of overall care				—

All the intercorrelations are positive and statistically significant. Hospitals scoring high on any one measure are also likely to score high on each of the remaining measures. The degree of relationship between any two of the four measures, however, varies considerably, depending on the particular measures viewed. The highest relationship obtains between the two measures of the quality of overall care; the correlations for these measures is .96. The smallest relationship obtains between the medical care measures and the nursing care measures; the correlation for these measures is .60.

Comments. (1) Georgopoulos and Mann's definition of effectiveness is identical to the one used in this handbook. The only difference is one of terms; Georgopoulos and Mann refer to "objectives," whereas this handbook refers to "goals." (2) The question used to collect information about "overall patient care" can be readily adapted for use in other organizations. If a university, whose goal is teaching, is studied, then the following question might be used to collect information:

> On the basis of your experience and information, how would you rate the quality of teaching that the students generally receive from this university? (Check one.)
>
> _____Overall teaching in this university is outstanding
>
> _____Excellent
>
> _____Very good
>
> _____Good
>
> _____Fair
>
> _____Rather poor
>
> _____Overall teaching in this university is poor

If the university also pursues a research goal, which is typically the case, then a similar question could also be devised for research. A question could be devised for each organizational goal. (3) Georgopoulos and Mann collected information from four categories of respondents: medical staff, nursing staff, technicians, and administrators. These individuals generally are competent to evaluate the adequacy of patient care and they have the opportunity to gain knowledge about it. Equivalent individuals could be selected for other organizations. In a university, for example, information about teaching could be collected from professors, teaching assistants, and selected administrators (department chairmen and academic deans mostly). A sample of students should also be directly questioned.[10] (4) Georgopoulos and Mann's measure of overall patient care relies on information collected by questionnaires and interviews, with the main reliance on the questionnaire. The researchers use documents to check the validity of their measure of medical care. However, documents could not be used as the main instrument of data collection because the documents of the ten hospitals were not sufficiently standardized. Georgopoulos and Mann are to be commended for their use of multiple means of data collection; many researchers study effectiveness by means of a single method of data collection. Further research, however, should make more extensive use of documents. Documents may not lend themselves readily to the construction of general measures of effectiveness; however, documents are ideal instruments to validate questionnaires and interviews. (5) The validity of Georgopoulos and Mann's measure appears to be adequate. Two strong notes of caution are in order, however. (a) The researchers note that the ten hospitals differ in the quality of the overall care they provide their patients; the range is from 1.99 to 2.94. This means that the hospitals range from "Excellent" to "Very good." This does not seem to be a large range! It is, however, difficult to evaluate these statistics until the same measure has been applied to other hospitals, especially some hospitals that are "known" to be "Rather poor" and "Poor." (b) The respondents Georgopoulos and Mann use, as the third comment indicates, are both competent and knowledgeable with respect to the evaluation of the adequacy of patient care. These respondents, however, also have a vested interest in highly evaluating the effectiveness of the hospitals. Their jobs, for example, may be threatened if they evaluate the effectiveness of the hospitals as low. The trustees of the hospitals, the representatives of the community, are to be informed about the results of the research. A high degree of professionalization can, to some extent, neutralize the vested interest of the respondents. Professionals, however, often exhibit a highly developed ability to mistake their interests for the welfare of their clients. In short, the researchers must make an exceptionally strong case for the validity of their measures when vested interests are at stake. Georgopoulos and Mann devote more care to the validity of their measure than do the vast majority of organizational researchers. However, in this particular case, additional information is needed. (6) The reliability of Georgopoulos and Mann's measure is adequate. This comment is based on their four questionnaire measures of effectiveness rather than on the single measure of overall patient care, the focus of this handbook. As is the case with respect to communication and coordination, the researchers exercise an uncommon care in the evaluation of the validity and reliability of their measures.

Source. Basil S. Georgopoulos and Floyd C. Mann, *The Community General Hospital* (New York: Macmillan, 1962), pp. 1–88 and 198–264.

NOTES

1. This definition of effectiveness comes from Amitai Etzioni, *Modern Organizations* (Englewood Cliffs, N.J.: Prentice-Hall, 1964), p. 8. See also Amitai Etzioni, *A Comparative Analysis of Complex Organizations* (New York: The Free Press of Glencoe, 1961), p. 78.
2. Efficiency is discussed in the concluding chapter of this handbook.
3. Etzioni, *Modern Organizations, op. cit.,* p. 6.
4. A more extended discussion of the "goal approach" and the "system resource approach" is found in James L. Price, "The Study of Organizational Effectiveness," *The Sociological Quarterly*, 13 (Winter, 1972), 3–15. This article contains a discussion of Gross' recent research on organizational goals. A more extended discussion of this research is Edward Gross and Paul V. Grambsch, *University Goals and Academic Power* (Washington, D.C.: American Council of Education, 1968).

    An excellent introduction to the problem of measuring effectiveness is *Assessment of Organizational Effectiveness*, ed. Jaisingh Ghorpade (Pacific Palisades, Calif.: Goodyear Publishing Company, 1971). Ghorpade has conducted major research on the subject of organizational effectiveness; his work is either contained or cited in his *Assessment of Organizational Effectiveness*.
5. *Ibid.*
6. *Ibid.* Selwyn Becker, in personal conversation, argues that it is impossible to construct a general measure of organizational effectiveness. He may well be correct. However, this is an issue to be settled empirically. A sensible strategy may be to research suggested general measures—such as the one advanced in this chapter—before drawing the conclusion that it is impossible to construct a general measure of organizational effectiveness.
7. Basil S. Georgopoulos and Floyd C. Mann, *The Community General Hospital* (New York: Macmillan, 1962), p. 271.
8. The italics are in the original version of the questionnaire.
9. The original version of the questionnaire has numbers, included within parentheses, immediately following each of the dashes. The numbers indicate the weights assigned to the different responses.
10. Georgopoulos and Mann asked the hospital personnel to report on the patients' evaluation of the quality of medical care they received from the hospital. It is best to ask the patients directly to evaluate the quality of medical care that they receive. Richard Hall, in personal communication, correctly suggests that client perceptions of effectiveness are an ignored dimension in the measurement of effectiveness. The patients in the hospital are, of course, its clients.

FORMALIZATION

13 _____

Definition. *Formalization* is the degree to which the norms of a social system are explicit.[1] An organization, for example, which compiles its norms in written form will generally have a higher degree of formalization than an organization which does not compile its norms in written form. The concept of formalization is discussed under such diverse labels as the following: "rules," "procedures," "degree of structure," "degree of task structure," "segmental participation," "programming," "ambiguity," "program specification," and "primary-secondary" relationships.

The terms used to define formalization sometimes refer to the use of written norms.[2] An organization, according to this set of terms, which compiles its norms in written form is more formalized than one which does not. However, formalization should not be equated with the use of written norms. The idea is the degree to which the norms are explicit. Organizations, as indicated in the preceding paragraph, which compile their norms in written form will generally have more explicit norms than organizations which do not have such compilations. But the norms of an organization—or any other social system— can be very explicit without ever being written. Written norms may be used as a measure of formalization; however, it would be unfortunate if formalization was restricted to the use of written norms.

The concept of formalization could be included under the concept of "primary-secondary" relationships. A characteristic of secondary relationships is their contractual nature; and the crucial feature of a contract is its degree of explicitness. An attempt is made in this handbook to consider separately the different analytical components of concepts like primary-secondary relationships.[3] For example, another common analytical component of primary-secondary relationships is the degree of operation by "merit" (sometimes referred to as "ascription-achievement")[4]; this handbook includes the "merit" component of primary-secondary relationships in the previous discussion of "distributive justice." Similarly, the "contractual" component of a primary-secondary relationship (sometimes referred to as "diffuseness-specificity")[5] is included in the idea of formalization.

Measurement. Extensive research on formalization has been done at the University of Wisconsin by Aiken and Hage and at the University of Aston (Birmingham, England) by Pugh, Hickson, and their colleagues. Both groups of researchers have collected their data by interviews. However, Aiken and Hage have relied more on the traditional type of survey, whereas Pugh, Hickson, and their colleagues have relied more on documentary data. Both approaches to the study of formalization are needed and are thus included in this handbook.

THE MEASURES

1. HAGE AND AIKEN

Description. The study investigates the determinants of routine technology.[6] The data upon which it is based were collected from 16 social welfare and health organizations located in a large midwestern metropolis in 1967. Ten organizations are private; six are either public or branches of public agencies. The 16 organizations are all the larger welfare organizations that provide rehabilitation, psychiatric services, and assistance to the mentally retarded. The organizations vary in size from 24 to over 600 persons. Interviews were conducted with 520 staff members. Respondents within each organization were selected by the following three criteria: (1) all executive directors and departmental heads; (2) in departments of less than ten members, one half of the staff was selected randomly; and (3) in departments of more than ten members, one third of the staff was selected randomly. Nonsupervisory administrative and maintenance personnel are not included in the study.

Definition. Formalization is one of the hypothesized determinants of routine technology; however, there is no definition of formalization in this article. Elsewhere, however, Hage and Aiken define formalization in terms of "the importance of rules." They state that

> Giving orders is only one method for creating a unified organizational effort. An organization could not continue for very long if each operation required a decision from those who have the responsibility to make them. Organizations need daily guidelines for their operations; these guidelines are furnished by *rules*, the repository of past experience.[7] (Emphasis supplied.)

Data Collection. The data were collected by means of interviews.[8] The following fifteen questions are used:

> I'm going to read a series of statements that may or may not be true for your job in (NAME OF ORGANIZATION). For each item I read, please answer as it applies to you and your organization; using the answer categories on this next card. (SHOW CARD 1)

CARD 1

1. Definitely true
2. More true than false
3. More false than true
4. Definitely false

	Defi- nitely true	More true than false	More false than true	Defi- nitely false
1. First, I feel that I am my own boss in most matters.	___	___	___	___
2. A person can make his own decisions here without checking with anybody else.	___	___	___	___
3. How things are done around here is left pretty much up to the person doing the work.	___	___	___	___
4. People here are allowed to do almost as they please.	___	___	___	___
5. Most people here make their own rules on the job.	___	___	___	___
6. The employees are constantly being checked on for rule violations.	___	___	___	___
7. People here feel as though they are constantly being watched to see that they obey all the rules.	___	___	___	___
8. There is no rules manual.	___	___	___	___
9. There is a complete written job description for my job.	___	___	___	___
10. Whatever situation arises, we have procedures to follow in dealing with it.	___	___	___	___
11. Everyone has a specific job to do.	___	___	___	___
12. Going through the proper channels is constantly stressed.	___	___	___	___
13. The organization keeps a written record of everyone's job performance.	___	___	___	___
14. We are to follow strict operating procedures at all times.	___	___	___	___
15. Whenever we have a problem, we are supposed to go to the same person for an answer.[9]	___	___	___	___

Computation. The five following measures are constructed from the 15 questions: job codification (Questions 1–5), rule observation (Questions 6–7), rule manual (Question 8), job descriptions (Question 9), specificity of job descriptions (Questions 10–15). Replies to these fifteen questions are scored from "1" (definitely true) to "4" (definitely false). A mean is constructed for each respondent for each of the five measures of formalization. The higher the mean (a "4" is the highest mean), the higher the formalization. The researchers report no ranges for the means of the five measures. Each respondent is then classified by "social position" and, based on the first mean, a second mean is computed for each social position in the organization for each of the five measures. A social position is defined by the level or stratum in the organization and the department or type of professional activity. For example, if an agency's professional staff consists of psychiatrists and social workers, each divided into two hierarchical levels, the agency has four social positions: supervisory psychiatrists, psychiatrists, supervisory social workers, and social workers. The organizational scores for each of the five measures are determined by computing an average of all social position means in the organization.

Validity. Hage and Aiken predicted a positive relationship between routine work and formalization, that is, the more routine the work, the greater the formalization. Significant relationships are found between routine work, on the one hand, and rule manual, job description, and specificity of job description, on the other. Nonsignificant relationships, although in the predicted directions, are found between routine work, on the one hand, and job codification and rule observation, on the other hand.

Reliability. The study contains no data relevant to reliability.

Comments. (1) Hage and Aiken's concept of formalization seems to be very similar to this handbook's. An organization in which rules are important—Hage and Aiken's definition of formalization—is probably an organization in which the norms are explicitly stated—this handbook's definition of formalization. A set of rules is one way for an organization to state its norms explicitly. (2) One of Hage and Aiken's five measures is "rule observation." This measure seems to be more relevant to visibility[10] than to the "importance of rules." The attempt to increase visibility by means of surveillance[11]—and thus to obtain a high degree of rule observation—seems to be analytically different from the extent to which the rules explicitly indicate preferred courses of action.[12] The researchers' other four measures appear relevant to the importance of rules. (3) The results with respect to validity are mixed. Three of the predictions are confirmed, whereas two are not. However, the results are more positive than negative because two of the relationships, although nonsignificant, are in the predicted direction. (4) The measures of formalization may be adequate with respect to reliability; however, in the absence of any relevant data, this handbook can but note that the reliability of the measures has not been demonstrated. This article is part of a large three-wave panel study conducted by Hage and Aiken, probably the only such type of organizational study in existence. Panel studies can easily provide test-retest coefficients, and it is possible that Hage and Aiken will provide these coefficients in future reports of their significant research.

Source. Jerald Hage and Michael Aiken, "Routine Technology, Social Structure, and Organizational Goals," *Administrative Science Quarterly*, 14 (September, 1969), 366–376.

Further Sources. 1. Michael Aiken and Jerald Hage, "Organizational Alienation," *American Sociological Review*, 31 (August, 1966), 497–507.

2. Jerald Hage and Michael Aiken, "Program Change and Organizational Properties," *Americal Journal of Sociology*, 72 (March, 1967), 503–519.

3. Jerald Hage and Michael Aiken, "Relationship of Centralization to Other Structural Properties," *Administrative Science Quarterly*, 12 (June, 1967), 72–92.

4. Jerald Hage and Michael Aiken, *Social Change in Complex Organizations* (New York: Random House, 1970).

5. Richard H. Hall, "An Empirical Study of Bureaucratic Dimensions and Their Relation to Other Organizational Characteristics" (unpublished Ph.D. dissertation, Columbus, The Ohio State University, 1961).[13]

6. Richard H. Hall, "The Concept of Bureaucracy: An Empirical Assessment," *American Journal of Sociology*, 69 (July, 1963), 32–40.

2. INKSON, PUGH, AND HICKSON

Description. The aim of this study is methodological; specifically, to develop a short form of an interview schedule to represent accurately the concepts of "context" and "structure" used in previous research by Inkson, Pugh, and Hickson.[14] A long form of the interview schedule was used in previous research on 52 organizations in the English Midlands. To develop the short form, the researchers studied 40 organizations which, like the previous 52, are located in the English Midlands. Twenty-four of these organizations are manufacturing firms, whereas 16 are service organizations. Most of the service organizations are government agencies. Table 13–1 contains the size distribution of the 40 organizations.

TABLE 13–1 Manufacturing and Service Organizations, by Size

Size	Manufacturing	Service
250–499	8	2
500–999	3	3
1,000–1,999	6	4
2,000–4,999	5	3
Over 5,000 employees	2	4

Definition. In this article the term "structuring of activities" is relevant to formalization. Another article by the researchers indicates that formalization, standardization, specialization, and vertical span are encompassed by "structuring of activities."[15] Formalization is defined as " . . . the extent to which rules, procedures, instructions, and communications are written."[16]

Data Collection. Interviews were used to collect the information to measure formalization. The following parts of the interview schedule are relevant:[17]

DOCUMENTATION (formalization of role-definition)

ARE THE FOLLOWING DOCUMENTS AVAILABLE?

Obtain copies whenever possible.

(The question is whether documents are available irrespective of whether they are actually used. A document is at minimum a single piece of paper with printed, typed, or otherwise reproduced content—not handwritten. Several copies of the same piece of paper may each score as separate documents if used for separate purposes (e.g., organization A may score 3 for unrelated pieces of paper, while organization B may score 3 for a docket of carbon copies each of which is detached for a particular purpose). The problem of a single piece of paper serving separate purposes has not arisen.)

DOCUMENTS

Written CONTRACTS OF EMPLOYMENT
(obtain copies for as many grades of employee as possible—for subsequent content analysis for information given above legally required minimum)

INFORMATION BOOKLETS
(an information booklet covers a general topic or topics, such as employment conditions or safety. It is not specific to a particular job, but it can be specific to a topic, e.g., pensions):

Which categories of employee are given booklets?

_____

_____

_____

Total number of different kinds of information booklet is   _____

ORGANIZATION CHART[18]
Obtain any chart that is available. Add to it, or if no chart, sketch one, should this be necessary to obtain adequate information.

How much of total organization is included?_____

Copies are given to:_____

_____

_____

Written OPERATING INSTRUCTIONS available to the direct worker (include instructions attached to equipment)	YES	NO
Written terms of reference or JOB DESCRIPTIONS for Direct 'workers'	YES	NO
Line (workflow) Superordinates	YES	NO
Staff (other than line superordinates)	YES	NO
Chief Executive	YES	NO
MANUAL OF PROCEDURES (or standing orders)	YES	NO

Written STATEMENT OF POLICIES (excluding minutes of governing bodies) YES NO
Written WORKFLOW ('production') SCHEDULE or programme   YES NO
Written RESEARCH PROGRAMME (listing intended research work) and/or RESEARCH REPORTS (reporting work done)   YES NO

Computation. The following scoring instructions are related to the interview schedule:[19]

For each of the items, circle the number representing the appropriate score and enter this number against the item in the score column.

Item	*Score*

Written contract of employment:
    none = 0
    written contract = 1[20]	

Information booklets given to:
    none = 0
    few employees = 1
    many = 2
    all = 3	

Number of information booklets:
    none = 0
    one = 1
    two = 2
    three = 3
    four or more = 4	

Organization chart given to:
    none = 0
    Chief executive only = 1
    C.E. plus one other executive = 2
    C.E. plus most/all department heads = 3	

Written operating instructions:
    not available to direct worker = 0
    available to direct worker = 1	

Written terms of reference or job descriptions for
  direct workers:
    not provided = 0
    provided = 1	

for line (workflow) superordinates:
    not provided = 0
    provided = 1	

for staff (other than line superordinates):
    not provided = 0
    provided = 1	

Item	Score

for chief executive:
  not provided = 0
  provided = 1	

Manual of procedures:
  none = 0
  manual = 1	

Written policies:
  none = 0
  written policies = 1	

Workflow ('production') schedule or programme:
  none = 0
  schedule = 1	

Written research programme or reports:
  none = 0
  programme or reports = 1	

Total Score =	

The larger the score, the greater the formalization. Ranges for the different organizations are not provided in the article.

Validity. (1) The short form of the interview schedule was applied to the 52 organizations previously studied by means of the long form. The correlation for structuring of activities for the different forms on the same sample is .97. (2) The previous study finds a positive relationship between structuring of activities, on the one hand, and size and workflow integration, on the other. The present study of 40 organizations finds similar relationships. (3) Fourteen of the 40 organizations of the present study were also included in the previous study of the 52 organizations. The field work for the first and second studies was carried out, respectively, in 1962–1964 and 1967–1968. Two sets of scores were thus obtained by two different instruments—a long form and a short form—for the same set of 14 organizations. The product-moment correlations between the two sets of scores is .87 for structuring of activities. (4) The two studies found the same range of organizational types. (5) The researchers, based on their previous study, formulated a development sequence that predicted an increase in the structuring of activities. This increase in structuring occurred in 39 organizations; in one organization structuring remained constant.

Reliability. An item analysis is carried out for the two aspects of context and the two aspects of structure. The general biserial correlation coefficient, originally developed by Brogden,[21] is used for this item analysis. The coefficient for structuring of activities is .71.

Comments. (1) Inkson, Pugh, and Hickson—like many researchers—define formalization in terms of written communication. As indicated in the introductory section of this chapter, an organization can have a high degree of "structuring of activities" without the use of written "rules, procedures, and instructions." Therefore, it seems best to define formalization in terms of the degree of explicitness with respect to norms (rules, procedures, and instructions are examples of norms) and to use written communication as a measure of this explicitness. (2) The earlier research on the 52 organizations in the English Midlands—the study which used a long form of the interview schedule—collected information about four aspects of formalization: role definition, information passing, recording of role performance, and overall formalization.[22] The present study of 40 organizations—which used the short form of the interview schedule—collected information about one aspect of formalization, role definition. The original version of the interview schedule, described in the previous section dealing with data collection, refers to FORMALIZATION OF ROLE-DEFINITION. In the long run, the researchers may find it desirable to design a short form that encompasses the four aspects of formalization. (3) In collecting their data, the researchers relied heavily on the use of documents. This emphasis is urgently needed in contemporary organizational research, which almost exclusively relies on the collection of data by means of surveys. Documents and surveys have different strengths and weaknesses and it is best to use both methods of data collection (plus observation) to complement each other rather than to rely almost exclusively on a single method. The researchers are to be especially applauded for their extensive use of documents. Inkson, Pugh, and Hickson collected their information about documents by means of an interview schedule. Eventually, researchers will want to construct their measures directly from the documents. (4) The information that the researchers provide about validity and reliability is very adequate with respect to structuring of activities. Few organizational studies are as careful in these matters as are Inkson, Pugh, and Hickson. However, formalization is but one aspect of structuring of activities (the other aspects are standardization, specialization, and vertical span) and separate information is not presented for formalization. Therefore, it is not possible to evaluate the validity and reliability of the measures of formalization.

Source. J. H. K. Inkson, D. S. Pugh, and D. J. Hickson, "Organization Context and Structure: An Abbreviated Replication," *Administrative Science Quarterly*, 15 (September, 1970), 318–329.

Further Sources. The Industrial Administration Research Unit of the University of Aston has published a large number of articles reporting the results of its research. Unfortunately, the published work of this Research Unit is not yet available in monograph form. However, the references at the end of the present article contain the major publications of the Research Unit.

NOTES

1. This definition is based on Peter M. Blau and W. Richard Scott, *Formal Organizations* (San Francisco: Chandler, 1962), p. 7. An excellent theoretical discussion of formalization is contained in D. J. Hickson, "A Convergence in Organization Theory," *Administrative Science Quarterly*, 11 (September, 1966), 224–237.

2. An example of formalization defined in terms of written records is D. S. Pugh, D. J. Hickson, C. R. Hinings, and C. Turner, "Dimensions of Organizational Structure," *Administrative Science Quarterly*, 13 (June, 1968), 65–105.

3. This handbook discusses the practice of separating the different analytical components of concepts in connection with "bureaucracy" in the chapter on the administrative staff and the concept of "organizational climate" in the chapter on alienation.

4. Ascription-achievement (sometimes referred to as "quality-performance") is one of Talcott Parsons' pattern variables. A clear discussion of the pattern variables is found in Harry M. Johnson, *Sociology* (New York: Harcourt, Brace, & World 1960), pp. 135–141.

5. Diffuseness-specificity is another of Parsons' pattern variables. See *Ibid*.

6. Another article from the study is used by this handbook for the concept of centralization.

7. Jerald Hage and Michael Aiken, *Social Change in Complex Organizations* (New York: Random House, 1970), p. 21.

8. The information with respect to data collection comes from three sources: 1) Jerald Hage and Michael Aiken, "Routine Technology, Social Structure, and Organizational Goals," *Administrative Science Quarterly*, 14 (September, 1969), 366–376; 2) Michael Aiken and Jerald Hage, "Organizational Interdependence and Intra-Organizational Structure," *American Sociological Review*, 33 (December, 1966), 912–930; and 3) a questionnaire kindly supplied by Jerald Hage and Michael Aiken. The first source is, of course, the article selected for its measurement of formalization.

9. The instrument in this handbook is not an exact reproduction of Hage and Aiken's. Three changes are made in the questions to simplify presentation. First and second, the numbering and sequence of the questions are changed. Third, the Hage and Aiken instrument contains some questions that do not collect data on formalization; these questions are not included. However, none of these changes is significant. The Hage and Aiken instrument also contains some instructions about probing that are not included in this handbook.

10. The concept of visibility is discussed in Robert K. Merton, *Social Theory and Social Structure* (Glencoe, Ill.: The Free Press, 1968), pp. 373–376.

11. Hage and Aiken refer, not to visibility and surveillance, but only to surveillance.

12. The concept of visibility is not used in organizational research and is, therefore, not included in this handbook. There is, however, a sizeable amount of organizational research relevant to visibility. Examples are research that describes "statistical records" and "close supervision" as mechanisms of control. However, this research does not explicitly use the concept of visibility.

13. The questions for Hage and Aiken's "job codification" and "rule observation" are derived by factor analysis from two scales used by Hall, "hierarchy of author-

ity" and "rules." Hall refers to these two scales in his much cited article on bureaucracy (Further Source No. 6). Hage and Aiken also derive a third scale ("hierarchy of authority") from Hall's two scales; this third scale is described in the chapter on centralization. Hall's two scales are described in his dissertation. The construction of the scales is described in Chapter Two of the dissertation; the instruments of data collection are found in Appendix V.

14. The same article is also used by this handbook in connection with autonomy.

15. Pugh, *op. cit.*, esp. pp. 100–102.

16. *Ibid.*, p. 75.

17. The interview schedule is supplied through the courtesy of D. J. Hickson, a senior member of the Industrial Administration Research Unit. That part of the interview schedule that is relevant to formalization is slightly simplified for the sake of clarity. Nothing essential is removed from the interview schedule. The lines are in the original version of the schedule.

18. Information about the organization chart is introduced at this point from another part of the schedule.

19. The scoring instructions are not contained in the source article; they accompany the interview schedule supplied by D. J. Hickson. The scoring instructions and the interview schedule are, of course, separate documents.

20. The original version of the schedule does not contain the "none = 0" and the "written contract = 1."

21. H. E. Brogden, "A New Coefficient: Applications to Biserial Correlation and to Estimation of Serial Efficiency," *Psychometrika*, 14 (September, 1949), 169–182.

22. Pugh, *op. cit.*, pp. 100–102.

INNOVATION

14

Definition. *Innovation* is the degree to which a social system is a first or early user of an idea among its set of similar social systems.[1] A business firm that is the first to produce a new product, a university that is the first to establish a new type of curriculum, a hospital that is the first to implement a new treatment program, a military establishment that is the first to develop a new weapons system—these are examples of innovation. In literature about organizations, material relevant to innovation is found in discussions of "social change," "adaptiveness," "flexibility," "bureaucratic ossification," "ritualism," and "program change."

Innovation is a less general term than social change, that is, any modification of the social structure and/or culture of a social system. All innovation is social change, but not all social change is innovation.

This handbook's restricted definition of innovation is not common in organizational literature. Innovation is customarily equated with change in most organizational literature.[2] However, this restricted definition provides a somewhat more homogeneous range of phenomena for study than does the customary definition. And it is usually easier to construct theory about relatively homogeneous phenomena.

Measurement. The first measure (Forehand) focuses on the innovative behavior of executives. Since executives are usually the major decision-makers in organizations, it makes sense to focus on their innovative behavior. A more general approach to innovation is required, however, because executive decisions to innovate must be implemented, and typically this implementation is performed by individuals who are not executives. The second and third measures (Patchen) are thus general measures of innovation.

THE MEASURES

1. FOREHAND

Description. This study investigates the use of innovative behavior as a partial criterion of executive performance. The executives whose behavior is described are 188 persons holding administrative positions in 30 agencies of the United States Government. Their grade levels range from 11 to 17, with a mean of 13.3. Eighty-seven executives describe their positions as "primarily line" and 101 executives describe their positions as "primarily staff."

Definition. "Innovative behavior," according to Forehand, "includes the development and consideration of novel solutions to administrative problems, and evaluation of them in terms of criteria broader than conformity to preexisting practice. . . ."[3]

Data Collection. Data about innovative behavior were obtained from questionnaires through which executives were described by their organizational associates. Two groups of raters (superiors and peers) and two methods for describing behavior (rating scales and forced-adjective comparisons) are used. The rating scales have less validity than the forced-adjective comparisons; therefore, only the forced-adjective comparisons are selected for discussion by this handbook. The following part of the questionnaire is used to collect information for the forced-adjective comparisons:

This part of the questionnaire is designed to permit a more explicit description of the *executive style* of the participant. On the following page are several pairs of adjectives. In each case both of the adjectives are complimentary when used to describe an individual, and either or both of them might be descriptive of a good executive. Here are two examples:

Decisive
Perceptive

Ambitious
Decisive

The task is to *select* and *underline* the *one* adjective of each pair which you think is more descriptive of the participant. For example, if you think that decisiveness is more characteristic of the participant than perceptiveness, you would underline the first adjective in the first pair; if you think that perceptiveness is more characteristic, you would underline the second adjective. Similarly, you would consider whether ambition or decisiveness is more characteristic of the participant, and mark the second pair accordingly.

The selection may be difficult, since all of the qualities are desirable. Please make a selection however, even though the choice is close. If you wish to express a reservation or make a comment, please do so in a marginal note.

Remember, UNDERLINE THE ADJECTIVE IN EACH PAIR WHICH YOU THINK IS MORE CHARACTERISTIC OF THE PARTICIPANT.

industrious	inquiring	dependable
dependable	independent	stable
inquiring	cooperative	prudent
cooperative	flexible	flexible
self-reliant	inquiring	independent
stable	stable	dependable

original dependable	original industrious	cooperative original
prudent independent	flexible stable	self-reliant industrious
original stable	self-reliant prudent	prudent inquiring
industrious prudent	cooperative prudent	self-reliant dependable
inquiring dependable	stable independent	independent cooperative
flexible industrious	flexible self-reliant	industrious inquiring
self-reliant original	original prudent	self-reliant cooperative
flexible independent	independent industrious	flexible dependable
stable cooperative		independent original

Computation. The Forced-Choice Innovation Measure is constructed from a list of five adjectives judged to be descriptive of innovative behavior (self-reliant, inquiring, flexible, original, independent) and five adjectives judged to be equally complimentary but unrelated to innovation (stable, industrious, prudent, dependable, cooperative). The 25 "cross list" pairs of adjectives, that is, pairs containing one adjective from each list (along with ten "dummy" intralist pairs), constitute the material presented to the rater. The score is the number of times an "innovative" adjective is selected over a "noninnovative" adjective. No ranges or averages are presented.

Validity. (1) The correlation between superiors' and peers' response to innovation, as measured by the Forced-Choice Innovation Measure, is sufficient to indicate that the raters' perceptions of the behavior it describes are to some degree congruent. (2) The major correlates of the measure, both within and across the two categories of raters (superiors and peers), are other measures of innovation, and ratings of attributes theoretically related to innovativeness. (3) The measure is significantly correlated with general effectiveness ratings only when raters report, by an independent measure, that they value innovative behavior highly. (4) Ratings are influenced by attitude and position of rater (supervisor or peer) and by organizational climate.

Reliability. The study contains no data relevant to reliability.

Comments. (1) Forehand limits innovation to the administrative component of organizations. However, this handbook defines innovation in such a way that both the administrative and productive components of an organization are included. In fact, the term is not restricted to organizations. This handbook's definition is more general, encompassing Forehand's so that his measure is relevant to the concept as defined here. (2) In terms of validity, it would, of course, be better if the ratings were not influenced by the attitude and position of the rater and by the climate of the organization. However, most of the data relevant to validity support the measure; therefore, the measure seems to have adequate validity.

Source. Garlie A. Forehand, "Assessments of Innovative Behavior: Partial Criteria for the Assessment of Executive Performance," *Journal of Applied Psychology*, 47 (June, 1963), 206–213. Forehand has deposited the following materials with the American Documentation Institute: a copy of the questionnaire containing the rating scales, the forced-choice assessment, and the raters' attitude measure; a copy of the Organizational Perceptions instrument; and a four-page paper which reports several supplementary analyses. Order Document No. 7503 from Auxiliary Publications Project, Photoduplication Service, Library of Congress, Washington 25, D.C. Remit in advance $2.00 for microfilm or $3.75 for photocopies and make checks payable to: Chief, Photoduplication Service, Library of Congress.

Further Sources. 1. H. Guetzkow, G. A. Forehand, and B. J. James, "Educational Influence on Administrative Judgment," *Administrative Science Quarterly*, 6 (March, 1962), 483–500.
2. Garlie A. Forehand and Harold Guetzkow, "Judgment and Decision-Making Activities of Government Executives as Described by Superiors and Co-Workers," *Management Science*, 8 (April, 1962), 359–370.

2. PATCHEN

Description. This study is concerned with the development of valid and reliable measures of motivation and morale. It was done primarily in five geographically separate units of the Tennessee Valley Authority and in three divisions of a private electronics company. Supplementary data for one measure were obtained from a company that manufactures household appliances. Many different types of employees are included: engineers in several specialties, operating personnel in automated power plants, clerical employees, salesmen, and semi-skilled production workers. The samples from the TVA, the electronics company, and the appliance company include, respectively, 834, 223, and 557 employees.

Definition. The study investigates five aspects of motivation and morale: job motivation, interest in work innovation, willingness to express disagreement with supervisors, attitude toward changes introduced into the job situation, and identification with the work organization. Handbook measure No. 2—the present measure—focuses on "interest in work innovation," whereas handbook measure No. 3—the next measure—focuses on "attitude toward changes introduced into the job situation." Interest in work innovation is defined as "finding new ways of doing things on the job."[4]

Data Collection. The following six questionnaire items are used to collect information about interest in work innovation:

1. In your kind of work, if a person tries to change his usual way of doing things, how does it generally turn out?

   (1)____Usually turns out worse; the tried and true methods work best in my work

   (3)____Usually doesn't make much difference

   (5)____Usually turns out better; our methods need improvement

2. Some people prefer doing a job in pretty much the same way because this way they can count on always doing a good job. Others like to go out of their way in order to think up new ways of doing things. How is it with you on your job?

   (1)____I always prefer doing things pretty much in the same way

   (2)____I mostly prefer doing things pretty much in the same way

   (4)____I mostly prefer doing things in new and different ways

   (5)____I always prefer doing things in new and different ways

3. How often do you try out, on your own, a better or faster way of doing something on the job?

   (5)____Once a week or more often

   (4)____Two or three times a month

   (3)____About once a month

   (2)____Every few months

   (1)____Rarely or never

4. How often do you get chances to try out your own ideas on your job, either before or after checking with your supervisor?

   (5)____Several times a week or more

(4)___About once a week

(3)___Several times a month

(2)___About once a month

(1)___Less than once a month

5. In my kind of job, it's usually better to let your supervisor worry about new or better ways of doing things.

(1)___Strongly agree

(2)___Mostly agree

(4)___Mostly disagree

(5)___Strongly disagree

6. How many times in the past year have you suggested to your supervisor a different or better way of doing something on the job?

(1)___Never had occasion to do this during the past year

(2)___Once or twice

(3)___About three times

(4)___About five times

(5)___Six to ten times

(6)___More than ten times had occasion to do this during the past year.

Computation. An Index of Interest in Work Innovation (Index A) is computed by averaging the scores obtained on each of these six items. The numbers in parentheses preceding each response category in the preceding section indicate the scores assigned to the response. A shorter index (Index B) based on the three best items (Questions 1, 5, and 6) is also computed for TVA employees. The following discussion focuses on Index A.

Validity. (1) Each employee's score on the Index of Interest in Work Innovation is compared to supervisors' rankings of this employee with respect to his "looking out for new ideas." The median correlation between index scores and supervisory rankings is .34 at TVA and .35 at the electronics company. (2) For all steam plants at the TVA taken together, the Index of Interest in Work Innovation scores of the employees who submitted formal written suggestions —as determined by an examination of official records—are significantly higher than the index scores of the employees who did not submit formal written suggestions. (3) Index scores are correlated with the number of formal suggestions TVA employees reported making during the three-year period preceding questionnaire administration. (4) Scores on the index are correlated with scores concerning aspects of the job situation and other relevant variables. Interest in work innovation has the strongest associations with job difficulty, identification with one's own occupation, general job motivation, and willingness to disagree with supervisors.

Reliability. (1) The correlations among the six questionnaire items are positive but low at TVA and somewhat higher at the electronics company. (2) The test-retest reliability of the index is .87 for individuals and .92 for groups at the electronics company. A period of one month separated administrations of the questionnaires.

Comments. (1) Patchen's definition of work innovation ("finding new ways of doing things on the job") is very similar to this handbook's definition of innovation ("first or early user of an idea among its set of similar social systems"). An organization whose members readily find new ways of doing things on the job is probably a first or early user of an idea among its set of organizations. (2) This handbook focuses on the six questions that Patchen used to collect information about interest in work innovation, Index A. With respect to Index B, Patchen states that " . . . the potential user who has limited questionnaire space available should note the references to the short three-item scale, which shows evidence of validity almost equal to the longer measure."[5] This second index is valuable because every questionnaire seems to have "limited space available." It would be helpful if more organizational researchers would shorten their measures, without, of course, too much loss of validity and reliability.[6] (3) The measures have very adequate validity and reliability. The material about validity is especially impressive. The use of data from formal records—the suggestion system—to check the validity of the questionnaire items is a valuable practice which should be more widely used by survey researchers. It would also be helpful if the Index of Interest in Work Innovation were correlated with organizations where the degree of actual work innovation had been measured by careful observation and by an extensive use of formal records. This extra data would make an impressive index even more impressive. Unlike most organizational researchers, Patchen devotes some time to the assessment of the reliability of his measure; this effort is especially appreciated.

Source. Martin Patchen, *Some Questionnaire Measures of Employee Motivation and Morale* (Ann Arbor, Mich.: Survey Research Center, University of Michigan, 1965), pp. 1–25.

Further Sources. 1. Martin Patchen, "Labor-Management Consultation at TVA: Its Impact on Employees," *Administrative Science Quarterly*, 10 (September, 1965), 149–174.

2. Martin Patchen, *Participation, Achievement, and Involvement on the Job* (Englewood Cliffs, N.J.: Prentice-Hall, 1970).[7]

3. PATCHEN

Description. This study is described in connection with the second measure; therefore, no further description is necessary.

Definition. Patchen discusses "acceptance of job changes" in the following terms:

> In an era of swift technological and administrative changes, the degree of employee acceptance versus resistance to change is of considerable importance to managers. From the standpoint of individual well-being, general resistance to change may also be important in that it may indicate that the person feels threatened by the change in some way. It seems desirable therefore to be able to assess the extent to which employees react favorably or unfavorably to changes in the job situation.[8]

Data Collection. The following five questionnaire items are used to collect information about acceptance of job changes:

1. Sometimes changes in the way a job is done are more trouble than they are worth because they create a lot of problems and confusion. How often do you feel that changes which have affected you and your job at (name of organization) have been like this?

    (1)___50% or more of the changes have been more trouble than they're worth

    (2)___About 40% of the changes

    (3)___About 25% of the changes

    (4)___About 15% of the changes

    (5)___Only 5% or fewer of the changes have been more trouble than they're worth

2. From time to time changes in policies, procedures, and equipment are introduced by the management. How often do these changes lead to better ways of doing things?

    (1)___Changes of this kind never improve things

    (2)___They seldom do

    (3)___About half of the time they do

    (4)___Most of the time they do

    (5)___Changes of this kind are always an improvement

3. How well do the various people in the plant or offices who are affected by these changes accept them?

    (1)___Very few of the people involved accept the changes

    (2)___Less than half do

    (3)___About half of them do

    (4)___Most of them do

    (5)___Practically all of the people involved accept the changes

4. In general, how do you *now* feel about changes during the past year that affected the way your job is done?

    (1)___Made things somewhat worse

    (2)___Not improved things at all

    (3)___Not improved things very much

    (4)___Improved things somewhat

    (5)___Been a big improvement

    ___There have been no changes in my job in the past year

5. During the past year when changes were introduced that affected the way your job is done, how did you feel about them *at first*?

At first I thought the changes would:

    (1)___Make things somewhat worse

    (2)___Not improve things at all

    (3)___Not improve things very much

    (4)___Improve things somewhat

    (5)___Be a big improvement

    ___There have been no changes in my job in the past year

Computation. The numbers in parentheses, preceding the responses to the five questions in the preceding section, indicate the scores assigned to each response. An Index of Acceptance of Job Changes is computed by summing the response scores for the five questions. No information is presented about the means or standard deviations.

Validity. (1) Scores on the Index of Acceptance of Job Changes have positive correlations with supervisors' ranking of each employee's acceptance of change in nine out of ten units at TVA and in both of the two units at the electronics company. Five of the nine positive correlations at TVA are statistically significant. (2) Scores on the index show strong correlations, for units, with certain aspects of the work situation to which acceptance of change might, theoretically, be expected to relate. In particular, acceptance of change scores are strongly related to employee participation in work decision-making at TVA.

Reliability. (1) Correlations among the five questions are positive but fairly small. (2) Test-retest reliability coefficients for the index, based on data from the electronics company, are .76 for individuals and .80 for groups. A period of one month separated administrations of the questionnaires.

Comments. (1) The Index of Acceptance of Job Changes focuses on essentially the same phenomena indicated by this handbook's definition of innovation. An organization whose members readily accept job changes is probably a first or early user of an idea among its set of organizations. (2) The presentation of means and standard deviations would facilitate comparative research using Patchen's measures. (3) The validity and reliability of this index is very adequate. Few organizational researchers evaluate the validity and reliability of their measures as carefully as Patchen. It would be helpful, however, to compare this index with indexes of organizations which had experienced different degrees of actual job changes, as determined by systematic observation and the study of official records.

Source. Martin Patchen, *Some Questionnaire Measures of Employee Motivation and Morale* (Ann Arbor, Mich.: Survey Research Center, University of Michigan, 1965), pp. 1–14 and 40–47.

Further Sources. 1. Martin Patchen, "Labor-Management Consultation at TVA: Its Impact on Employees," *Administrative Science Quarterly*, 10 (September, 1965), 149–174.
2. Martin Patchen, *Participation, Achievement, and Involvement on the Job* (Englewood Cliffs, N.J.: Prentice-Hall, 1970).[9]

ADDITIONAL READINGS

1. Jerald Hage and Michael Aiken, "Program Change and Organizational Properties," *American Journal of Sociology*, 72 (March, 1967), 503–519.
2. Jerald Hage and Michael Aiken, *Social Change in Complex Organizations* (New York: Random House, 1970).

NOTES

1. This definition of innovation is based on Selwyn W. Becker and Thomas L. Whisler, "The Innovative Organization: A Selective View of Current Theory and

Research," *Journal of Business*, 40 (October, 1967), 462–469 (esp. p. 463). Also relevant is Selwyn W. Becker and Frank Stafford, "Some Determinants of Organizational Success," *Journal of Business*, 40 (October, 1967), 511–518.

2. Becker and Whisler, *op. cit.*, p. 463.

3. Garlie A. Forehand, "Assessments of Innovative Behavior: Partial Criteria for the Assessment of Executive Performance," *Journal of Applied Psychology*, 47 (June, 1963), p. 206.

4. Martin Patchen, *Some Questionnaire Measures of Employee Motivation and Morale* (Ann Arbor, Mich.: Survey Research Center, University of Michigan, 1965), p. 3.

5. *Ibid.*, p. 25.

6. A concern with the development of shorter instruments also motivates the study by J. H. K. Inkson, D. S. Pugh, and D. J. Hickson, "Organization Context and Structure: An Abbreviated Replication," *Administrative Science Quarterly*, 15 (September, 1970), 318–329.

7. This book came to the attention of the author of this handbook too late to be included in this edition.

8. Patchen, *op. cit.*, p. 40.

9. See footnote number seven.

MECHANIZATION

15

Definition. *Mechanization* is the degree to which a social system uses inanimate sources of energy.[1] Among organizations, for example, the automated factory, computer, crane, fork-lift truck, power tool, electric typewriter, gasoline engine, diesel engine—all are illustrations of mechanization. The concept of mechanization is commonly discussed under such labels as "automation," "industrialization," and "technology."

Although there is a large literature dealing with technology, this handbook has no chapter devoted to the topic. A sizeable amount of this literature, however, focuses on the degree to which a social system uses inanimate sources of energy and the degree to which role performance in the system is repetitive. And this focus is encompassed by this handbook's mechanization and routinization. A later chapter deals with routinization, that is, repetitiveness of role performance. The referents for technology are basically in this handbook, although under different labels.[2]

The use of tools and equipment is not an aspect of mechanization.[3] The use of the horse-drawn plow, for example, is not mechanization because the energy source is animate (the horse). However, the use of a tractor to plow a field is an example of mechanization because its source of energy is inanimate (a gasoline or diesel engine). It is only when the tools and equipment depend on inanimate sources of energy—and the particular source is not important—that they are discussed in the context of mechanization.

Studies of mechanization in organizations commonly focus on the production system. ("Work system" and "economy" are other terms that refer to the production system.)[4] This encourages the study of an automated assembly of engines for automobiles—to cite one illustration—but ignores the use of computers in the offices of the same factory. There is no reason, from the perspective of this handbook, why mechanization should be limited to the production system of an organization. The use of computers in an administrative office is as much an example of mechanization as the use of automated equipment in a production line. Therefore, this handbook defines mechanization as the degree to which a social system, not just its productive component, uses inanimate sources of energy.

Measurement.[5] The first measure of mechanization (Inkson, Pugh, and Hickson) is the best in the organizational literature. However, because of its recent publication, it has not received wide usage. The second measure (Melman) is probably the most widely used of the remaining measures of mechanization.

Melman's measure of mechanization, installed horsepower per wage earner, is used to study organizations and societies. This handbook's preference for measures that use the organization as the unit of analysis (a preference discussed in the introductory chapter) does not mean the exclusion of measures that can be used with different units of analysis. To prefer organizational measures is to insist on measures that have been used to study organizations, and Melman's measure of mechanization meets this standard.

THE MEASURES

1. INKSON, PUGH, AND HICKSON

Description. The aim of this study is methodological: to develop a short form of an interview schedule to represent accurately the concepts of "context" and "structure" used in previous research.[6] A long form of the interview schedule was used in previous research on 52 organizations in the English Midlands. To develop the short form, the researchers studied 40 organizations which, like the previous 52, are located in the English Midlands. Twenty-four of these organizations are manufacturing firms, whereas 16 are service organizations. Most of the service organizations are government agencies. The 40 organizations range in size from under 500 employees to over 5,000 employees.

Definition. "Workflow integration" is the contextual concept relevant to mechanization. Workflow integration is defined as " . . . the degree of *automated*, continuous, fixed-sequence operation. . . ."[7] (Emphasis supplied.) Mechanization ("automation") is thus a component of workflow integration.

Data Collection. The following part of the interview schedule is used to collect information about the automated component of workflow integration:[8]

For guidance consult the examples below from the Amber and Amber[9] classification:

HAND TOOLS—shovel, knife, pliers, axe, crowbar, hammer, scissors, wrench file, handsaw, bellows, paintbrush, trowel, etc.

POWERED MACHINES AND TOOLS—snag grinder, cement trowelling machine, portable floor polisher, electric hand-drill, drillpress, air hammer, etc.

SINGLE-CYCLE AUTOMATICS AND SELF-FEEDING MACHINES—pipe threading machines, radial drill, electro-erosion machine, precision boring machine (without accessory automatic control system), machine tools, such as grinder, planer, mill, shaper, lathe, etc.

AUTOMATICS WHICH REPEAT CYCLES—engine production lines, self-feed press lines, automatic copying lathe, automatic gear hobbers, automatic assembly of switches, etc.

SELF-MEASURING AND ADJUSTING BY FEED-BACK—feedback from product, automatic sizing grinders, size-controlled honing machines, dynamic balancing, colour matching or blending, level control, etc.

COMPUTER CONTROL—rate-of-feed cutting, machinability control, maintaining pH, error compensation, turbine fuel control, etc.

TECHNOLOGY

WHAT IS THE MOST AUTOMATIC PIECE OF EQUIPMENT?
WHAT DOES IT DO?

IN GENERAL, THE WORK IS DONE BY

Ring the highest number that applies
Which of the following categories most accurately describes:
(a) the BULK of the equipment used by the organization in its workflow
(b) the most AUTOMATIC piece of equipment used by the organization on its workflow (ignore thermostatic governors)

	(a) *the bulk of equipment*	(b) *the most automatic*
Handtools and manual machines	0	0
Powered machines and tools	1	1
Single-cycle automatics and self-feeding machines	2	2
Automatics which repeat the cycles (all ENERGY mechanized)	3	3
Self-measuring and adjusting by feedback	4	4
Computer controlled	5	5

Additional information about these six classes of equipment is provided in the coding instructions for the interview schedule.[10] This information is important because this part of the interview schedule is based on an accurate classification of the equipment in the 40 organizations. The following should assist in classification of the equipment.[11]

(1) *Hand tools and manual machines*.[12] These tools are without self-action properties. The tools do not replace human energy or basic control, but may include built-in guides and measurements. They increase the workers' efficiency, but do not replace the workers. These tools include all muscle-energized machines. The tools give mechanical advantages, but do not replace man's energy. The following are simple machines: lever, inclined plane, wheel and axle, screw, pulley, and wedge. Examples of hand tools, not included on the interview schedule, are as follows: block and tackle, pencil sharpener, bow and arrow, bicycle, typewriter, churn, wheelbarrow, tire-pump, desk stapler, jack, hand lawn mower, and hand loom.

(2) *Powered machines and tools*. These machines and tools replace human muscles. The machine action and control is completely dependent upon the operator. These machines and tools use mechanical energy (windmill, water-horse, steam engine, electric motor), but operators position the work and machine for desired action. Examples of powered machines and tools, not included on the interview schedule, are as follows: power lawn mower, spray gun, and belt sander.

(3) *Single-cycle automatics and self-feeding machines*. These machines

mechanize human dexterity. They complete actions that have been initiated by operators. Operators must set up, load, initiate action, adjust, and unload.

(4) *Automatics that repeat cycles.* This type of machine mechanizes all energy. The mechanized human attribute is diligence. These machines carry out routine instructions without aid by operators. They start cycles and repeat actions automatically. These machines load, go through a sequence of operations, and unload to the next station or machine. They have open loop (not self-corrective) performance. They obey internal (fixed) or external (variable) programs, such as cams, tapes, or cards. Transfer machines and "Detroit" automation are examples of this type of machine. Examples of automatics that repeat cycles, but that are not included on the interview schedule, are as follows: television, relays, locks, valves, machines for making springs, bottles, hinges, chain, cartons, doughnuts, automatic packaging, and machines that are not self-correcting (record-playback and numerical programmed).

(5) *Self-measuring and adjusting by feedback.* These machines increasingly mechanize information activities. Judgment is the human attribute mechanized. These machines measure and compare results to obtain desired size or position and adjust to minimize any error. The following positional feedback examples are not included on the interview schedule: pattern tracing flame cutter, sero-assisted follower control, feedback control of machine tool table, saddle and spindle, and tape controlled machines (only if self-correcting).

(6) *Computer control.* Evaluation is the human attribute mechanized. These machines are cognizant of multiple factors on which machine or process performance is predicated; they evaluate and reconcile by means of computer operations to determine proper control action.

Computation. The score is from "0" to "5." Hand tools and manual machines are scored "0," whereas computer controlled machines are scored "5." Two scores are assigned, one for the bulk of the equipment and another for the most automatic piece of equipment. The two scores are summed to obtain a single score.[13] The higher the score, the greater the mechanization. The researchers present no information about the concentration or dispersion of these scores.

Validity. (1) The short form of the interview schedule was applied to the 52 organizations previously studied by means of the long form of the interview schedule. The correlation for workflow integration for the two forms on the same sample is .96. (2) The previous study finds a positive relationship between structuring of activities and workflow integration; the present study of 40 organizations finds a similar relationship. (3) Fourteen of the 40 organizations were also included in the previous study of 52 organizations. Two sets of scores are thus obtained by two different instruments for the same set of 14 organizations. The two sets of scores for workflow integration show very little, if any, change. (4) A typology of organizations is developed on the basis of the previous study. The present study finds the same range of types as the earlier one, thereby establishing a consistent typology.

Reliability. An item analysis is carried out for the two aspects of context and the two aspects of structure. The general biserial correlation coefficient, originally developed by Brogden,[14] is used for the item analysis. The coefficient for workflow integration (an aspect of context) is .96.

Comments. (1) Inkson, Pugh, and Hickson focus on mechanization of the production system (they term it the "workflow") of the organization.[15] They also view mechanization as one aspect of "workflow integration" which, in turn, is viewed as a "contextual" concept. This handbook sees mechanization as the degree to which a social system, not just its productive component, uses inanimate sources of energy; it also sees mechanization as a separate analytical concept rather than as a segment of more general concepts, such as workflow integration and context. (2) The interview schedule, if supplemented by the coding instructions, provides sufficient information to replicate. This ability to replicate is especially commendable in view of the difficulty of collecting the complicated type of information required for the measurement of mechanization. (3) The scoring instructions do not indicate explicitly whether or not the two sets of scores—one for the bulk of the equipment and the other for the most mechanized piece of equipment—are to be summed to obtain a final mechanization score. It would also have been helpful if the researchers had indicated the concentration and dispersion of the scores. Scores for concentration and dispersion provide a basis for comparison with other studies which will use the interview schedule developed by Inkson, Pugh, and Hickson. However, organizational researchers do not generally provide measures of concentration and dispersion. (4) The evidence for the validity and reliability of workflow integration is very adequate. Few studies evidence as much care in these critical areas as Inkson, Pugh, and Hickson. Unfortunately, however, mechanization is but one component of workflow integration, and separate evidence is not presented for the mechanization component. Therefore, it is impossible to evaluate the validity and reliability of the researchers' measure of mechanization.

Source. J. H. K. Inkson, D. S. Pugh, and D. J. Hickson, "Organization Context and Structure: An Abbreviated Replication," *Administrative Science Quarterly*, 15 (September, 1970), 318–329.

Further Sources. The Industrial Administration Research Unit of the University of Aston has published a large number of articles reporting the results of its research. Unfortunately, the published work of the Research Unit is not yet available in monograph form. However, the references at the end of the present article contain the major publications of the Research Unit.

2. MELMAN

Description. This study investigates the determinants of industrial labor productivity. There are two parts to the investigation. The first part consists of a study of the motor vehicle and allied metal products industry in Great

Britain. The primary focus is on 20 plants in the motor vehicle industry. The second part consists of a comparative study of Great Britain, United States, Finland, France, Germany, Hungary, Netherlands, Norway, Poland, Sweden, U.S.S.R., Canada, and Japan. The primary focus of the second part is on Great Britain and the United States. This handbook summarizes the information from the second part of Melman's study.

Definition. Melman refers to mechanization as the degree to which nonmanual sources of energy are used in the production process.

Data Collection. The data for the second part of Melman's study consists of a secondary analysis of data collected by other researchers and government agencies. Therefore, Melman does not reproduce the instrument for collecting the data.

Computation. Melman uses "installed horsepower per wage-earner" to measure mechanization. The greater the installed horsepower, the greater the mechanization. The concentration and distribution of the installed horsepower for the different countries is not presented.

Validity. (1) and (2) Melman predicated that the ratio of alternative labor to machine cost would be a determinant of mechanization. He also predicated a direct relationship between mechanization and labor productivity, that is, the greater the mechanization, the greater the labor productivity. Both of these predictions are confirmed.

Reliability. The study contains no data relevant to reliability.

Comments. (1) Melman, like many organization researchers, defines mechanization in terms of the production process, whereas this handbook views any use of inanimate source of energy, whether in production or administration, as illustrative of mechanization. (2) It would be helpful had Melman indicated in some detail exactly how a researcher collects information about the installed horsepower per wage earner. This information is probably found in records. Organizations maintain vast files, however, and the researcher who wants to replicate Melman's study requires more detailed instructions for the location of these records. (3) The secondary analysis feature of the study is admirable; more research of this type is needed to use the vast amount of existing organizational data. However, a secondary analysis complicates the task of reproducing the instrument of data collection. And replication is hindered to the extent that other researchers cannot use identical methods of data collection. It is unreasonable to expect a secondary analysis to reproduce the instruments used in the original research, especially when the original research consists of a series of studies, as in Melman's study. The problem of reproducing instruments of data collection is discussed in the concluding chapter of this handbook. (4) The relationship between installed horsepower per wage earner and amount of kilowatts used per wage earner is relevant because the second measure is often used by researchers.[16] Melman states that .74545 kilowatts are needed to power one horsepower for one hour.[17] Therefore, the installed horsepower per wage earner can be obtained by multiplying the kilowatts used per wage earner hour by .74545. This handbook does not include the second measure—the amount of kilowatts used per wage earner— because it can be obtained from the first. Installed horsepower is the measure selected for inclusion because of its wide use. (5) Comparison with future studies would be facilitated had Melman presented the concentration and distribution of the installed horsepower scores. This presentation would, of course, have lengthened his book. (6) Confirmation of his predictions con- tributes to the validity of his measure. However, Melman is careful to point out that installed horsepower as a measure of mechanization has been criti- cized by Jerome and Thorp.[18] The data relevant to the measure, at the present, lead to the conclusion that its validity has been inadequately demonstrated. (7) Since he presents no data on reliability, Melman fails to demonstrate the reliability of installed horsepower as a measure of mechanization.

Source. Seymour Melman, *Dynamic Factors in Industrial Productivity* (Oxford, Eng.: Basil Blackwell, 1956).

Further Source. Seymour Melman, *Decision-Making and Productivity* (Oxford, Eng.: Basil Blackwell, 1958).

ADDITIONAL READING

1. Robert Blauner, *Alienation and Freedom* (Chicago: The University of Chicago Press, 1964).

NOTES

1. This definition of mechanization comes from William A. Faunce, *Problems of an Industrial Society* (New York: McGraw-Hill, 1968), pp. 42–44. Faunce refers to "power" rather than to "energy."

2. Parallels for this handbook's treatment of technology are found in the discussions of bureaucracy, organizational climate, and primary-secondary relationships in the chapters devoted, respectively, to administrative staff, alienation, and formalization.

   The most important recent empirical research on technology has probably been conducted in England. The following research is especially significant: Tom Burns and G. M. Stalker, *The Management of Innovation* (Chicago: Quadrangle, 1961); David J. Hickson, D. S. Pugh, and Diana C. Pheysey, "Operations Technology and Organization Structure: An Empirical Reappraisal," *Adminis- trative Science Quarterly*, 14 (September, 1969), 378–397; and Joan Woodward, *Industrial Organization* (London: Oxford, 1965). The most important recent theoretical work on technology has probably been done by Perrow. His most influential work in this area is Charles Perrow, "A Framework for the Comparative Analysis of Organizations," *American Sociological Review*, 32 (April, 1967), 194–208.

3. Jerome includes the use of tools and equipment as an aspect of mechanization. See Harry Jerome, *Mechanization in Industry* (New York: National Bureau of Economic Research, 1934), pp. 41–42. However, most of the data in Jerome's book is based on a definition of mechanization very similar to that used by this handbook.

4. The two measures of mechanization selected for this chapter focus on the production system.

5. The best general discussion of the measurement of mechanization is found in Jerome, *op. cit.*

6. This handbook also uses the study to illustrate measures of autonomy and formalization.

7. J. H. K. Inkson, D. S. Pugh, and D. J. Hickson, "Organization Context and Structure: An Abbreviated Replication," *Administrative Science Quarterly*, 15 (September, 1970), p. 319.

8. The interview schedule is supplied through the courtesy of D. J. Hickson, a senior member of the Industrial Administration Research Unit. That part of the interview schedule relevant for mechanization is slightly simplified for the sake of clarity. The lines are in the original version of the interview schedule.

9. The reference is to George H. Amber and Paul S. Amber, *Anatomy of Automation* (Englewood Cliffs, N. J.: Prentice-Hall, 1962).

10. The coding instructions (termed "Writing-up Schedule") are also supplied through the courtesy of D. J. Hickson.

11. This information about the classification of the equipment follows quite closely the material contained in the coding instructions. One result is that there is some redundancy.

12. The interview schedule refers to "hand tools"; however, the coding instructions refer to "hand tools and manual machines."

13. It is not clear whether or not these two scores are summed to obtain a single score.

14. H. E. Brogden, "A New Coefficient: Applications to Biserial Correlation and to Estimation of Serial Efficiency," *Psychometrika*, 14 (September, 1949), 169–182.

15. D. S. Pugh, D. J. Hickson, C. R. Hinings, and C. Turner, "Dimensions of Organizational Structure," *Administrative Science Quarterly*, 13 (June, 1968), 65–105.

16. See, for example, Seymour Melman, *Decision-Making and Productivity* (Oxford, Eng.: Basil Blackwell, 1958).

17. Seymour Melman, *Dynamic Factors in Industrial Productivity* (Oxford, Eng.: Basil Blackwell, 1956), p. 110.

18. Jerome, *op. cit.* and Willard L. Thorp, "Horsepower Statistics for Manufacturers," *Journal of the American Statistical Association*, 24 (March, 1929), 376–385.

MOTIVATION

16

Definition. *Motivation* is the degree to which the members of a social system are willing to work.[1] "Dedication," "commitment," "effort," "involvement," "central life interests," "organizational climate"[2]—these are some of the terms used to discuss the concept of motivation in organizational literature.

Motivation is distinguished from satisfaction (Chapter 19 discusses the concept of satisfaction). Motivation is also distinguished from alienation. Both are social psychological concepts; however, "willingness to work" is conceptually different from "powerlessness" (this handbook's definition of alienation). Motivation and satisfaction are commonly distinguished in the organizational literature;[3] the concept of motivation, however, is sometimes referred to as alienation.[4]

Measurement. The two measures of motivation (Lodahl–Kejner and Patchen) are designed to measure motivation as a social psychological concept, that is, both measures are based on subjective data. It is a common practice in organizational literature to measure the concept of motivation by objective data, such as absenteeism and turnover.[5] However, this handbook distinguishes structural concepts, such as absenteeism and turnover, from social psychological concepts, such as motivation. Distinctions at the conceptual level must be paralleled by distinctions at the measurement level.

THE MEASURES

1. LODAHL AND KEJNER

Description. The purpose of this study is to define job involvement, develop a scale for measuring it, gather evidence on the validity and reliability of the scale, and to learn something about the nature of job involvement through its correlation with other job attitudes. Three groups of subjects were studied: (1) 137 nursing personnel (head nurses, staff nurses—Registered Nurses— practical nurses, nurse aides, and orderlies) in a large general hospital; (2) 70 engineers working in an advanced development laboratory; and (3) 46 second-year graduate students in business administration.

Definition. Job involvement is defined ". . . as the degree to which a person's work performance affects his self-esteem. . . ."[6]

Data Collection. The data were collected by means of the following 20 questionnaire items:

1. I'll stay overtime to finish a job, even if I'm not paid for it.
2. You can measure a person pretty well by how good a job he does.
3. The major satisfaction in my life comes from my job.
4. For me, mornings at work really fly by.
5. I usually show up for work a little early, to get things ready.
6. The most important things that happen to me involve my work.
7. Sometimes I lie awake at night thinking ahead to the next day's work.
8. I'm really a perfectionist about my work.
9. I feel depressed when I fail at something connected with my job.
10. I have other activities more important than my work.
11. I live, eat, and breathe my job.
12. I would probably keep working even if I didn't need the money.
13. Quite often I feel like staying home from work instead of coming in.
14. To me, my work is only a small part of who I am.
15. I am very much involved personally in my work.
16. I avoid taking on extra duties and responsibilities in my work.
17. I used to be more ambitious about my work than I am now.
18. Most things in life are more important than work.
19. I used to care more about my work, but now other things are more important to me.
20. Sometimes I'd like to kick myself for the mistakes I make in my work.

Four categories of response are provided: strongly agree, agree, disagree, and strongly disagree. The article does not indicate the exact format for these four categories. If space is at a premium, a six-item scale which consists of the following questions can be used: 3, 6, 8, 11, 15, and 18.

Computation. The four categories of response are scored from "1" (strongly agree) to "4" (strongly disagree). The total involvement score is the summation of the 20 questions. The higher the score, the lower the involvement. The means and standard deviations, respectively, for the three groups of subjects are as follows: nurses (43.37 and 6.52), engineers (42.62 and 7.83), and students (48.06 and 9.56).

Validity. (1) Analysis of variance performed on the data indicate that the three groups of subjects differ significantly from each other ($F = 4.87, p < .01$). (2) Four sets of data are used to assess the relation of job involvement to other variables. The result is a series of "plausible correlations" with these other variables.

Reliability. The split-half reliability of the scale is computed by calculating product-moment correlation coefficients between halves of the scale, using odd-even items as the split. The split-half correlations, corrected by means of the Spearman-Brown formula, are as follows for the three groups of subjects: nurses (.72), engineers (.80), and students (.89).

Comments. (1) Lodahl and Kejner's concept of job involvement ("degree to which a person's work performance affects his self-esteem") is different from this handbook's concept of motivation ("degree to which a person is willing to work"). However, the basic concepts seem to be related. A person whose work performance strongly affects his self-esteem is also probably a person characterized by a strong willingness to work. Therefore, Lodahl's and Kejner's measures are relevant to this handbook's concept of motivation. (The measures used by the researchers appear to be more relevant to motivation as defined by this handbook than their terminology would indicate.) (2) Lodahl and Kejner do not present the exact format of the four categories of responses to their 20 questions. It would have taken very little space to reproduce this format; such reproduction, while not a major point, would make possible replication of the study by other researchers. (3) The researchers devoted time and effort to the development of the short six-item scale. This is appreciated since space is always at a premium on questionnaires.[7] (4) Lodahl and Kejner score their scale in such a way that a high score signifies low motivation. It would be less confusing if the scoring were reversed, that is, if a high score signified high motivation. (5) The researchers present means and standard deviations for their measure; these statistics constitute baselines with which future research can be meaningfully compared. The presentation of means and standard deviations should be a routine procedure; unfortunately, such is not the case in organizational research. (6) The validity and reliability of the scale appears to be adequate. Since most organizational research does not assess the reliability of its measures, the researchers' concern with reliability is exemplary.

Source. Thomas M. Lodahl and Mathilde Kejner, "The Definition and Measurement of Job Involvement," *Journal of Applied Psychology*, 49 (February, 1965), 24–33.

Further Sources. 1. R. Anderson, "Activity Preferences and Leadership Behavior of Head Nurses," *Journal of Nursing Research*, 13 (Summer, 1964), 239–243.

2. Paul S. Goodman, "The Measurement of an Individual's Organizational Map," *Administrative Science Quarterly*, 13 (September, 1968), 246–265.

3. Paul Goodman, J. Furcon, and J. Rose, "Examination of Some Measures of Creative Ability by the Multitrait-Multimethod Matrix," *Journal of Applied Psychology*, 53 (June, 1969), 240–243.

4. Thomas M. Lodahl, "Patterns of Job Attitudes in Two Assembly Technologies," *Administrative Science Quarterly*, 8 (March, 1964), 482–519.

2. Patchen

Description. This study is concerned with the development of valid and reliable measures of motivation and morale. The study was done primarily in five geographically separate units of the Tennessee Valley Authority and in three divisions of a private electronics company. Supplementary data for one measure were obtained from a company which manufactures household appliances. Many different types of employees are covered: engineers in several specialties, operating personnel in automated power plants, clerical employees, salesmen, and semi-skilled production workers. The TVA, electronics company, and appliance company samples, respectively, include 843, 223, and 557 employees.

Definition. Job motivation refers to "... general devotion of energy to job tasks."[8]

Data Collection. The following four questionnaire items are used to collect data about job motivation:

1. On most days on your job, how often does time seem to drag for you?

    (1)___About half the day or more

    (2)___About one-third of the day

    (3)___About one-quarter of the day

    (4)___About one-eighth of the day

    (5)___Time never seems to drag

2. Some people are completely involved in their job—they are absorbed in it night and day. For other people, their job is simply one of several interests. How involved do you feel in your job?

    (1)___Very little involved; my other interests are more absorbing

    (2)___Slightly involved

    (3)___Moderately involved; my job and my other interests are equally absorbing to me

    (4)___Strongly involved

    (5)___Very strongly involved; my work is the most absorbing interest in my life

3. How often do you do some extra work for your job which isn't really required of you?

(5)____Almost every day

(4)____Several times a week

(3)____About once a week

(2)____Once every few weeks

(1)____About once a month or less[9]

4. Would you say you work harder, less hard, or about the same as other people doing your type of work at (name of organization)?

(5)____Much harder than most others

(4)____A little harder than most others

(3)____About the same as most others

(2)____A little less hard than most others

(1)____Much less hard than most others[10]

Computations. The numbers in parentheses in the preceding questions indicate the scores assigned to each response. Three indices are constructed: Index A, based on the first two questions; Index B, based on the answers to the four questions; and Index C, based on the answers to the first three questions. The scores for a respondent are averaged. The concentration and dispersion of the scores are not indicated.

Validity. (1) Index A generally has only a slight correlation with supervisory rankings of each employee's "concern for doing a good job" at the TVA. Index B generally has a more marked association with supervisors' ratings of "concern for doing a good job" at the electronics company. (2) The relation of average job motivation index scores to group absence rates is generally substantial; this is especially true for the TVA steam plants, where Index A is used, and for the appliance company, where Index C is used. Data on the relation of index scores to absence for individuals come mainly from TVA. In several parts of the TVA, there are significant negative associations (as predicted) between scores on Index A and the number of absences, though the size of these associations is not as great for individuals as for groups. (3) For a small number of individuals at the electronics company, scores on Index B correlate positively with production volume. Index C scores for work units at the appliance company have small positive relationships to supervisors' rating of several aspects of cost efficiency; are slightly related to the ratings of work quality; and are not correlated with ratings of efficiency in meeting schedules. Index scores for work units at the appliance company also have generally small but positive correlations in the expected direction with grievances, work accidents, number of suggestions submitted, and number of suggestions installed. (4) A comparison of different occupational groups at the electronics company shows predicted differences in the distribution of responses for Index B. A group of high-level salesmen and a group of engineering personnel show much higher positive motivation than a group of production workers. (5) Scores on Index A show, for groups, a number of theoretically predictable associations with aspects of the work situation. The strongest of these associations are with perceived opportunities for achievement on the job, control over work methods, and identification with one's own occupation.

Reliability. The test-retest reliability coefficients for the electronics company is .80 for individual scores and .83 for group scores. A period of one month separated administration of the questionnaires.

Comments. (1) Patchen's terms, like those of Lodahl and Kejner, are different from those used in this handbook. However, if one examines Patchen's four questions, and especially the third and fourth questions, it seems as if the concept that Patchen has in mind for "general devotion of energy to job tasks" is quite similar to the concept that this handbook has in mind for "willingness to work." The terms are different but the ideas are very similar. (2) It would be helpful for comparative research if Patchen had provided measures of concentration and dispersion. (3) Patchen is not explicit about how total scores for his respondents are calculated. The different indices in his study are generally computed by summing the individual responses. However, he uses an average for the first index in the book. His usage seems to indicate an average score for job motivation.[11] (4) The validity and reliability of the measures are adequate. The following comments by Patchen are appropriate in this context:

> In general, the data show that the indices of job motivation have fairly good ability to distinguish among individuals or groups when there is considerable variation in index scores and/or on the criteria being predicted. The indices show less ability to detect fine differences within units where job motivation is relatively homogeneous. The indices appear, therefore, to be of greater use in the former situation.

> Of the three indices used, Index B is probably best for use in distinguishing among individuals in the same unit or same type of unit. Index C is probably best for use in characterizing groups. Finally, it should be noted that additional reliability evidence is needed for Indices B and C. Additional items for the indices may also be desirable.[12]

Source. Martin Patchen, *Some Questionnaire Measures of Employee Motivation and Morale* (Ann Arbor, Mich.: Survey Research Center, University of Michigan, 1965), pp. 1–14 and 26–39.

Further Sources. 1. Martin Patchen, "Participation in Decision-Making and Motivation: What is the Relation?" *Personnel Administration*, 27 (November–December, 1964), 24–31.

2. Martin Patchen, "Labor-Management Consultation at TVA: Its Impact on

Employees," *Administrative Science Quarterly*, 10 (September, 1965), 149–174.

3. Martin Patchen, *Participation, Achievement, and Involvement on the Job* (Englewood Cliffs, N.J.: Prentice-Hall, 1970).[13]

ADDITIONAL READINGS

1. Robert Dubin, "Industrial Workers' Worlds: A Study of the 'Central Life Interests' of Industrial Workers," *Social Problems*, 3 (January, 1956), 131–142.[14]
2. Louis H. Orzack, "Work as a 'Central Life Interest' of Professionals," *Social Problems*, 7 (Fall, 1959), 125–132.
3. Donald C. Pelz and Frank M. Andrews, *Scientists in Organizations* (New York: Wiley, 1966), pp. 80–89.
4. Victor H. Vroom, "Ego-Involvement, Job Satisfaction, and Job Performance," *Personnel Psychology*, 15 (Summer, 1962), 159–177.

NOTES

1. John P. Robinson, Robert Athanasiou, Kendra B. Head, *Measures of Occupational Attitudes and Occupational Characteristics* (Ann Arbor, Mich.: Survey Research Center, University of Michigan, 1969), p. 79.
2. The concept of "organizational climate" is discussed in the chapter on alienation.
3. The following sources distinguish motivation and satisfaction: Mason Haire, Edwin E. Ghiselli, and Lyman W. Porter, *Managerial Thinking* (New York: Wiley, 1966), p. 73; Nancy C. Morse, *Satisfactions in the White-Collar Job* (Ann Arbor, Mich.: Survey Research Center, 1953), pp. 11–12; Donald C. Pelz and Frank M. Andrews, *Scientists in Organizations* (New York: Wiley, 1966), pp. 80–89; Robinson *et al., op. cit*; and Arnold S. Tannenbaum, *Social Psychology of the Work Organization* (Belmont, Calif.: Wadsworth, 1966), pp. 36–37.
4. Alienation is referred to as "commitment to work" in William A. Faunce, *Problems of an Industrial Society* (New York: McGraw-Hill, 1968), p. 149. Faunce, however, does not generally refer to alienation in this manner.
5. An example of the use of objective data (accidents, sickness, and absences) to measure a subjective concept ("withdrawal from work") is J. M. M. Hill and E. L. Trist, *Industrial Accidents, Sickness, and other Absences* (London: Tavistock, 1962).
6. Thomas M. Lodahl and Mathilde Kejner, "The Definition and Measurement of Job Involvement," *Journal of Applied Psychology*, 49 (February, 1965), p. 25.
7. The researchers also present information about the reliability of the six-item scale.
8. Martin Patchen, *Some Questionnaire Measures of Employee Motivation and Morale* (Ann Arbor, Mich.: Survey Research Center, University of Michigan, 1965), p. 26.
9. This question is used in the electronics company and in the appliance company, but not at TVA.

10. This question is used in the electronics company and in the appliance company, but not at TVA.
11. See Patchen, *op. cit.*, p. 39 (esp. the first line).
12. *Ibid.*, p. 39.
13. This study came to this handbook's attention too late to be included.
14. The Dubin and Orzack readings should be viewed as a unit because Orzack tests Dubin's "central life interest" idea in a professional setting.

BASES OF POWER

17 _____

Definition. Measures, focusing on the distribution of power, are presented in connection with autonomy and centralization. Autonomy examines this distribution from the perspective of the organization and its environment, whereas centralization examines the distribution of power within the organization. *Bases of power*, however, are the source of an individual's capacity to obtain performance from other individuals.[1] Different sources of power are distinguished. An individual (sometimes referred to as a "power wielder") may exercise power over other individuals (sometimes referred to as "power recipients") because of his control of sanctions, the respect accorded his knowledge, the existence of norms which legitimate his exercise of power, and because of his personal attractiveness. Material relevant to the bases of power often appears in discussions of Weber's classic typology of authority and Etzioni's widely cited typology of organizations.[2]

Measurement. Most of the empirical work with respect to the bases of power stems from the work of French and Raven, whose major intellectual influence was the ideas of Kurt Lewin.[3] Max Weber's ideas about the bases of power, which are widely cited by organizational researchers, have not stimulated measurement research comparable in quality to the work of French and Raven. The measure selected (Bachman) is in the tradition of French and Raven's research on the bases of power.

THE MEASURE

BACHMAN

Description. This research attempts to provide some useful guidelines for college administrators and to explore the parallels between administrative process in higher education and those in other kinds of organizations, especially industrial ones. The respondents selected for study consist of full-time faculty members at each of 12 liberal arts colleges belonging to a regional association of colleges. Faculty size at the 12 colleges ranges from 67 to 173, with a median of 92 and a mean of 101. The sample consists of 685 faculty members.

Definition. Bases of influence refers to the reasons for doing things suggested by a superior.

Data Collection. The following questionnaire item is used to collect information about the bases of the academic dean's influence over the respondents:

> Listed below are five reasons generally given by people when they are asked *why* they do the things their superiors suggest or want them to do.[4] Please read all five carefully. Then number them according to their importance to you as reasons for doing the things your academic dean suggests or wants you to do. Give rank "1" to the most important factor, "2" to the next, etc.
>
> A. I respect him personally, and want to act in a way that merits his respect and admiration.
> B. I respect his competence and judgment about things with which he is more experienced than I.
> C. He can give special help and benefits to those who cooperate with him.
> D. He can apply pressure or penalize those who do not cooperate.
> E. He has a legitimate right, considering his position, to expect that his suggestions will be carried out.

These "five reasons" are designed by Bachman to collect information about French and Raven's five different bases of powers. The five bases, and the corresponding responses, are as follows: referent (Response A), expert (Response B), reward (Response C), coercive (Response D), and legitimate (Response E).

Computation. The scores assigned are indicated on the questionnaire item reproduced in the preceding section. Means and standard deviations are computed for the respondents, as discrete individuals ($N = 685$), and as members of colleges ($N = 12$). Table 17–1 presents these means and standard deviations for the bases of dean's influence.

TABLE 17–1 Bases of Dean's Influence, Means, and Standard Deviations

	M Rating ($N = 685$)	*SD among individuals* ($N = 685$)	*SD among college Ms* ($N = 685$)
Referent	2.48	1.09	0.19
Expert	1.94	1.15	0.38
Reward	3.67	0.96	0.16
Coercive	4.40	1.07	0.26
Legitimate	2.40	1.14	0.20

The lower the score for the bases of influence ("1" and "5" are, respectively, the lowest and highest possible scores), the more important is the particular basis of influence being ranked.

Validity. (1) Satisfaction with the academic dean is higher when the dean's influence is based on expertise and personal attractiveness (the expert and referent bases of influence) rather than when the dean's influence is based on legitimacy and the use of sanctions (the reward and coercive bases of influence). This finding corresponds to the results of a previous study of account executives and office managers.[5] (2) In the previous study of account executives and office managers, legitimate influence is consistently rated most important. In the present study, on the other hand, expertise is considered the most important basis of the dean's influence, with legitimate influence given a second level of priority. As might be predicted, college faculty members are clearly less likely than account executives and office managers to see themselves as subordinates in a hierarchy.

Reliability. The study contains no data relevant to reliability.

Comments. (1) Bachman's "bases of influence" corresponds to this handbook's "bases of power." It is fairly common in organizational literature to indicate the same concept by such terms as "power," "influence," and "control."[6] This handbook uses the term power because it is used more widely than either influence or control. (2) Bachman's questionnaire item refers to the "academic dean" and will thus have to be modified when used to study other types of organizations. (3) The lower the score for the bases of influence, the more important is the particular basis of influence being ranked. It may have been somewhat less confusing to the reader to have reversed this scoring, that is, to have made "5" (rather than "1") the most important ranking. (4) Bachman's presentation of means and standard deviations will provide a baseline for future replications. The use of a measure should, at the minimum, be accompanied by means and standard deviations. (5) The validity of the measure appears to be adequate, whereas the reliability is inadequate. No measures of reliability could be located in any of the studies on the bases of power which stem from the work of French and Raven.

Source. Jerald G. Bachman, "Faculty Satisfaction and the Dean's Influence: An Organizational Study of Twelve Liberal Arts Colleges," *Journal of Applied Psychology*, 52 (February, 1968), 55–61.

Further Sources. 1. Jerald G. Bachman, Clagett G. Smith, and Jonathan A. Slesinger, "Control, Performance, and Satisfaction: An Analysis of Structural and Individual Effects," *Journal of Personality and Social Psychology*, 4 (August, 1966), 127–136.

2. Jerald G. Bachman, David G. Bowers, and Philip M. Marcus, "Bases of Supervisory Power: A Comparative Study in Five Organizational Settings," in *Control in Organizations*, ed. Arnold S. Tannenbaum (New York: McGraw-Hill, 1968), pp. 229–238.

3. Dorwin Cartwright, "Influence, Leadership, Control," in *Handbook of*

Organizations, ed. James G. March (Chicago: Rand McNally, 1965), pp. 1–47.

4. John R. P. French, Jr. and Richard Snyder, "Leadership and Interpersonal Power," in *Studies in Social Power*, ed. Dorwin Cartwright (Ann Arbor, Mich.: Institute for Social Research, University of Michigan, 1959), pp. 118–149.

5. John R. P. French, Jr. and Bertram Raven, "The Bases of Social Power," in *Studies in Social Power*, ed. Dorwin Cartwright (Ann Arbor, Mich.: Institute for Social Research, University of Michigan, 1959), pp. 150–167.

6. John R. P. French, Jr., H. William Morrison, and George Levinger, "Coercive Power and Forces Affecting Conformity," *Journal of Abnormal and Social Psychology*, 61 (July, 1960), 93–101.

7. Robert L. Kahn, Donald M. Wolfe, Robert P. Quinn, and J. Diedrick Snoek, *Organizational Stress* (New York: Wiley, 1964).

8. Bertram H. Raven and John R. P. French, Jr., "Legitimate Power, Coercive Power, and Observability in Social Influence," *Sociometry*, 21 (June, 1958), 83–97.

9. Bertram H. Raven, "Social Influence on Opinions and the Communication of Related Content," *Journal of Abnormal and Social Psychology*, 58 (January, 1959), 119–128.

10. Bertram H. Raven and John R. P. French, Jr., "Group Support, Legitimate Power, and Social Influence," *Journal of Personality*, 26 (September, 1958), 400–409.

11. Ezra Stotland and Alvin Zander, "Effects of Public and Private Failure on Self-Evaluation," *Journal of Abnormal and Social Psychology*, 56 (March, 1958), 223–229.

12. Donald I. Warren, "Power, Visibility, and Conformity in Formal Organizations," *American Sociological Review*, 33 (December, 1968), 951–970.

13. ——, "The Effects of Power Bases and Peer Groups on Conformity in Formal Organizations," *Administrative Science Quarterly*, 14 (December, 1969), 544–556.

14. Alvin Zander and Theodore Curtis, "Effects of Social Power on Aspiration Setting and Striving," *Journal of Abnormal and Social Psychology*, 64 (January, 1962), 63–74.

ADDITIONAL READINGS

1. Fred E. Fiedler, *A Theory of Leadership Effectiveness* (New York: McGraw-Hill, 1967), p. 281.

2. Robert L. Peabody, "Perceptions of Organizational Authority," *Administrative Science Quarterly*, 6 (March, 1962), 463–482.

3. Robert L. Peabody, *Organizational Authority* (New York: Atherton, 1964).

NOTES

1. This definition is based on Jerald G. Bachman, David G. Bowers, and Philip M. Marcus, "Bases of Supervisory Power: A Comparative Study in Five Organizational Settings," in *Control in Organizations*, ed. Arnold S. Tannenbaum (New York: McGraw-Hill, 1968), p. 229.

2. The basic sources for Weber's typology of authority are Max Weber, *The Theory of Social and Economic Organization* (New York: Oxford, 1947), pp. 329–341 and Max Weber, *From Max Weber: Essays in Sociology* (New York: Oxford, 1946), pp. 196–244. Also very helpful is Reinhard Bendix, *Max Weber* (Garden City, N. Y.: Doubleday, 1960), pp. 289–459. The source of Etzioni's typology is Amitai Etzioni, *A Comparative Analysis of Complex Organizations* (New York: Free Press of Glencoe, 1961), pp. 3–67. Also relevant is Amitai Etzioni, *Modern Organizations* (Englewood Cliffs, N. J.: Prentice-Hall, 1964), pp. 58–67.

3. The most influential of French and Raven's work is John R. P. French, Jr. and Bertram Raven, "The Bases of Social Power," in *Studies in Social Power*, ed. Dorwin Cartwright (Ann Arbor, Mich.: Institute for Social Research, University of Michigan, 1959), pp. 150–167.

4. The emphasis is found in the original.

5. Jerald G. Bachman, Clagett G. Smith, and Jonathan A. Slesinger, "Control, Performance, and Satisfaction: An Analysis of Structural and Individual Effects," *Journal of Personality and Social Psychology*, 4 (August, 1966), 127–136.

6. Bachman equates influence and control. See Jerald G. Bachman, "Faculty Satisfaction and the Dean's Influence: An Organizational Study of Twelve Liberal Arts Colleges," *Journal of Applied Psychology*, 52 (February, 1968), p. 55.

ROUTINIZATION

18 _____

Definition. *Routinization* is the degree to which role performance in a social system is repetitive.[1] In an organization, for example, the degree of routinization is closely linked to different occupations. Blue-collar occupations are generally more routinized than are white-collar occupations. Among blue-collar occupations, craft occupations have a lower degree of routinization than semi-skilled and unskilled occupations. Among white-collar occupations, the managerial and professional occupations have a lower degree of routinization than secretarial and clerical occupations. The concept of routinization is discussed under many labels in organizational literature: "technology," "standardization," "technological complexity," "programmed decision-making," "complexity," and "professionalization."

The degree of professionalization is often used to characterize organizations;[2] however, this handbook has no separate chapter devoted to professionalization. The frame of reference used in this handbook is applicable to all types of social systems. In short, the concepts are analytical. Professionalization, however, refers, not to a *social system*, such as an organization, but to an *occupation*.[3] Since an occupation is not a social system, this handbook does not devote a separate chapter to professionalization. When organizations are characterized concerning their degree of professionalization, the reference, in the terms of this handbook, is basically to their degree of routinization. This handbook deals basically with the referent of professionalization, albeit, under the label of routinization.

The concept of routinization should not be restricted to the production system of an organization.[4] As in the illustrations in the first paragraph, the concept can be used to indicate role performance in either the production system or the administration system. Routinization, like mechanization, refers to all the components of a social system.

Measurement. There has been little measurement research with respect to routinization. The research of Hage and Aiken is the exception to this generalization; therefore, one of their articles is selected for this handbook.

THE MEASURE

HAGE AND AIKEN

Description. This study investigates the relationship between technology, social structure, and goals. The component of technology investigated is "routineness of work." The data upon which this study is based were gathered in 16 social welfare and health organizations located in a large midwestern metropolis in 1967. Ten organizations are private; six are either public or branches of public agencies. These are all large welfare organizations that provide rehabilitation, psychiatric services, and assistance for the mentally retarded. Interviews were conducted with 520 staff members. Respondents within each organization were selected by the following criteria: (1) all executive directors and department heads; (2) in departments of less than ten members, one-half of the staff was selected randomly; (3) in departments of more than ten members, one-third of the staff was selected randomly. Interviews were not conducted with nonsupervisory administrative and maintenance personnel.

Definition. Routineness of work refers to " . . . the degree to which organizational members have non-uniform work activities. . . ."[5]

Data Collection. Five questions were used in the interviews to collect the data to measure routinization. The five questions have two different formats on the interview schedule.[6] The first question is as follows:

> 1.[7] Would you describe your job as being highly routine, somewhat routine, somewhat non-routine, or highly non-routine?[8]

Highly Routine	Somewhat Routine	Somewhat Non-routine	Highly Non-routine

The remaining four questions[9] are as follows:

> I'm going to read a series of statements that may or may not be true for your job in (NAME OF ORGANIZATION). For each item I read, please answer as it applies to you and your organization, using the answer categories on this next card. (SHOW CARD 1)

CARD I

CARD I	Definitely true	More true than false	More false than true	Definitely false
1. Definitely true				
2. More true than false				
3. More false than true				
4. Definitely false				

> 2. People here do the same job in the same way every day.

    _____   _____   _____   _____

	Definitely true	More true than false	More false than true	Definitely false
3. One thing people like around here is the variety of work.	_____	_____	_____	_____
4. Most jobs have something new happening every day.	_____	_____	_____	_____
5. There is something different to do every day.[10]	_____	_____	_____	_____

Computation. The first question is scored from "1" (highly non-routine) to "4" (highly routine). The remaining four questions are also scored from "1" (definitely true) to "4" (definitely false).[11] An average score on these five questions is computed for each respondent. Each respondent is then classified by "social position" and a second mean is computed for each social position. "... A social position," according to Hage and Aiken, "was defined ... by level and department. For example, if an organization's professional staff consisted of two departments—psychiatric and social work—and two levels—supervisors and caseworkers—there were four social positions in the organization."[12] These four social positions would be as follows: supervisory psychiatrist, psychiatrist, supervisory caseworkers, and caseworkers. The organizational score is determined by computing the average of all social position means in the organization. Table 18–1 presents the means and ranges for scores of degree of routineness in different types of organizations.

TABLE 18–1   Means and Ranges for Scores of Degree of Routineness in Different Types of Organizations

Type of Organization	Number	Mean	Range
Family agencies	6	1.83	1.31–2.46
Rehabilitation centers	3	1.80	1.59–1.94
Residential treatment homes	3	1.73	1.46–1.90
Mental hospitals	3	1.73	1.63–1.82
Department of special education	1	1.64	1.64

The lowest possible score is "1" (highly non-routine) and the highest possible score is "4" (highly routine).

Validity. (1) Since these organizations provide psychological, psychiatric, and rehabilitation service, it could be anticipated that their scores would tend more toward non-routineness. The scores in Table 18–1 indicate that this is the case; none of the means is larger than "2." (2) As might be anticipated, the higher the occupational level within each organization, the more likely the job occupant is to report that his job is very non-routine. Hage and Aiken do not present the scores for these different occupational levels. (3) The social structure of organizations with more routine work are found to be more centralized, more formalized, and to have less professionally-trained staffs; however, no relationship with stratification is found. Organizations with routine work are further found to emphasize goals of efficiency and the quantity of clients served, not innovativeness, satisfaction, or quality of client services. These findings basically confirmed predictions made by the researchers.

Reliability. The study contains no data relevant to reliability.

Comments. (1) Hage and Aiken's concept of "routineness of work" corresponds very closely to this handbook's concept of "routinization." It is clear, for example, that "uniform" and "repetitive" refer to the same type of role performance. It is also clear that Hage and Aiken do not limit routineness of work to the production system of an organization; their concept is applicable to both the production system and the administrative system. Hage and Aiken's ideas are not identical with those of this handbook, however. They include "professionalization" as part of "complexity," whereas this handbook includes most of the referent of professionalization under routinization.[13] Hage and Aiken also view routineness of work under the more general term "technology." As Hage and Aiken carefully note, technology includes different analytical concepts, among them routinization and mechanization, which are treated separately in this handbook.[14] (2) Hage and Aiken's means and ranges should facilitate comparisons with further research which uses their measures. It would have been helpful had they also presented a single mean for the 16 organizations. Standard deviations, by type of organization and for all organizations, would also have been useful for comparative research. (3) It would be easier for the reader had Hage and Aiken presented their scoring in this article rather than in another article.[15]

Source. Jerald Hage and Michael Aiken, "Routine Technology, Social Structure, and Organization Goals," *Administrative Science Quarterly*, 14 (September, 1969), 366–375.

Further Sources. 1. Michael Aiken and Jerald Hage, "Organizational Interdependence and Intra-Organizational Structure," *American Sociological Review*, 33 (December, 1968), 912–930.
2. Richard H. Hall, "An Empirical Study of Bureaucratic Dimensions and Their Relation to Other Organizational Characteristics" (unpublished Ph.D. dissertation, Columbus, The Ohio State University, 1961).[16]
3. Richard H. Hall, "Intraorganizational Structural Variation," *Administrative Science Quarterly*, 7 (December, 1962), 295–308.

4. Richard H. Hall, "The Concept of Bureaucracy: An Empirical Assessment," *American Journal of Sociology*, 69 (July, 1963), 32–40.

ADDITIONAL READINGS

1. Fred E. Fiedler, *A Theory of Leadership Effectiveness* (New York: McGraw-Hill, 1967), pp. 282–291.
2. D. S. Pugh, D. J. Hickson, C. R. Hinings, and C. Turner, "Dimensions of Organizational Structure," *Administrative Science Quarterly*, 13 (June, 1968), 65–105.
3. Arthur N. Turner and Paul R. Lawrence, *Industrial Jobs and the Worker* (Boston: Graduate School of Business Administration, Harvard, 1965).

NOTES

1. Two very helpful articles dealing with the concept of routinization are Eugene Litwak, "Models of Bureaucracy Which Permit Conflict," *American Journal of Sociology*, 67 (September, 1961), 177–184 and Charles Perrow, "A Framework for the Comparative Analysis of Organizations," *American Sociological Review*, 32 (April, 1967), 194–208. The term "routinization" comes from the work of Max Weber.

2. Blau and his colleagues, for example, commonly refer to the degree of professionalization of an organization. See Peter M. Blau, Wolf V. Heydebrand, and Robert E. Stauffer, "The Structure of Small Bureaucracies," *American Sociological Review*, 31 (April, 1966), 179–191 (esp. 181–182). Most of their research is cited under "Additional Readings" in the chapter on complexity.

3. An excellent introduction to the literature on professions is Richard H. Hall, *Occupations and the Social Structure* (Englewood Cliffs, N. J.: Prentice-Hall, 1969), pp. 70–137. The first sentence is instructive:

   Profession is probably the most widely used and commonly known *occupational* category and refers to the *occupational* class most readily identified as a type of *occupation* by the public at large. . . . (Emphasis added with respect to "occupational" and "occupation.")

   This quotation from Hall's book is not intended to imply his support for this handbook's approach to professionalization. His opinion on this point is unknown to the author of this handbook. Not cited in Hall's book is an excellent measurement article by Hickson and Thomas. See D. J. Hickson and M. W. Thomas, "Professionalization in Britain: A Preliminary Measurement," *Sociology*, 3 (January, 1969), 37–53.

4. Perrow, in *op. cit.*, seems to restrict routinization to the production system of an organization.

5. Michael Aiken and Jerald Hage, "Organizational Interdependence and Intra-Organizational Structure," *American Sociological Review*, 33 (December, 1968), p. 927.

6. The relevant parts of the interview schedule are not reproduced in the article but are supplied through the courtesy of Jerald Hage.

7. The numbers in this handbook differ from those on the original version of the interview schedule.

8. The original version of the interview schedule also contains instructions for probing.

9. This handbook selects from the interview schedule only the four questions which collect data for the measurement of routinization. The interview schedule, at this point, also includes questions to collect information for the measurement of centralization and formalization.

10. The original version of the interview schedule, at this point, instructs the interviewer to "RECORD COMMENTS, BUT DO NOT PROBE."

11. This computation information comes from Aiken and Hage, *op. cit.*, p. 927.

12. Jerald Hage and Michael Aiken, "Routine Technology, Social Structure, and Organization Goals," *Administrative Science Quarterly*, 14 (September, 1969), p. 368.

13. Part of what Hage and Aiken mean by complexity is also included in this handbook's concept of complexity.

14. The procedure followed with respect to "technology" is also followed with respect to "bureaucracy," "organizational climate," and "primary-secondary" social relationships. These concepts are discussed, respectively, in the chapters on administrative staff, alienation, and formalization. The discussion of technology in the chapter on mechanization is also relevant to the material in this chapter.

15. Aiken and Hage, *op. cit.*

16. The last four questions used by Hage and Aiken come from Hall's dissertation where they are part of his "division of labor" scale. Hall's scale, used in his much cited article on bureaucracy (Further Source No. 4), is described in his dissertation. The construction of the scale is described in the second chapter of the dissertation; the instrument of data collection is found in Appendix V.

SATISFACTION

19 _____

Definition. *Satisfaction* is the degree to which the members of a social system have a positive affective orientation toward membership in the system.[1] Members who have a positive affective orientation are satisfied, whereas members who have a negative affective orientation are dissatisfied. The organizational literature commonly distinguishes various dimensions of satisfaction, such as work, supervision, pay, promotion, and co-workers.[2] Thus it is possible to have different degrees of satisfaction for the different dimensions. Data pertinent to satisfaction are found in discussions of "morale,"[3] "identification," "job attitudes," "boredom," "cohesion," "solidarity," "loyalty," "integration," and "organizational climate."

"Satisfaction" is often distinguished from "general satisfaction."[4] The latter term refers to satisfaction with "life in general." The concepts of this handbook are applicable to any social system: one can be satisfied with membership in an organization, community, society, family, or peer group. The concepts, in short, are analytical. It is only the measures which are focused on a specific type of social system, the organization. The referent for general satisfaction, however, is more general than the referent for satisfaction. General satisfaction has no social system as its unit of analysis. Although all the concepts of the handbook are analytical, some type of social system is used as the unit of analysis for each of the concepts. The relationship between satisfaction and general satisfaction should be explored;[5] meanwhile, the less general referent is used in this handbook.

The "Herzberg controversy" has raised important issues in the definition and measurement of satisfaction. The traditional point of view assumes that the same dimensions are capable of producing either satisfaction or dissatisfaction: a high amount of the dimension produces satisfaction, whereas a low amount of the dimension produces dissatisfaction. Herzberg and his colleagues have challenged the traditional point of view. They have argued that certain dimensions in the work situation (termed "satisfiers") are capable of producing satisfaction, but play an extremely small part in producing dissatisfaction; on the other hand, other dimensions in the work situation (termed "dissatisfiers") are capable of producing dissatisfaction, but do not generally lead to satisfaction. The Herzberg study cites the dimensions of work, responsibility, and advancement as the major satisfiers, whereas company policy and administration, supervision (both technical and interpersonal relationships), working conditions, and pay are cited as the major dissatisfiers.

There has been an immense amount of research devoted to testing the "two-factor theory" advanced by Herzberg and his colleagues. Several authors have carefully reviewed this literature and have attempted to evaluate the evidence. The conclusion advanced by Smith and Cranny seems to be dominant at the present time; they state that

> Herzberg must be given credit for highlighting the essential multidimensionality of satisfaction. *The weight of recent evidence, however, is against his two-factor oversimplification.*[6] (Emphasis supplied.)

This handbook adopts the traditional concept of satisfaction; therefore, it is assumed that the same organizational dimension can produce either satisfaction or dissatisfaction.

Material relevant to satisfaction is found in discussions of "cohesion," "solidarity," "loyalty," and "integration." The latter four terms seem to be referring to essentially the same concept; "cohesion" is probably the most common.[7] *The position of this handbook is that the concepts of satisfaction and cohesion are very similar.* The most widely used definition of cohesiveness is stated well in Back's article: ". . . cohesiveness is the *attraction* of membership in a group for its members. . . ."[8] (Emphasis supplied.) Back then indicates three bases for the attractiveness of a group:

> Individuals may want to belong to a group because they like the other members, because being a member of a group may be attractive in itself (for example, it may be an honor to belong to it), or because the group may mediate goals which are important for the members. . . .[9]

The measurement of cohesion emphasizes, generally by some form of friendship choice, the first basis of attraction, that is, the liking of other members. Satisfaction with "supervision" and "co-workers" are dimensions of the term and seem to encompass most of what is meant by liking "the other members" of a group.[10] The most commonly emphasized basis of attraction is thus explored, by use of different terms, in the study of satisfaction. Members of an organization can also be satisfied with its prestige and goals, Back's second and third bases of attraction. These dimensions of satisfaction are not generally explored; however, there is no reason why they could not be explored in the same manner as "supervision" and "co-workers." To assert that a group is highly attractive to its members is to assert that the members have a very positive affective orientation toward membership in the group. "Attraction" and "affective orientation" seem to have basically the same referent.

This handbook distinguishes alienation and satisfaction. Both are social psychological concepts, that is, they refer to internal orientations. However, the perception of "powerlessness"—this handbook's definition of alienation —has a cognitive reference, whereas satisfaction has an affective reference. The cognitive and affective components of internal orientations are commonly distinguished in social psychological research.[11] The term alienation, however, is often used in the literature to refer to the concept of satisfaction, as defined by this handbook.

Measurement. There are at least five excellent measures of satisfaction that could be selected. Satisfaction is the only concept for which there is an abundance of excellent measures. The strategy of this handbook, in the face of this unusual embarrassment of riches, is to select measures that illustrate different approaches.

There are two approaches to the measurement of satisfaction in organizational literature.[12] One approach is to collect information about general satisfaction with membership in the organization. The other approach is to collect information about specific dimensions of satisfaction, such as work, supervision, pay, promotion, and co-workers. The first measure (Brayfield and Rothe) illustrates the general approach; the second measure (Porter and Lawler) and the third measure (Smith, Kendall, and Hulin) illustrate the specific approach.[13]

Although the second and third measures illustrate the specific approach, they differ in two significant ways. The Porter and Lawler measure is based on Maslow's categorization of needs[14] and measures satisfaction in terms of the difference between actual and anticipated fulfillment. The Smith, Kendall, and Hulin measure is based on no explicit theory and measures satisfaction in terms of actual fulfillment. The second and third measures, despite their common focus on specific dimensions of satisfaction, thus provide quite different approaches.

Absenteeism and turnover are commonly used measures of satisfaction.[15] They are not used as measures of satisfaction by this handbook because they are structural concepts rather than social psychological concepts. Absenteeism has already been defined in terms of failure to report for scheduled work; there is thus no reference to internal orientation in this definition.[16] Turnover is also defined in structural terms in the discussion of succession. This handbook makes no explicit attempt to classify its frame of reference into structural and social psychological concepts; it is not apparent how such an explicit classification would be useful. However, the definition and measurement work of the handbook has been informed by the common distinction between structural concepts and social psychological concepts.

THE MEASURES

1. BRAYFIELD AND ROTHE

Description. The purpose of this study is to develop an index of job satisfaction. Different groups were used in the development of the index; however, the final version of the index was administered to two samples. One sample consists of 231 female office employees in typing, stenographic, clerical, and accounting positions. These office employees are mostly young, unmarried girls without dependents. The average girl in the sample has completed 12 years of schooling. She has been on her present job for more than one year and has been employed by the company for one and three-fourths years. The second sample consists of 91 adult night school students in classes in Personnel Psychology at the University of Minnesota during 1945 and 1946. The group includes 49 males and 42 females. The age range is from 22 to 54 with a median of 35 years. Practically the entire sample is engaged in either clerical, semi-professional, professional, or managerial occupations.

Definition. There is no explicit definition of job satisfaction in the article. However, the questionnaire refers to "how people feel about different jobs."[17] The feelings range from highly satisfied to lowly satisfied.

Data Collection. The data were collected by means of the following questionnaire items:

Some jobs are more interesting and satisfying than others. We want to know how people feel about different jobs. This blank contains 18 statements about jobs. You are to cross out the phrase below each statement which best describes how you feel about your present job. There are no right or wrong answers. We should like your honest opinion on each one of the statements. Work out the sample item numbered (0).

0. There are some conditions concerning my job that could be improved.
   STRONGLY AGREE AGREE UNDECIDED DISAGREE STRONGLY DISAGREE[18]
1. My job is like a hobby to me.
2. My job is usually interesting enough to keep me from getting bored.
3. It seems that my friends are more interested in their jobs.
4. I consider my job rather unpleasant.
5. I enjoy my work more than my leisure time.
6. I am often bored with my job.
7. I feel fairly well satisfied with my present job.
8. Most of the time I have to force myself to go to work.
9. I am satisfied with my job for the time being.
10. I feel that my job is no more interesting than others I could get.
11. I definitely dislike my work.
12. I feel that I am happier in my work than most other people.
13. Most days I am enthusiastic about my work.
14. Each day of work seems like it will never end.
15. I like my job better than the average worker does.
16. My job is pretty uninteresting.
17. I find real enjoyment in my work.
18. I am disappointed that I ever took this job.

Computation. The five responses are scored from "1" to "5". The scoring varies with the format of the question. Questions 1, 2, 5, 7, 9, 12, 13, 15, and 17 are scored in the following manner: Strongly Agree ("5"), Agree ("4"), Undecided ("3"), Disagree ("2"), and Strongly Disagree ("1"). The remaining questions are scored in the following manner: Strongly Agree ("1"), Agree ("2"), Undecided ("3"), Disagree ("4"), and Strongly Disagree ("5"). The scores for the 18 items are summed. The larger the score, the higher the satisfaction. The scores range from 18 (low satisfaction) to 90 (high satisfaction). The range of scores for the sample of female office employees is 35 to 87; the mean score is 63.8 with a standard deviation of 9.4. The range of scores for the adult night school students is 29 to 89; the mean score is 70.4 with a standard deviation of 13.2.

Validity. (1) The adult night school students are divided into two categories, those employed in personnel occupations and those not employed in personnel occupations. Since the night school course was concerned with Personnel Psychology, it was assumed that the students employed in personnel occupations would be more satisfied with their jobs than the students not employed in personnel jobs. This assumption is confirmed by the data. (2) The adult night school students also completed a measure of job satisfaction developed by Hoppock in the early 1930's.[19] The product-moment correlation between scores on the Hoppock blank (Form 11) and the Brayfield–Rothe index is .92.[20]

Reliability. The odd-even product-moment reliability coefficient computed for the sample of female office employees is .77, which is corrected by the Spearman-Brown formula to .87.

Comments. (1) Brayfield and Rothe's implicit definition of satisfaction seems to correspond quite closely to this handbook's definition of satisfaction. The way the members of the organization "feel" about their jobs—Brayfield and Rothe's implicit definition—seems to have essentially the same referent as the degree of "affective" orientation toward the organization—this handbook's definition. "Feel" and "affect" are often used interchangeably in organizational literature. (2) The computational section indicates that the scoring varies with the format of the question. However, Brayfield and Rothe do not indicate the exact procedure. The scoring for the different questions is relatively easy to determine, but it would have been helpful if Brayfield and Rothe had explicitly indicated the scoring for the reader. (3) The presentation of the means, standard deviations, and ranges for the scores is helpful. Organizational researchers would do well to emulate this aspect of Brayfield and Rothe's research. (4) The index appears to have adequate validity and reliability. It is gratifying to note that, unlike most organizational researchers, Brayfield and Rothe explicitly confront the problems of validity and reliability.

Source. Arthur H. Brayfield and Harold F. Rothe, "An Index of Job Satisfaction," *Journal of Applied Psychology*, 35 (October, 1951), 307–311.

Further Sources. 1. Philip Ash, "The SRA Employee Inventory—A Statistical Analysis," *Personnel Psychology*, 7 (Autumn, 1954), 337–363.
2. Arthur H. Brayfield, Richard V. Wells, and Marvin W. Strate, "Interrelationships Among Measures of Job Satisfaction and General Satisfaction," *Journal of Applied Psychology*, 41 (August, 1957), 201–205.
3. Robert B. Ewen, "Weighting Components of Job Satisfaction," *Journal of Applied Psychology*, 51 (February, 1967), 68–73.

2. PORTER AND LAWLER

Description. This study, carried out in seven organizations, investigates the relationship between attitudes and behavior; the specific focus is upon job attitudes and job behavior. Three of the organizations are divisions of state governments; the other four are privately-owned manufacturing and utility companies. The sample from these seven organizations consists of 563 middle-level and lower-level managers.

Definition. "Satisfaction," according to Porter and Lawler, "is defined as the extent to which rewards actually received meet or exceed the perceived equitable level of rewards. The greater the failure of actual rewards to meet or exceed perceived equitable rewards, the more dissatisfied a person is considered to be in a given situation."[21]

Data Collection. The following questionnaire items are used to collect the data:
On the following pages will be listed several characteristics of qualities connected with your own management position. For each such characteristic, you will be asked to give three ratings.

a) How much of the characteristic is there now connected with your management position?
b) How much of the characteristic do you think should be connected with your managerial position?
c) How important is this position characteristic to you?
Each rating will be on a seven-point scale, which will look like this:
(minimum)   1   2   3   4   5   6   7   (maximum)

You are to circle the number on the scale that represents the amount of the characteristic being rated. Low numbers represent low or minimum amounts, and high numbers represent high or maximum amounts. If you think there is "very little" or "none" of the characteristic presently associated with the position, you would circle numeral 1. If you think there is "just a little," you would circle numeral 2, and so on. If you think there is a "great deal but not a maximum amount," you would circle numeral 6. For each scale, circle only one number.

Please do not omit any scales.

1. The feeling of self-esteem a person gets from being in my management position:

   a) How much is there now?   (min) 1 2 3 4 5 6 7 (max)
   b) How much should there be?   1 2 3 4 5 6 7
   c) How important is this to me?   1 2 3 4 5 6 7[22]

2. The authority connected with my management position:
3. The opportunity for personal growth and development in my management position:
4. The prestige of my management position inside the company (that is, the regard received from others in the company):
5. The opportunity for independent thought and action in my management position:
6. The feeling of security in my management position:
7. The feeling of self-fulfillment a person gets from being in my management position (that is, the feeling of being able to use one's own unique capabilities, realizing one's potentialities):
8. The prestige of my management position outside the company (that is, the regard received from others not in the company):
9. The feeling of worthwhile accomplishment in my management position:
10. The opportunity, in my management position, to give help to other people:
11. The opportunity, in my management position, for participating in the setting of goals:
12. The opportunity, in my management position, for participation in the determination of methods and procedures:
13. The opportunity to develop close friendships in my management position:

Computation. A respondent's satisfaction score is calculated by subtracting the score on response (a) from the score on response (b). The lower the score, the higher the satisfaction. The most satisfied respondent receives a score of "0," whereas the most dissatisfied respondent receives a score of "6."[23] Separate scores are calculated for the following five "need categories";[24] Security (No. 6),[25] Social (Nos. 10 and 13), Esteem (Nos. 1, 4, and 8), Autonomy (Nos. 2, 5, 11, and 12), Self-Realization (Nos. 3, 7, and 9). Means are calculated for each of these five need categories. Porter and Lawler do not present the means and standard deviations for the five need categories; however, they do present ranges for each.[26]

Validity. Two propositions related to satisfaction were advanced by Porter and Lawler prior to their research. First, they predicted that ratings of the quality of an individual's performance by his superior would be related as strongly or more strongly to his expressed degree of need fulfillment as compared to his degree of need satisfaction. The second prediction was that an individual's own ratings of the quality of his job performance would be related more strongly to his expressed degree of need fulfillment than to his degree of need satisfaction. The first proposition is not confirmed; the results show that performance differences among managers are about equally associated with satisfaction as they are with fulfillment. These results, however, are not significantly in the opposite direction from that predicted. The second proposition is confirmed.

Reliability. The study contains no data relevant to reliability.

Comments. (1) Porter and Lawler's definition mostly indicates the sources of satisfaction rather than the concept of satisfaction. "The extent to which rewards actually received meet or exceed the perceived equitable level of rewards" —Porter and Lawler's definition of satisfaction—indicates why individuals become satisfied (the rewards received meet or exceed the perceived equitable level), but does not indicate the orientational referent for the term: whether, for example, the referent is cognitive or affective. But Porter and Lawler's implied concept of satisfaction seems to be consistent with this handbook's. The term "need" used by Porter and Lawler is sometimes used very similarly to this handbook's "affect." (2) One of the outstanding features of Porter and Lawler's study is that they study satisfaction as a part of an explicit theory indicating relationships between attitudes and behavior.[27] The reader is thus spared the torture of abstracting an implicit theory from a mass of empirical data. (3) The researchers state that 13 questionnaire items are used to collect information about satisfaction;[28] the previous section on data collection contains the list of the 13 questionnaire items. However, Appendix II, which reproduces the questionnaire, contains 15 items. It is not too difficult to locate the 13 questionnaire items used to collect the data about satisfaction; the items are available in another study.[29] However, the location of these items consumes time; it would be simpler if such tasks were performed by those who conduct the research. (4) The 13 items used by the researchers are directed to the occupants of managerial roles. Note, for example, the continued reference to "my management position." This terminology will have to be modified for use with occupants of nonmanagerial roles. (5) Porter and Lawler indirectly collect their data about satisfaction. Rather than directly asking the respondents to indicate their degree of satisfaction—as do most investigations of satisfaction—Porter and Lawler collect data about actual and anticipated fulfillment. Satisfaction is the difference between actual and anticipated fulfillment. It is not a good practice to collect data for a concept by any single procedure. Therefore, Porter and Lawler's indirect collection of data provides a good supplement to the more common direct collection of data. (6) Porter and Lawler do not give complete scoring instructions for their 13 questionnaire items. They state that the difference in answers between the second alternative (the perceived equitable amount) and the first alternative (reality) of these 13 questions is taken as the measure of satisfaction. However, they do not state that these differences are used to calculate means; this part of the scoring is available in another study.[30] Complete scoring instructions should accompany the report of research. (7) Porter and Lawler score their data in such a way that a low score equals a high degree of satisfaction. It might be less confusing had the scoring been devised in such a way that a low score indicates low satisfaction. (8) The researchers presented ranges for their scores; the inclusion of means and standard deviations would also have been helpful. (9) The previous comments have been mostly critical of Porter and Lawler's research. These comments, it should be emphasized, make no basic criticism of Porter and Lawler's research; for the most part they suggest minor modifications. The major virtue of this research, and a virtue that can easily be lost to view in a handbook of organizational measurement, is that it investigates satisfaction as one component of an explicit theory of the relationship between job attitudes and job behavior. Most research on satisfaction is not guided by the theoretical sophistication demonstrated by Porter and Lawler.

Source. Lyman W. Porter and Edward E. Lawler, III, *Managerial Attitudes and Performance* (Homewood, Ill.: Irwin, 1968), pp. 1–55 and 120–150.

Further Sources. The bibliography at the end of Porter and Lawler's book contains further sources. A guide to these sources is found at the top of page 131. The following article, however, is relevant, but is not included in the book: Edward E. Lawler, III, "Managers' Attitudes Toward How Their Pay Is and Should be Determined," *Journal of Applied Psychology*, 50 (August, 1966), 273–279.

3. SMITH, KENDALL, AND HULIN

Description. The researchers' purpose is to develop measures of job satisfaction and retirement satisfaction. This handbook focuses on the measure of job satisfaction. Four studies, using a total of 988 subjects, were used to develop the measures. A final study using 2662 subjects was conducted to obtain average satisfaction scores. These studies are carefully described by Smith, Kendall, and Hulin.

Definition. Job satisfaction is defined as ". . . the feelings a worker has about his job. . . ."[31] Five dimensions of job satisfaction are distinguished: work, supervision, pay, promotions, and co-workers.

Data Collection. The data were collected by means of a questionnaire. Five scales are used to collect data about the five dimensions of job satisfaction. Each is presented on a separate page. The instructions and responses for the "work" dimension of satisfaction are as follows:

Think of your present work. What is it like most of the time? In the blank beside each word given below, write

_y_ for "YES" if it describes your work
_n_ for "NO" if it does not describe it
_?_ if you cannot decide

Similar instructions and identical responses are provided for the other four dimensions (supervision, pay, promotions, and co-workers).[32] The words used to describe the five dimensions of satisfaction are as follows:

WORK
Y Fascinating
N Routine
Y Satisfying
N Boring
Y Good
Y Creative
Y Respected
N Hot
Y Pleasant
Y Useful
N Tiresome
Y Healthful
Y Challenging
N On your feet
N Frustrating
N Simple
N Endless
Y Gives a sense of
   accomplishment

PAY
Y Income adequate for normal
   expenses
Y Satisfactory profit sharing
N Barely live on income
N Bad
Y Income provides luxuries
N Insecure
N Less than I deserve
Y Highly paid
N Underpaid

PROMOTIONS
Y Good opportunity for
   advancement
N Opportunity somewhat limited
Y Promotion on ability
N Dead-end job
Y Good chance for promotion
N Unfair promotion policy
N Infrequent promotions
Y Regular promotions
Y Fairly good chance for
   promotions

SUPERVISION
Y Asks my advice
N Hard to please
N Impolite
Y Praises good work
Y Tactful
Y Influential
Y Up-to-date
N Doesn't supervise enough
N Quick tempered
Y Tells me where I stand

CO-WORKERS
Y Stimulating
N Boring
N Slow
Y Ambitious
N Stupid
Y Responsible
Y Fast
Y Intelligent
N Easy to make enemies
N Talk too much

SUPERVISION

N Annoying
N Stubborn
Y Knows job well
N Bad
Y Intelligent
Y Leaves me on my own
N Lazy
Y Around when needed

CO-WORKERS

Y Smart
N Lazy
N Unpleasant
N No privacy
Y Active
N Narrow interests
Y Loyal
N Hard to meet

Computation. The response shown beside each item in the preceding section is the one scored in the positive direction for each scale. Under Work, for example, if the respondent places a "Y" beside "fascinating," then this item is scored in a positive direction. Conversely, if the respondent places an "N" beside "fascinating," then this item is scored in a negative direction. The scoring for the different responses are as follows: Yes to a positive item ("3"); No to a negative item ("3"); ? to any item ("1"); Yes to a negative item ("0"); and No to a positive item ("0"). The scores are summed for each of the five dimensions. Smith, Kendall and Hulin refer to their measure as the "Job Descriptive Index." The researchers present means and standard deviations for the Job Descriptive Index for large samples of men and women pooled across all companies studied; these statistics are contained in Table 19–1.

TABLE 19–1 Means and Standard Deviations for Male and Female Employees Pooled Across 21 Plants

| | | Male | | | Female | |
| | | | Standard | | | Standard |
Scale	N	Mean	Deviation	N	Mean	Deviation
Work	1971	36.57	10.54	638	35.74	9.88
Pay	1966	29.90	14.53	635	27.90	13.65
Promotions	1945	22.06	15.77	634	17.77	13.38
Supervision	1951	41.10	10.58	636	41.13	10.05
Co-Workers	1928	43.49	10.02	636	42.09	10.51

Validity. Smith, Kendall, and Hulin assess convergent and discriminant validity by means of the multitrait-multimethod matrix.[33] The results show consistent convergent and discriminant validity.

Reliability. The estimated split-half correlation coefficients, using a sample of 80 male employees from two electronics plants, are shown in Table 19-2.

Comments. (1) "The feelings a worker has about his job"—the Smith, Kendall, and Hulin definition of job satisfaction—is very similar to this handbook's

TABLE 19–2   Split-Half Correlation Coefficients

Scale	Correlation of Random Split-Halves	Correlations Corrected to Full Length by Spearman-Brown Formula
Work	.73	.84
Pay	.67	.80
Promotions	.75	.86
Supervision	.77	.87
Co-Workers	.78	.88

"degree of positive affective orientation toward membership in the system." The different dimensions of job satisfaction used by the researchers encompasses most aspects of system membership. Organizational researchers often use "feelings" and "affect" interchangeably.[34] (2) The reader may have noticed that Smith, Kendall, and Hulin have no statistic for overall satisfaction. The lack of such a statistic is consistent with the dimensional approach to the study of job satisfaction used by the researchers. (3) Smith, Kendall, and Hulin include means, standard deviations, and averages (termed "norms" by the researchers) for the Job Descriptive Index. These data should greatly facilitate comparative research. (4) Vroom's evaluation of the Job Descriptive Index is sound; he states that the index ". . . is without doubt the most carefully constructed measure of job satisfaction in existence today. . . ."[35]

Source. Patricia C. Smith, Lorne M. Kendall, and Charles L. Hulin, *The Measurement of Satisfaction in Work and Retirement* (Chicago: Rand McNally, 1969).

The following request by the researchers is relevant:

> . . . researchers wishing to use these scales in their own work are asked to inform the senior author of their intentions and to request permission for use. In this way we hope to be able to cumulate further statistics on the JDI [Job Descriptive Index].[36]

Dr. Smith is the senior author; she is a member of the Department of Psychology, Bowling Green State University, Bowling Green, Ohio.

Further Sources. Published studies by Smith and her colleagues are cited in the references at the end of the book by Smith, Kendall, and Hulin. The following sources are relevant, but are not cited in the book:

1. Robert B. Ewen, Charles L. Hulin, Patricia C. Smith, and Edwin A. Locke, "An Empirical Test of the Herzberg Two-Factor Theory," *Journal of Applied Psychology*, 50 (December, 1966), 544–550.
2. Charles L. Hulin, "Job Satisfaction and Turnover in a Female Clerical Population," *Journal of Applied Psychology*, 50 (August, 1966), 280–285.
3. Charles L. Hulin, "Effects of Changes in Job-Satisfaction Levels on Employee Turnover," *Journal of Applied Psychology*, 52 (April, 1968), 122–126.

4. Charles L. Hulin, "Source of Variation in Job and Life Satisfaction: The Role of Community and Job-Related Variables," *Journal of Applied Psychology*, 53 (August, 1969), 279–291.

5. Edwin A. Locke, "The Relationship of Task Success to Task Liking and Satisfaction," *Journal of Applied Psychology*, 49 (October, 1965), 379–385.

6. Thomas M. Lodahl and Mathilde Kejner, "The Definition and Measurement of Job Involvement," *Journal of Applied Psychology*, 49 (February, 1965), 24–33.

ADDITIONAL READINGS

The two most important measures that have been excluded from this handbook are the Minnesota Satisfaction Questionnaire and the SRA Attitude Survey (formerly, the "SRA Employee Inventory"). "SRA" refers to Science Research Associates. References are included for both of these measures.

The choice was between the three following measures: Job Descriptive Index, The Minnesota Satisfaction Questionnaire, and the SRA Attitude Survey. The measures of satisfaction developed by Brayfield–Rothe and Porter–Lawler are sufficiently different from these three measures to be included in this handbook. The Job Descriptive Index is given preference over the Minnesota Satisfaction Questionnaire and the SRA Attitude Survey because, as the statement by Vroom in the comments indicates, it is the most carefully constructed measure of job satisfaction in existence today.

Measures of cohesion are also included because, as indicated in the introduction to this chapter, this handbook takes the position that "cohesion" and "satisfaction" have essentially the same referent.[37]

1. Philip Ash, "The SRA Employee Inventory: A Statistical Analysis," *Personnel Psychology*, 7 (Autumn, 1954), 337–364.[38]

2. Melany E. Baehr, "A Simplified Procedure for the Measurement of Employee Attitudes," *Journal of Applied Psychology*, 37 (June, 1953), 163–167.

3. Melany E. Baehr, "A Factorial Study of the SRA Employee Inventory," *Personnel Psychology*, 7 (Autumn, 1954), 319–336.

4. Melany E. Baehr, "A Reply to R. J. Wherry Concerning 'An Orthogonal Re-Rotation of the Baehr and Ash Studies of the SRA Employee Inventory,' " *Personnel Psychology*, 9 (Spring, 1956), 81–92.

5. Melany E. Baehr and Richard Renck, "The Definition and Measurement of Employee Morale," *Administrative Science Quarterly*, 3 (September, 1958), 157–184.

6. Ellen L. Betz, "Need-Reinforcer Correspondence As a Predictor of Job Satisfaction," *Personnel and Guidance Journal*, 47 (May, 1969), 878–883.[39]

7. Arthur H. Brayfield, Richard V. Wells, and Marvin W. Strate, "Interrelationships Among Measures of Job Satisfaction and General Satisfaction," *Journal of Applied Psychology*, 41 (August, 1957), 201–205.

8. Robert K. Burns, L. L. Thurstone, David G. Moore, and Melany E. Baehr, *General Manual for the SRA Employee Inventory* (Chicago: Science Research Associates, 1952). The "SRA Employee Inventory" is now termed the "SRA Attitude Survey." Information about the survey, plus legal permission to use the survey, can be obtained from Science Research Associates, 259 East Erie Street, Chicago, Illinois 60611. The above cited manual is the place to begin if one wishes to use the SRA Attitude Survey.

9. Robert E. Carlson, Rene V. Dawis, George W. England, and Lloyd H. Lofquist, *The Measurement of Employment Satisfaction* (Minneapolis, Minn.: Industrial Relations Center, University of Minnesota, 1962).

10. Zile S. Dabas, "The Dimensions of Morale: An Item Factorization of the SRA Employee Inventory," *Personnel Psychology*, 11 (Summer, 1958), 217–234.

11. Rene V. Dawis, George W. England, and Lloyd H. Lofquist, *A Theory of Work Adjustment* (Minneapolis, Minn.: Industrial Relations Center, University of Minnesota, 1964).

12. George B. Graen, Rene V. Dawis, and David J. Weiss, "Need Type and Job Satisfaction Among Industrial Research Scientists," *Journal of Applied Psychology*, 52 (August, 1968), 286–289.

13. Lester M. Libo, *Measuring Group Cohesiveness* (Ann Arbor, Mich.: Survey Research Center, University of Michigan, 1953).[40]

14. Seymour M. Lipset, Martin A. Trow, and James S. Coleman, *Union Democracy* (Glencoe, Ill.: The Free Press, 1956), pp. 69–140. The reference is to the Social Relations Index whose composition and scoring are described on p. 437.

15. David G. Moore and Robert K. Burns, "How Good Is Morale?" *Factory*, 114 (February, 1956), 130–136.

16. Stanley E. Seashore, *Group Cohesiveness in the Industrial Work Group* (Ann Arbor, Mich.: Survey Research Center, University of Michigan, 1954).

17. Sergio Talacchi, "Organizational Size, Individual Attitudes and Behavior," *Administrative Science Quarterly*, 5 (December, 1960), 398–420.

18. David J. Weiss, Rene V. Dawis, George W. England, and Lloyd H. Lofquist, *Construct Validation Studies of the Minnesota Importance Questionnaire* (Minneapolis, Minn.: Industrial Relations Center, University of Minnesota, 1964).

19. David J. Weiss, Rene V. Dawis, George W. England, and Lloyd H. Lofquist, *Manual for the Minnesota Satisfaction Questionnaire* (Minneapolis, Minn.: Industrial Relations Center, University of Minnesota, 1967). Use of the Minnesota Satisfaction Questionnaire requires legal permission from the Industrial Relations Center. Unpublished papers relevant to the questionnaire can also be obtained from the center. This

manual is the place to begin if one wishes to use the Minnesota Satisfaction Questionnaire.

20. P. F. Wernimont, "Intrinsic and Extrinsic Factors in Job Satisfaction," *Journal of Applied Psychology*, 50 (February, 1966), 41–50.

21. Robert J. Wherry, "An Orthogonal Re-Rotation of the Baehr and Ash Studies of the SRA Employee Inventory," *Personnel Psychology*," (Autumn, 1954), 365–380.

22. Robert J. Wherry, "A Reply to Baehr's Reply on Rotation of the SRA Inventory Studies," *Personnel Psychology*, 9 (Spring, 1956), 93–99.

23. Robert J. Wherry, "Factor Analysis of Morale Data: Reliability and Validity," *Personnel Psychology*, 11 (Spring, 1958), 78–89.

NOTES

1. Helpful discussions of the concept of satisfaction are provided by Robert M. Guion, "The Problem of Terminology," *Personnel Psychology*, 11 (Spring, 1958), 59–64 and Victor H. Vroom, *Work and Motivation* (New York: Wiley, 1964), pp. 99–105. The Guion article is part of a symposium devoted to industrial morale.

2. These dimensions of satisfaction come from Patricia C. Smith, Lorne M. Kendall, and Charles L. Hulin, *The Measurement of Satisfaction in Work and Retirement* (Chicago: Rand McNally, 1969), p. 83. Other researchers use similar dimensions of satisfaction.

3. Some organizational researchers distinguish morale from satisfaction. An example is Raymond A. Katzell, "Measurement of Morale," *Personnel Psychology*, 11 (Spring, 1958), 71–78. (The Katzell article is part of a symposium devoted to industrial morale.) Most organizational researchers, however, do not distinguish morale from satisfaction.

4. Satisfaction and general satisfaction are distinguished in the following sources: Arthur H. Brayfield, Richard V. Wells, Marvin W. Strate, "Interrelationships Among Measures of Job Satisfaction and General Satisfaction," *Journal of Applied Psychology*, 41 (August, 1957), 201–205; Darrell E. Roach, "Dimensions of Employee Morale," *Personnel Psychology*, 11 (Autumn, 1958), 419–431; and Joseph Weitz, "A Neglected Concept in the Study of Job Satisfaction," *Personnel Psychology*, 5 (Autumn, 1952), 201–205.

5. The relationship between satisfaction and general satisfaction is investigated in *ibid.*

6. Patricia C. Smith and C. J. Cranny, "Psychology of Men at Work," *Annual Review of Psychology*, 19 (1968), p. 471. The following reviews of the literature relevant to the two-factor theory also basically support the Smith and Cranny position: Ronald J. Burke, "Are Herzberg's Motivators and Hygienes Unidimensional?" *Journal of Applied Psychology*, 50 (August, 1966), 317–321; Bonnie Carroll, *Job Satisfaction* (Ithaca, N. Y.: New York State School of Industrial and Labor Relations, Key Issues Series—No. 3, 1969), pp. 6–7; Marvin D. Dunnette, John P. Campbell, and Milton D. Hakel, "Factors Contributing to Job Satisfaction and Job Dissatisfaction in Six Occupational Groups," *Organiza-*

tional Behavior and Human Performance, 2 (May, 1967), 143–174; Robert J. House and Lawrence A. Wignor, "Herzberg's Dual-Factor Theory of Job Satisfaction and Motivation: A Review of the Evidence and a Criticism," *Personnel Psychology*, 20 (Winter, 1967), 369–389; Lyman W. Porter, "Personnel Management," *Annual Review of Psychology*, 17 (1966), 395–422; Vroom, *op. cit.*, pp. 126–129.

The Smith and Cranny position is not supported by Orlando Behling, George Labovitz, and Richard Kosmo, "The Herzberg Controversy: A Critical Reappraisal," *Academy of Management Journal*, 11 (March, 1968), 99–108; David A. Whitsett and Erik K. Winslow, "An Analysis of Studies Critical of the Motivator-Hygiene Theory," *Personnel Psychology*, 20 (Winter, 1967), 391–415; and Erik K. Winslow and David A. Whitsett, "Dual Factor Theory: A Reply to House and Wignor," *Personnel Psychology*, 21 (Spring, 1968), 55–62.

7. Researchers with sociological backgrounds seem to prefer the term "solidarity," whereas researchers with psychological-social psychological backgrounds seem to prefer the term "cohesion." Integration is sometimes used as a synonym for solidarity-cohesion; however, integration also has a diversity of other uses, among which are "consensus," "centralization" (viewed in terms of participation), and "order."

8. Kurt W. Back, "Influence Through Social Communication," *Journal of Abnormal and Social Psychology*, 46 (January, 1951), 9–23. The following sources also use a definition of cohesion very similar to Back's: Leonard Berkowitz, "Group Standards, Cohesiveness, and Productivity," *Human Relations*, 7 (November, 1954), 509–519; Leonard Berkowitz, "Group Norms among Bomber Crews: Patterns of Perceived Crew Attitudes, 'Actual' Crew Attitudes, and Crew Liking Related to Aircrew Effectiveness in Far Eastern Combat," *Sociometry*, 19 (September, 1956), 141–153; Dorwin Cartwright and Alvin Zander, "Introduction," in *Group Dynamics*, ed. Dorwin Cartwright and Alvin Zander (Evanston, Ill.: Row, Peterson, 1953), pp. 73–91; Leon Festinger, Stanley Schachter, and Kurt Back, *Social Pressures in Informal Groups* (Stanford, Calif.: Stanford, 1950); James E. Dittes, "Attractiveness of Group as Function of Self-Esteem and Acceptance by Group," *Journal of Abnormal and Social Psychology*, 59 (July, 1959), 77–82; and John Downing, "Cohesiveness, Perception, and Values," *Human Relations*, 11 (May, 1958), 157–166. The major source is the study by Festinger, Schachter, and Back.

The definition of cohesion advanced by Festinger and his colleagues is criticized in the following articles: John G. Darley, Neal Gross, and William E. Martin, "Studies of Group Behavior: Stability, Change, and Interrelations of Psychometric and Sociometric Variables," *Journal of Abnormal and Social Psychology*, 46 (October, 1951), 565–576; Neal Gross and William E. Martin, "On Group Cohesiveness," *American Journal of Sociology*, 57 (May, 1952), 546–554; Neal Gross, William E. Martin, and John G. Darley, "Studies of Group Behavior: Leadership Structures in Small Organized Groups," *Journal of Abnormal and Social Psychology*, 48 (July, 1953), 429–432; and William E. Martin, John G. Darley, and Neal Gross, "Studies of Group Behavior: Methodological Problems in the Study of Interrelationships of Group Members," *Educational and Psychological Measurement*, 12 (Winter, 1952), 533–553.

9. Back, *op. cit.*, p. 9.

10. Supervision and co-workers, as dimensions of satisfaction, come from Smith *et al.*, *op. cit.*

11. Harry S. Upshaw, "Attitude Measurement," in *Methodology in Social Research*, ed. Hubert M. Blalock, Jr. and Ann B. Blalock (New York: McGraw-Hill, 1968), pp. 60–111 (esp. p. 71).

12. These two approaches are described in Brayfield *et al.*, *op. cit.*

13. The Minnesota Satisfaction Questionnaire and the SRA Attitude Survey, both of which are discussed under Additional Readings at the end of the chapter, also illustrate the specific approach to the measurement of satisfaction.

14. A. H. Maslow, *Motivation and Personality* (New York: Harper, 1954).

15. Some examples of the use of absenteeism and turnover as measures of satisfaction are found in Daniel Katz and Robert L. Kahn, *The Social Psychology of Organizations* (New York: Wiley, 1966), pp. 375–376 and Vroom, *op. cit.*, pp. 176–177.

16. The reference is to the previous chapter on absenteeism.

17. Arthur H. Brayfield and Harold F. Rothe, "An Index of Job Satisfaction," *Journal of Applied Psychology*, 35 (October, 1951), p. 309.

18. Each of the 18 questions uses this same set of responses.

19. R. Hoppock, *Job Satisfaction* (New York: Harper, 1935).

20. Brayfield and Rothe also suggest that their index has face validity and note that there is a high degree of consistency among the judges in the construction of the index. See Brayfield and Rothe, *op. cit.*, p. 310. The two items of data relevant to the validity of the Brayfield and Rothe index which are written up in this handbook make a stronger case for the validity of the index than this material about face validity and the consistency of the judges.

21. Lyman W. Porter and Edward E. Lawler, III, *Managerial Attitudes and Performance* (Homewood, Ill.: Irwin, 1968), p. 31.

22. Each of the 13 questions uses this set of responses.

23. Porter and Lawler note that "In the very small percentage of cases where 'should be' responses were less than 'is now' responses, the differences in that direction were arbitrarily treated as indicating even less dissatisfaction than zero differences." Porter and Lawler, *op. cit.*, p. 132.

24. These are Maslow's "need categories." See Maslow, *op. cit.*

25. The numbers within the parentheses indicate the numbers of the questions in the preceding section on data collection.

26. The ranges are not included in this handbook because they vary for the different propositions which Porter and Lawler test.

27. Porter and Lawler, *op. cit.*, pp. 15–40.

28. *Ibid.*, p. 131.

29. Lyman W. Porter, "Job Attitudes in Management: I. Perceived Deficiencies in Need Fulfillment as a Function of Job Level," *Journal of Applied Psychology*, 46 (December, 1962), 375–384.

30. *Ibid.*

31. Smith *et al.*, *op. cit.*, p. 6.

32. There are some small variations in the instructions for the other four dimensions

(supervision, pay, promotion, and co-workers). The reader is advised, in this instance, to obtain a copy of the original version of the questionnaire.

33. This technique is developed by D. T. Campbell and D. W. Fiske, "Convergent and Discriminant Validation by the Multitrait-Multimethod Matrix," *Psychological Bulletin*, 56 (March, 1959), 81–105.

34. Smith, Kendall, and Hulin also use the term "affect." See Smith *et al., op. cit.*, p. 87.

35. Vroom, *op. cit.*, p. 100.

36. Smith *et al., op. cit.*, p. 82.

37. Additional measures of satisfaction, not cited in the handbook, can be found in John P. Robinson, Robert Athanasiou, and Kendra B. Head, *Measures of Occupational Attitudes and Occupational Characteristics* (Ann Arbor, Mich.: Survey Research Center, 1969), pp. 99–185 (esp. pp. 99–143).

38. The following readings refer to the SRA Attitude Survey: Nos. 1–5, 7, 8, 10, 15, 17, and 21–23.

39. The following readings refer to the Minnesota Satisfaction Questionnaire: Nos. 6, 9, 11, 12, 18, 19.

40. The following readings refer to sources containing measures of cohesion: Nos. 13, 14, and 16.

Definition. *Size* is the scale of operations of a social system.[1] In an organization, for example, the scale of operations is indicated by such observables as the number of personnel, the amount of assets, and the degree of expenditures.

The organizational literature generally defines size in terms of the number of personnel, expressed either as "members" or "employees."[2] Because of its more general nature, members is a more accurate term than employees. Both voluntary associations and administrative organizations have members, but voluntary associations typically have few employees. Employees is the more common term, however, because organizational researchers mostly study administrative organizations.

The number of personnel is not the best way to define the concept of size.[3] An organization can be quite large in size, but due to a very high degree of mechanization, for example, have relatively few personnel. It seems preferable to define size in terms of scale of operations, and to use number of personnel as one indicator of scale.

The concept of size advanced by this handbook is implicit in much organizational research. Many researchers who investigate size cite a series of measures but offer no definition to encompass these measures. Melman's classic paper on administrative staff, for example, cites the five following measures of size: number of production personnel, total assets, average number of wage-earners per establishment, average value added by manufacture per establishment, and net sales. However, he offers no definition to encompass these five measures.[4] This handbook suggests that size, defined in terms of scale of operations, encompasses the measures of size commonly used in organizational literature.

Measurement. Few organizational studies provide assistance in the measurement of size. Even when the studies cite a series of measures, close examination usually indicates that what the studies have provided are a series of computations; the methods of data collection are typically not specified. An exception to this pattern is the study (Schoenherr and Fritz) selected for inclusion in this handbook.

THE MEASURE

SCHOENHERR AND FRITZ

Description. The purpose of the research reported in this paper is to design and apply suitable methods for systematic comparisons of large numbers of organizations. An attempt is made to get away from the traditional case study approach with its focus on a very small number of organizations. The United States Employment Security Agency is the organization selected for study. This organization consists of 54 autonomous and independent state agencies; there are an average of 40 local offices in each state. All the agencies, except that in Guam, are included in the study.[5] The total number of local offices in the study is 2,386, representing all the offices in the 50 states, plus those in the District of Columbia, Puerto Rico, and the Virgin Islands. Information was collected from the following four key informants in the central offices of each agency: the agency director or his deputy, the division heads in charge of the two major divisions, and the chief of the personnel division. The study was conducted by the Comparative Organization Research Program at the University of Chicago.[6]

Definition. Size is defined as the ". . . total number of actual personnel. . . ."[7] Most of the studies conducted by the Comparative Organization Research Program define size in terms of the number of employees;[8] therefore, the "number of actual personnel" probably means the "number of employees."

Data Collection. The data were collected by means of interviews and self-administered questionnaires. The interviewers spent eight to ten hours in each central office. Personnel listings, records, manning tables, and organizational charts were obtained from the four key informants. Information about size was obtained from "an official payroll printout."

Computation. The number of employees on the official payroll printout are counted to determine the size of the organizations. The larger the number of employees, the larger the size.

Validity. The article contains none of the customary data relevant to validity. The researchers, however, devised a series of techniques to achieve accuracy in the extraction of the data obtained by the interviews and the questionnaires; these techniques are carefully described in the article.

Reliability. The article contains no data relevant to reliability.

Comments. (1) The number of employees—the apparent definition of size used by Schoenherr and Fritz—is narrower than this handbook's scale of operations. However, as previously indicated, the number of employees can be used as a measure of the scale of operations. (2) Payroll records often distinguish between full-time and part-time employees; therefore, it would have been helpful had the researchers explicitly indicated whether or not their sample consists of full-time and/or part-time employees.[9] (3) The researchers indicate exactly how the data about size were collected. Most organizational research which investigates size has nothing that corresponds to Schoenherr and Fritz's "official payroll printouts." (4) The researchers' extensive use of documents is especially impressive. The long-term development of organizational theory requires the use of multiple methods of data collection, that is, surveys, observations, and documents. An advantage in studying organizations is the large number of available documents, and it is encouraging to see this source of data used by Schoenherr and Fritz. (5) Payrolls often fluctuate greatly during the course of a year;[10] therefore, it would have been helpful had the researchers indicated how their computations took this fact into account.

Source. Richard A. Schoenherr and Judith Fritz, "Some New Techniques in Organization Research," *Public Personnel Review*, 28 (July, 1967), 156–161.

Further Sources. 1. Peter M. Blau, "The Hierarchy of Authority in Organizations," *American Journal of Sociology*, 73 (January, 1968), 453–467.

2. Peter M. Blau, Wolf V. Heydebrand, and Robert E. Stauffer, "The Structure of Small Bureaucracies," *American Sociological Review*, 31 (April, 1966), 179–191.

3. Marshall W. Meyer, "Centralization and Decentralization of Authority in Departments of Finance," *Municipal Finance*, 40 (August, 1967), 41–45.

4. ——, "Two Authority Structures of Bureaucratic Organization," *Administrative Science Quarterly*, 13 (September, 1968), 211–228.

5. ——, "Automation and Bureaucratic Structure," *American Journal of Sociology*, 74 (November, 1968), 256–264.

6. ——, "Expertness and the Span of Control," *American Sociological Review*, 33 (December, 1968), 944–951.

7. Robert E. Stauffer, Peter M. Blau, and Wolf V. Heydebrand, "Organizational Complexities of Public Personnel Agencies," *Public Personnel Review*, 27 (April, 1966), 83–87.

ADDITIONAL READINGS

1. Eugene Haas, Richard H. Hall, and Norman J. Johnson, "The Size of the Supportive Component in Organizations: A Multi-Organizational Analysis," *Social Forces*, 42 (October, 1963), 9–17.[11]

2. Mason Haire, Edwin E. Ghiselli, and Lyman W. Porter, *Managerial Thinking* (New York: Wiley, 1966).[12]

3. Richard H. Hall, J. Eugene Haas, and Norman J. Johnson, "Organiza-

tional Size, Complexity, and Formalization," *American Sociological Review*, 32 (December, 1967), 903–912.

4. Bernard P. Indik, *Organization Size and Member Participation* (unpublished Ph.D. dissertation, Ann Arbor, University of Michigan, 1961).

5. ——, "Some Effects of Organization Size on Member Attitudes and Behavior," *Human Relations*, 16 (November, 1963), 369–384.

6. ——, "Organization Size and Supervision Ratio," *Administrative Science Quarterly*, 9 (December, 1964), 301–312.

7. ——, "Organization Size and Member Participation," *Human Relations*, 18 (November, 1965), 339–350.[13]

8. J. H. K. Inkson, D. S. Pugh, and D. J. Hickson, "Organization Context and Structure: An Abbreviated Replication," *Administrative Science Quarterly*, 15 (September, 1970), 318–329.[14]

9. Lyman W. Porter, "Job Attitudes in Management: IV. Perceived Deficiencies in Need Fulfillment as a Function of Size of Company," *Journal of Applied Psychology*, 47 (December, 1963), 386–397.

10. D. S. Pugh, D. J. Hickson, C. R. Hinings, and C. Turner, "The Context of Organization Structures," *Administrative Science Quarterly*, 14 (March, 1969), 91–114.[15]

NOTES

1. The term "scale of operations" is frequently used in discussions of size by organizational researchers who are economists. See, for example, Seymour Melman, *Dynamic Factors in Industrial Productivity* (Oxford, England: Basil Blackwell, 1956), p. 53.

2. The following sources define size as the number of members: Theodore Caplow, "Organizational Size," *Administrative Science Quarterly*, 1 (March, 1957), 484–505; Theodore Caplow, *Principles of Organization* (New York: Harcourt, Brace, & World, 1964), pp. 25–36; Richard H. Hall, J. Eugene Haas, and Norman J. Johnson, "Organizational Size, Complexity, and Formalization," *American Sociological Review*, 32 (December, 1967), 903–912; Bernard P. Indik, "Some Effects of Organization Size on Member Attitudes and Behavior," *Human Relations*, 16 (November, 1963), 369–384: Bernard P. Indik, "Organization Size and Supervision Ratio," *Administrative Science Quarterly*, 9 (December, 1964), 301–312; and Bernard P. Indik, "Organization Size and Member Participation," *Human Relations*, 18 (November, 1965), 339–350.

   The following sources define size as the number of employees: Peter M. Blau, "The Hierarchy of Authority in Organizations," *American Journal of Sociology*, 73 (January, 1968), 453–467; Jerald Hage and Michael Aiken, "Program Change and Organizational Properties: A Comparative Analysis," *American Journal of Sociology*, 72 (March, 1967), 503–519; Kerr Inkson, Roy Payne, and Derek Pugh, "Extending the Occupational Environment: The Measurement of Organizations," *Occupational Psychology*, 41 (January, 1967), 33–47; Lyman W. Porter and Edward E. Lawler, III, "The Effects of 'Tall' Versus 'Flat' Organization Structures on Managerial Job Satisfaction," *Personnel Psychology*, 17

(Summer, 1964), 135–148; and Sergio Talacchi, "Organization Size, Individual Attitudes and Behavior," *Administrative Science Quarterly*, 5 (December, 1960), 398–420.

3. Few organizational researchers have criticized size defined in terms of numbers of personnel. Two exceptions are T. E. Chester, *A Study of Post-War Growth in Management Organizations* (Paris, France: European Productivity Agency of the Organization for European Economic Cooperation, EPA Project No. 347, 1961), pp. 24–25 and Gerald Gordon and Selywn Becker, "Organizational Size and Managerial Succession: A Re-examination," *American Journal of Sociology*, 70 (September, 1964), 215–225.

4. Seymour Melman, "The Rise of Administrative Overhead in the Manufacturing Industries of the United States, 1899–1947," *Oxford Economic Papers* (*New Series*), 3 (January, 1951), p. 75 (also pp. 68–70 and 83). The following sources also list a series of measures of size without definition: Alfred D. Chandler, Jr., *Strategy and Structure* (Garden City, N.Y.: Doubleday, 1962), p. 61; G. E. Delehanty, *Nonproduction Workers in U.S. Manufacturing* (Amsterdam, Holland: North-Holland, 1968), p. 147; Oscar Grusky, "Corporate Size, Bureaucratization, and Managerial Succession," *American Journal of Sociology*, 67 (November, 1961), 261–269 (esp. p. 262); Wilbur G. Lewellen, *Executive Compensation in Large Industrial Corporations* (New York: Columbia, 1968), pp. 111 and 240; and David R. Roberts, *Executive Compensation* (Glencoe, Ill.: Free Press, 1959), pp. 11, 36, and 51.

5. The agency in Guam is not included because of its small size.

6. Additional studies conducted by the Comparative Organization Research Program are cited under "Further Sources" at the end of the chapter. Not cited under Further Sources because it appeared too late to be included in this handbook is Peter M. Blau and Richard A. Schoenherr, *The Structure of Organizations* (New York: Basic Books, 1971).

7. Richard A. Schoenherr and Judith Fritz, "Some New Techniques in Organization Research," *Public Personnel Review*, 28 (July, 1967), p. 160.

8. See, for example, Blau, *op. cit.*, and Marshall W. Meyer "Centralization and Decentralization of Authority in Departments of Finance," *Municipal Finance*, 40 (August, 1967), 41–45.

9. Very few organizational researchers who define size in terms of the number of employees specifically indicate the full-time and/or part-time nature of the employees. The following three sources are exceptions: Hall *et al.*, *op. cit.*; Indik, *Human Relations*, 16 (November, 1963), *op. cit.*; and Indik *Administrative Science Quarterly*, *op. cit.* Hall and his colleagues even devised a technique to convert part-time or voluntary members into "full-time equivalent" members. See Hall *et al.*, *op. cit.*, p. 905.

10. Some data about fluctuations during the course of a year are contained in Public Health Service, *Hospital Personnel* (Washington, D.C.: Superintendent of Documents, Public Health Service Publication No. 930-C-9, 1964), p. 40.

11. Additional Readings No. 1 and No. 3 should be viewed as a unit.

12. Additional Readings No. 2 and No. 9 should be viewed as a unit.

13. This article by Indik is based on his dissertation. The dissertation is included among the Additional Readings because it contains some measurement informa-

tion about size which Indik does not include in his article. See especially page 46 of the dissertation.

14. The instrument for the collection of data about size is not reproduced in the article. D. J. Hickson, a senior researcher associated with the Industrial Administration Research Unit, generously made available the instrument so it could be examined for possible inclusion within this handbook. Additional Readings No. 8 and No. 10 should be viewed as a unit.

15. This article by Pugh and his colleagues presents data which compare different measures of size. Additional data of this type are very much needed concerning size.

SPAN OF CONTROL

21 _____

Definition. *Span of control* refers to the number of members managed by the average administrator. The nature of this "management" will vary greatly for different types of occupations and for different types of organizations. In a factory, for example, the management of blue-collar workers by the foremen will be considerably different than the management of middle-level executives by the top executives. In a basic research laboratory, on the other hand, the management of scientists by a research administrator will be greatly different than the management of middle-level executives by the top executives in a factory. Though the nature of the management varies, managers of different types of occupational members in different types of organizations are still responsible for decision-making, coordination, and control. Thus it is appropriate to use the span of control concept in these different situations.

The terms "superordinates" and "subordinates"—or some close equivalents—are typically used to define span of control.[1] These terms are not used by this handbook because they apply less readily to professional and non-professional organizations.[2] The research administrator alluded to in the preceding paragraph is in some respects a "superordinate" with respect to the scientists working in the research laboratory. The research administrator, for example, will exercise considerable power with respect to the scientists' expenditure of money. In this way the relationship bears some resemblance to the typical superordinate-subordinate relationship in business firms and government agencies. However, there are some important respects in which the research administrator is not a "superordinate" of the scientists in the laboratory. The research administrator, for example, is often not competent to evaluate adequately the technical role performance of the scientists; this evaluation is the basic responsibility of other scientists who have a colleague, rather than a superordinate-subordinate, relationship with each other. To define span of control in terms of "management of members by an administrator"—as this handbook does—is to indicate a concept which is more readily applicable to professional and nonprofessional organizations.

Span of control must be distinguished from administrative staff and centralization.[3] As previously indicated, administrative staff refers to the full-time career members of a social system who basically perform the activities that indirectly contribute to its primary output. Most of these indirect activities involve decision-making, coordination, and control. The span of control, as previously defined, refers to the number of members managed by the average administrator. It is thus possible to calculate the span of control for the organization as a unit, or for a segment within the organization, such as the administrative staff members or the production staff members.

Centralization refers to the degree to which power is concentrated among the members of a social system. An organization may be highly centralized with a low span of control, that is, with a small number of members managed by the average administrator. On the other hand, an organization may be lowly centralized with a high span of control, that is, with a large number of members managed by the average administrator. The two concepts may usually be negatively related, that is, high centralization may usually be associated with a low span of control. Whether this is the case or not, the two concepts are analytically distinct and should be distinguished.

Measurement. One of the most careful studies of the span of control is the research conducted by Healey, whose work research is reviewed here.

THE MEASURE

HEALEY

Description. This study has two purposes: (1) to determine the degree to which, in practice, executives adhere to the theoretical span of control; and (2) to analyze the use of certain selected media of coordination and control by chief executives. The first purpose is the major concern of this handbook. The sample is limited to executives of Ohio manufacturing establishments that have 100 or more employees. The study covers almost one-third of these establishments. A total of 620 usable questionnaires were returned by the manufacturing establishments—445 from main-plant executives and 175 from branch-plant managers.

Definition. The span of control is defined as ". . . the number of immediate subordinates of the chief executive, usually the president, of a main plant or the number of immediate subordinates of the chief executive, usually the manager, of a branch plant."[4]

Data Collection. The following questionnaire item is used to obtain information about the span of control:

1. Please indicate the principal function or functional title, e.g., sales manager, of each of your immediate subordinates in the blanks provided on the chart on page 182.

Computation. The subordinates listed on the questionnaire blanks are counted. For the main plants, the range in the number of immediate subordinates is from 1 to 17. The most common number of subordinates reported is 6. For

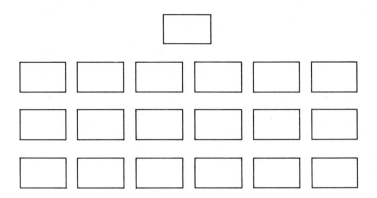

the branch plants, the range in the number of subordinates is from 1 to 24. The most common number reporting to the branch-plant manager is 6. These ranges and modes include cases where the chief executives and the managers have assistants (single "executive vice-presidents" in the study). The researcher also presents a separate set of data in which these assistants are excluded.

Validity. The organizational literature reviewed by Healey advocated a span of control ranging from 3 through 8. In Healey's study, a span of 3 through 8 is used by 76.3 percent of the main-plant executives and 70.3 percent of the branch-plant executives.[5] Therefore, the span of control in practice generally agrees with the advocated span of control.[6]

Reliability. The study contains no data relevant to reliability.

Comments. (1) Healey's "number of immediate subordinates" has essentially the same referent as this handbook's "number of members managed by the average administrator." Were Healey to study basic research laboratories rather than manufacturing establishments, his "superordinate-subordinate" terminology, as indicated in the introductory comments, would be somewhat less applicable. (2) The importance of considering "assistants" in calculating the span of control is noted by a number of researchers.[7] Healey is aware of this point and fortunately takes it into consideration in his computations. (3) Healey presents ranges and modes; this is helpful and should facilitate comparative research. The presentation of standard deviations would also have been helpful. (4) Healey's study focuses on the top executives of the manufacturing establishments; therefore, of necessity, he does not compute the span of control for the entire organization or for segments, such as middle-management and lower-management. Since the span of control varies for the different levels in the hierarchy of authority,[8] it is necessary to calculate the span of control for the different levels when the organization is the unit of analysis.[9]

Source. James H. Healey, *Executive Coordination and Control* (Columbus, Ohio: Bureau of Business Research, The Ohio State University, 1956), pp. 1–29, 61–118, and 240–263.

Further Source. James H. Healey, "Coordination and Control of Executive Functions," *Personnel*, 33 (September, 1956), 106–117.

ADDITIONAL READING

1. Thomas L. Whisler, Harold Meyer, Bernard H. Baum, and Peter F. Sorensen, Jr., "Centralization of Organizational Control: An Empirical Study of Its Meaning and Measurement," in *Control in Organizations*, ed. Arnold S. Tannenbaum (New York: McGraw-Hill, 1968), pp. 283–305.

NOTES

1. The following sources use the terms "superordinates" and "subordinates"—or some close equivalents—to define span of control: C. W. Barkdull, "Span of Control—A Method of Evaluation," *Michigan Business Review*, 15 (May, 1963), 25–32; Gerald D. Bell, "Determinants of Span of Control," *American Journal of Sociology*, 73 (July, 1967), 100–109; Ernest Dale, *Planning and Developing the Company Organization Structure* (New York: American Management Association, 1952), pp. 69–73; Alan C. Filley, "Decisions and Research in Staff Utilization," *Academy of Management Journal*, 6 (September, 1963), 220–231; Allen Janger, "Analyzing the Span of Control," *Management Record*, 22 (July–August, 1960), 7–10; J. L. Meij, "The Span of Control—Fact and Fundamental Principle," *Advanced Management*, 22 (February, 1957), 14–16; Jon G. Udell, "An Empirical Test of Hypotheses Relating to Span of Control," *Administrative Science Quarterly*, 12 (December, 1967), 420–439; Lyndall F. Urwick, "The Span of Control—Some Facts About the Fables," *Advanced Management*, 21 (November, 1956), 5–15; and Joan Woodward, *Management and Technology* (London, England: Her Majesty's Stationery Office, 1958), p. 9.

2. The distinction between professional organizations and nonprofessional organizations is found in Amitai Etzioni, *Modern Organizations* (Englewood Cliffs, N.J.: Prentice-Hall, 1964), pp. 75–93.

3. Some organizational researchers equate span of control and centralization. An example is Dale, *op. cit.*, p. 72. If span of control and centralization are different concepts, as this handbook suggests, then the measures of span of control should not be used as measures of centralization. An example of the use of measures of span of control for centralization is Thomas L. Whisler, Harold Meyer, Bernard H. Baum, and Peter F. Sorensen, Jr., "Centralization of Organizational Control: An Empirical Study of Its Meaning and Measurement," in *Control in Organizations*, ed. Arnold S. Tannenbaum (New York: McGraw-Hill, 1968), pp. 283–305.

4. James H. Healey, *Executive Coordination and Control* (Columbus, Ohio: Bureau of Business Research, The Ohio State University, 1956), p. 7.

5. Although assistants to these executives are included in this set of calculations, Healey presents a separate set in which they are excluded. When the assistants are

excluded, the findings conform even more closely to the span of control advocated in the literature reviewed by Healey.

6. Nine conclusions about the span of control are presented in Healey, *op. cit.*, pp. 241–246. Only one of these conclusions presents data which are relevant to validity.

7. The following sources note the importance of assistants in calculating the span of control: Barkdull, *op. cit.*; T. E. Chester, *A Study of Post-War Growth in Management Organizations* (Paris, France: European Productivity Agency of the Organization for European Economic Cooperation, EPA Project No. 347, 1961), p. 29; Filley, *op. cit.*; Udell, *op. cit.*; and Lyndall F. Urwick, "The Manager's Span of Control," *Harvard Business Review*, 34 (May–June, 1956), 39–47.

8. William M. Evan, "Indices of the Hierarchical Structure of Industrial Organizations," *Management Science*, 9 (April, 1963), 468–477.

9. The span of control is calculated for different levels in Gerald G. Fisch, "Stretching the Span of Management, *Harvard Business Review*, 41 (September–October, 1963), 74–85; Woodward, *op. cit.*, and Joan Woodward, *Industrial Organization* (London, England: Oxford, 1965).

SUCCESSION

.

22 _____

Definition. *Succession* is the degree of membership movement through the roles of a social system.[1] The retirement of a chief executive, the firing of a middle-level manager, the termination of a blue-collar worker, the promotion of a middle-level manager to a top-level executive position, the promotion of a blue-collar worker to foreman, the acquisition of new members—all are examples of organizational succession. Material relevant to succession is found in discussions of "mobility," "vertical mobility," "migration," "wastage," and "turnover."

Two types of succession can be distinguished. If a member leaves one organizational role for another role within the same organization, then this might be termed *internal succession*. The promotion examples cited in the preceding paragraph illustrate internal succession. If a member leaves one organizational role for another role within a different organization—moves across the membership boundary of the organization—then this might be termed *external succession*. External succession includes movement into and out of the organization. "Turnover" is the most common term for external succession.

Most studies of organizational succession focus on the movement of top-level executives out of the organization, that is, on "executive turnover."[2] This type of succession should, of course, be the subject of considerable attention because of the critical importance of these top-level executives to the operation of the organization. However, the concept of succession should not be limited to executive turnover.[3] Movement of executives within the organization is also encompassed by the concept. Similarly, nonexecutive, as well as executive roles, are the objects of concern. The terms used to refer to executive turnover actually imply a broad referent for the concept. If there is "administrative succession,"[4] to select but one of the terms, then by implication there must also be "nonadministrative succession."

Studies on turnover commonly make no reference to succession and studies of succession commonly make no reference to turnover,[5] but since turnover is one type of succession it is obvious that the bodies of organizational literature are related.

Measurement. Most measures of succession focus on turnover, that is, on external succession.[6] The "separation rate" is the most common measure of turnover used in organizational literature;[7] the second selection (Levine) illustrates it. The separation rate has been severely criticized by a number of researchers[8] and several alternate measures have been proposed; the second selection also contains one of these alternate measures.[9] The first selection (Kriesberg) contains a measure which collects data about the general concept of succession.

THE MEASURES

1. KRIESBERG

Description. This study, conducted by the National Opinion Research Center, attempts to test a hypothesized relationship between size and succession. The NORC study is concerned with the relations between public health and mental health personnel and programs at the state and local level. There are three classes of respondents: (1) heads of state public health departments and heads of state community and/or institutional mental health programs; (2) heads of local public health departments and heads of local mental health departments or centers; and (3) other state officials responsible for special public health, community-based mental health, and hospital-based mental health programs. Kriesberg's secondary analysis of the NORC data excludes these "other state officials." His sample consists of 115 public officials.

Definition. Succession is not defined in the study. However, the study tests Grusky's proposition, which links administrative succession directly to the size of the organization. Grusky defines administrative succession as ". . . the process by which key officials are replaced. . . ."[10] Like Grusky, Kriesberg focuses his study on a sample of "key officials." Therefore, it is reasonable to assume that Kriesberg uses Grusky's definition of administrative succession.

Data Collection. The following question was used by interviewers to collect information about succession:[11]

How many years have you been employed in your present job?

    Fewer than two years......................1
    2–4   years 2
    5–9   years 3
    10–14 years 4
    15–19 years 5
    20–24 years 6
    25–29 years 7
    30 or more years.........................8[12]

Apparently the interviewer circled the amount of time indicated by the respondent.

Computation. The measure of succession is the number of years an official had been in his present position. Three categories of computations are performed: percentage less than five years, percentage five–nine years, and percentage ten or more years. The article presents no averages or standard deviations; instead, the three categories of percentages are presented for different classifications of the respondents.

Validity. The results indicate that heads of large public health or of large mental health departments tend to have been in their present position for a shorter period of time than heads of small departments. These results are similar to those reported by Grusky.

Reliability. The article contains no data relevant to reliability.

Comments. (1) Kriesberg's administrative succession ("the process by which key officials are replaced") is one component of this handbook's concept of succession ("the degree of membership movement through the roles of a social system"). "Key officials" are but one type of member who moves through the roles of an organization. Kriesberg and Grusky, like most researchers who study succession, focus on the movement of top executives ("key officials"). (2) Many organizational researchers, in the interest of brevity, do not reproduce the actual questionnaire or interview items used to collect information for their computations. This practice is understandable but it hinders the replication of findings (this is discussed in the concluding chapter of this handbook). Although Kriesberg does not present his interview items in the article, he generously made available a copy of the original study which contained a copy of the interview schedule. (3) Kriesberg is one of the few researchers to collect data measuring the general concept of succession. Most organizational research, as previously indicated, either measures internal or external succession. (4) Comparative research with respect to Kriesberg's data would be facilitated had he included averages and standard deviations among his computations. (5) Kriesberg's measure will present a misleading indication of the degree of succession if the organization has recently experienced a change in the number of positions. A rapid increase in the number of positions, for example, will considerably lower the degree of succession since the new positions will require new incumbents. Researchers who use Kriesberg's measure should be aware of this possible source of distortion. The next two measures avoid this possible source of distortion by using rates rather than calculating the number of years an official has been in his present position, the Kriesberg measure.

Source. Louis Kriesberg, "Careers, Organization Size, and Succession," *American Journal of Sociology*, 68 (November, 1962), 355–359.

2. AND 3. LEVINE

Description. This study investigates turnover among nursing personnel in general hospitals. Fifty-one nonfederal, general hospitals were studied. The hospitals are located in Illinois, Indiana, Michigan, New Jersey, New York, and Ohio. Fourteen of the hospitals are "government," 18 are "church," and 19 are "other."[13] Thirty-one of the hospitals have between 100 and 199 daily average number of patients, 11 have between 200 and 299 patients, and 9 have between 300 and 499 patients. There are four categories of nursing personnel: (1) nursing administrators, supervisors, and head nurses; (2) professional staff nurses; (3) practical nurses; and (4) nursing aides, attendants, and orderlies. There were 9,419 full-time nursing personnel employed by the 51 hospitals at the beginning of the year for which the data were collected.

Definition. The study implicitly defines turnover as the "number of terminations of employment during a specified period of time."

Data Collection. Levine does not provide a copy of the instrument used to collect the data about turnover. He merely states that the hospitals provided two kinds of turnover figures:

> ... first, they reported for each type of nursing position the number who quit their jobs during the 12-month period, January 1, 1955 to December 31, 1955, among those who were on the payroll on January 1. The other figure was the number who quit during this 12-month period among those who came on the payroll after January 1, 1955.[14]

The hospitals distinguish between voluntary and involuntary terminations; however, the number of involuntary terminations is so small that Levine does not use the distinction.

Computation. Levine computes two measures of annual turnover. The first is the "turnover rate," which indicates the total number of persons who resigned during the year as a percentage of the average number of personnel employed during the year. The number employed at the beginning of the year, plus the number employed at the end of the year, divided by two, equals the average number of personnel employed during the year. The second measure of annual turnover computed is the "instability rate," which indicates the percentage of personnel on the payroll at the beginning of the year who quit during the year. The two computations are intended to supplement each other. The turnover rate and the instability rate for the 51 hospitals are, respectively, 57.5 percent and 35.7 percent. There are no averages or standard deviations for the two rates.

Validity. Levine indicates that the turnover rate varies by size of the hospital: the larger hospitals have a higher turnover rate. Levine's data also indicate (he does not state the matter in exactly these terms) that the administrators (nursing administrators, supervisors, and head nurses) have lower turnover rates than the nonadministrators (professional staff, nurses, practical nurses, nursing aides, attendants, and orderlies). These findings correspond to what other researchers have found with respect to the turnover rate.[15]

Reliability. The article contains no data relevant to reliability.

Comments. (1) Levine's concept of turnover ("the number of terminations of employment") is one type of succession ("the membership movement through the roles of a social system"). Levine focuses on the outward movement of full-time personnel through the nursing roles of one type of social system, a general hospital. Since his concept of turnover can be subsumed under this handbook's concept of succession, Levine's measures of turnover are relevant to this handbook's concept of succession. (2) Replication of his findings would be facilitated had Levine presented the instrument he used to collect the data from the hospitals. Fortunately, however, Levine carefully describes the type of data that the hospitals provided—full-time or part-time, voluntary or involuntary terminations, the exact time period for the data, and so forth. This descriptive information should facilitate replication. (3) Levine's methods of data collection will have to be modified to study succession in voluntary associations. There are few "terminations of employment" in voluntary associations because such organizations typically have few "employees." Voluntary associations have "members" and "roles" and there is some movement of the members through some of the roles. Data about this movement, however, cannot be collected by descriptions about the "number of terminations of employment." The study of succession has not been often applied to voluntary associations; therefore, Levine cannot be faulted for his focus on one type of administrative organization, a general hospital. (4) Levine computes the average number of personnel employed during the year by adding the number employed at the beginning of the year to the number employed at the end of the year and dividing by two. Other researchers compute these averages differently. (5) Comparative research with Levine's two measures of turnover would have been facilitated had he also presented averages and standard deviations. Unfortunately, the presentation of these statistics is not well established in organizational research.

Source. Eugene Levine, "Turnover Among Nursing Personnel in General Hospitals," *Hospitals*, 31 (September 5, 1957), 50–53 and 138–140.

Further Source. Eugene Levine and Stuart Wright, "New Ways to Measure Personnel Turnover in Hospitals," *Hospitals*, 31 (August 1, 1957), 38–42.

ADDITIONAL READINGS

1. Frederick J. Gaudet, *Labor Turnover* (New York: American Management Association, 1960), pp. 13–36.[16]
2. Magnus Hedberg, "The Turnover of Labor in Industry, an Actuarial Study," *Acta Sociologica* 5 (1960), 129–143.[17]
3. Magnus Hedberg, *The Process of Labor Turnover* (Stockholm, Sweden: The Swedish Council for Personnel Administration, 1967).

4. J. M. M. Hill, "A Note on Labor Turnover in an Iron and Steel Works," *Human Relations*, 6 (February, 1953), 79–87.[18]

5. J. M. M. Hill and E. L. Trist, *Industrial Accidents, Sickness, and other Absences* (London: Tavistock, 1959).

6. K. F. Lane and J. E. Andrew, "A Method of Labor Turnover Analysis," *Journal of the Royal Statistical Society*, Series A, Part 3, Vol. 118 (1955), 296–323.

7. Edward E. Lawler, III, "Managers' Perception of Their Subordinates' Pay and of Their Superiors' Pay," *Personnel Psychology*, 18 (Winter, 1965), 413–422.[19]

8. Lyman W. Porter and Edward E. Lawler, III, *Managerial Attitudes and Performance* (Homewood, Ill.: Irwin, 1968).

9. A. K. Rice, J. M. M. Hill, and E. L. Trist, "The Representation of Labor Turnover as a Social Process," *Human Relations*, 3 (November, 1950), 349–372.

10. A. K. Rice, "An Approach to Problems of Labor Turnover: A Case Study," *British Management Review*, 2 (1953), 19–47.

11. H. Silcock, "The Phenomenon of Labor Turnover," *Journal of the Royal Statistical Society*, Series A, Part 4, Vol. 117 (1954), 429–440.

12. F. H. Spratling and F. J. Lloyd, "Personnel Statistics and Sickness—Absence Statistics," *Journal of the Institute of Actuaries*, 77, Part 2, 346 (1951), 196–243.

13. Gordon S. Watkins, Paul A. Dodd, Wayne L. McNaughton, and Paul Prasow, *The Management of Personnel and Labor Relations* (New York: McGraw-Hill, 1950), pp. 343–374.

NOTES

1. This definition comes from Donald B. Trow, "Membership Succession and Team Performance," *Human Relations*, 13 (August, 1960), 259–269 (esp. p. 259).

2. The following studies of succession focus on executive turnover: Richard O. Carlson, "Succession and Performance Among School Superintendents," *Administrative Science Quarterly*, 6 (September, 1961), 210–227; Richard O. Carlson, *Executive Succession and Organizational Change* (Chicago: Midwest Administration Center, University of Chicago, 1962); Gerald Gordon and Selwyn Becker, "Organizational Size and Managerial Succession: A Re-examination," *American Journal of Sociology*, 70 (September, 1964), 215–222; Alvin W. Gouldner, *Patterns of Industrial Bureaucracy* (Glencoe, Ill.: The Free Press, 1954); Oscar Grusky, "Role Conflict in Organization: A Study of Prison Camp Officials," *Administrative Science Quarterly*, 3 (March, 1959), 452–472; Oscar Grusky, "Managerial Succession and Organizational Effectiveness," *American Journal of Sociology*, 69 (July, 1963), 21–31; Robert H. Guest, *Organizational Change* (Homewood, Ill.: Irwin, 1962); Joel Kotin and Myron R. Sharaf, "Intrastaff Controversy at a State Mental Hospital: An Analysis of Ideological Issues," *Psychiatry*, 30 (February, 1967), 16–29; Joel Kotin and Myron R. Sharaf,

"Management Succession and Administrative Style," *Psychiatry*, 30 (August, 1967), 237–248; Louis Kriesberg, "Careers, Organization Size, and Succession," *American Journal of Sociology*, 68 (November, 1962), 355–359; Robert Perrucci and Richard A. Mannweiler, "Organization Size, Complexity, and Administrative Succession in Higher Education," *The Sociological Quarterly*, 9 (Summer, 1968), 343–355; Trow, *op. cit.*; and Donald B. Trow, "Executive Succession in Small Companies," *Administrative Science Quarterly*, 6 (September, 1961), 228–239.

3. Levenson suggests that a general concept of succession should be used. See Bernard Levenson, "Bureaucratic Succession," in *Complex Organizations*, ed. Amitai Etzioni (New York: Holt, Rinehart, and Winston, 1961), pp. 362–375.

4. In addition to "administrative succession," the literature also refers to "managerial succession" and "executive succession."

5. An exception is Oscar Grusky, "The Effects of Succession: A Comparative Study of Military and Business Organization," in *The New Military*, ed. Morris Janowitz (New York: Russell Sage, 1964), pp. 83–117.

6. The best single discussion of the measurement of turnover is Frederick J. Gaudet, *Labor Turnover* (New York: American Management Association, Research Study 39, 1960). An excellent source of the literature on turnover is Frederick J. Gaudet, *The Literature on Labor Turnover* (N.Y.: Industrial Relations Newsletter, 1960). The Federal Government publishes an immense literature about turnover. Some of this literature is cited in James L. Price, *Annotated Bibliography of Federal Government Publications Presenting Data About Organizations* (Iowa City, Iowa: Center for Labor and Management, University of Iowa, Monograph Series No. 6, 1967).

7. The importance of the separation rate as a measure of turnover is noted in the following sources: Geoffrey Y. Cornog, "The Personnel Turnover Concept: A Reappraisal," *Public Administration Review*, 17 (Autumn, 1957), 247–256; Gaudet, *Labor Turnover, op. cit.*, pp. 14–15; Magnus Hedberg, "The Turnover of Labor in Industry, an Actuarial Study," *Acta Sociologica*, 5 (1960), 129–143; Eugene Levine and Stuart Wright, "New Ways to Measure Personnel Turnover in Hospitals," *Hospitals*, 31 (August 1, 1957), 38–42; and William E. Mosher, J. Donald Kingsley, and O. Glenn Stahl, *Public Personnel Administration* (New York: Harper, 1950), pp. 185–198.

8. The following sources contain criticisms of the separation rate: Hedberg, *op. cit.*; K. F. Lane and J. E. Andrew, "A Method of Labor Turnover Analysis," *Journal of the Royal Statistical Society*, Series A, Part 3, Vol. 118, (1955), 296–323; Levine and Wright, *op. cit.*; H. Silcock, "The Phenomenon of Labor Turnover," *Journal of the Royal Statistical Society*, Series A, Part 4, Vol. 117 (1954), 429–440; A. K. Rice, J. M. M. Hill, and E. L. Trist, "The Representation of Labor Turnover as a Social Process," *Human Relations*, 3 (November, 1950), 349–372; and F. H. Spratling and F. J. Lloyd, "Personnel Statistics and Sickness—Absence Statistics," *Journal of the Institute of Actuaries*, 77, Part 2, 346 (1951), 196–243.

9. Most of the alternative measures of turnover are very complex and it is doubtful whether such measures will ever be used widely. The measure proposed by Levine is the simplest of these alternative measures.

10. Oscar Grusky, "Corporate Size, Bureaucratization, and Managerial Succession," *American Journal of Sociology*, 67 (November, 1961), 261–269 (esp. p. 261).

11. This question is not reproduced in Kriesberg's article. A copy of the study from which this question came was supplied through the courtesy of Louis Kriesberg.

12. The original version of the questionnaire has an IBM number, to precode the responses, immediately preceding each of the eight numbers.

13. Levine does not indicate the types of hospitals included under "other."

14. Levine, *op. cit.*, pp. 50–51.

15. Hedberg, *op. cit.*, (esp. pp. 129–130).

16. The most frequently used measures of turnover are the separation rate and the accession rate. These two rates are described in Additional Readings Nos. 1 and 13 and are used in a study by Hedberg (No. 3).

17. The following Additional Readings contain criticisms of the separation rate—the most commonly used measure of turnover—and propose alternative measures: Nos. 2, 6, 9, 11, and 12.

18. The following Additional Readings should be treated as a unit: Nos. 4, 5, 9, and 10. The research reported in these readings has been conducted in England and constitutes some of the most theoretically and methodologically sophisticated treatments of turnover in the organizational literature.

19. This article has a measure that can be used for the general concept of succession rather than for internal or external succession. The calculations are presented on p. 415; however, the instrument of data collection is found on p. 189 of Additional Reading No. 8.

CONCLUSION

There are several courses of action that might be taken to improve the measures used in the study of organizations. This final chapter presents these suggestions under three headings: theory, research, and administration.

THEORY

A problem encountered in the compilation of this handbook was the existence of very impressive organizational measures for which no precise concept could be discerned. An illustration of this problem is provided by the Ohio State studies of leadership.[1] The two terms most often used by the Ohio State researchers are "consideration" and "initiating structure." Consideration and initiating structure can be used to describe either supervisory behavior or opinion about supervisors. The point of this section can be illustrated by an examination of the measurement of supervisory behavior with respect to initiating structure.

Table 23–1 lists the 20 questionnaire items used by the Ohio State researchers to collect data about initiating structure[2] and also indicates the concepts in this handbook that are most pertinent to the questionnaire items. The respondents are requested to describe the extent to which the 20 items describe the behavior of their supervisors.

TABLE 23–1 Questionnaire Items Used to Collect Data about Supervisory Behavior, Classified by this Handbook's Frame of Reference

Item	Classification
1.[3] He encourages overtime work	Motivation
2. He tries out his new ideas	Innovation
3. He rules with an iron hand	Centralization
4. He criticizes poor work	Distributive Justice
5. He talks about how much should be done	Motivation
6. He encourages slow working foremen to greater effort	Motivation
7. He waits for his foremen to push new ideas before he does	Innovation
8. He assigns people under him to particular tasks	Formalization
9. He asks for sacrifices from his foremen for the good of the entire department	Motivation

Item	Classification
10. He insists that his foremen follow standard ways of doing things on every detail	Routinization
11. He sees to it that people under him are working up to their limits	Motivation
12. He offers new approaches to problems	Innovation
13. He insists that he be informed on decisions made by foremen under him	Communication
14. He lets others do their work the way they think best	Centralization
15. He stresses being ahead of competing work groups	Motivation
16. He "needles" foremen under him for greater effort	Motivation
17. He decides in detail what shall be done and how it shall be done	Formalization
18. He emphasizes meeting of deadlines	Motivation
19. He asks foremen who have slow groups to get more out of their groups	Motivation
20. He emphasizes the quantity of work	Motivation

The 20 questionnaire items seem to collect information about seven of this handbook's concepts. With seven available alternatives, initiating structure could not be assigned to any single concept, and therefore was not included in this handbook.[4] This is unfortunate because an immense amount of methodologically impressive research has been conducted with respect to the Ohio State studies of leadership and the problem could have been avoided had these concepts been defined in a precise manner.[5] To suggest that concepts be precise is to argue for careful theoretical work. In the Introduction to his book on theory construction, A. L. Stinchcombe makes some comments which may be appropriate at this point. He says:

> Given the purpose of showing how empirical derivations can be obtained from many different theories, I am inevitably drawn into making statements about the world in substantive fields in which I am massively ignorant. But for a social theorist ignorance is more excusable than vagueness. Other investigators can easily show that I am wrong if I am sufficiently precise. They will have much more difficulty showing by investigation what, precisely, I mean if I am vague. I hope not to be forced to weasel out with, 'But I didn't really mean that.' *Social theorists should prefer to be wrong than misunderstood. Being misunderstood shows sloppy theoretical work.*[6] (Emphasis supplied.)

Organizational researchers would do well to comply with the norms that Stinchcombe imposes on himself.

RESEARCH

A Research Model. The primary purpose of this handbook is to promote standardization of the measures used in the study of organizations. The strategy is that standardization will be promoted by making existing measures available in a compact, orderly, and precise manner. Researchers who are investigating the same concept are not likely to use the same measure if they must independently search for measures through a voluminous, chaotic, and ambiguous literature. The ease of locating measures should promote standardization.

A handbook, however, is limited in what it can do to promote standardization. Researchers must ultimately be persuaded that the measures included in a handbook are good measures before they will use them. No amount of compactness, orderliness, and precision will persuade a researcher to use an inferior measure. Therefore, the main long-run effort to promote standardization must be based on measurement research.

A model for this type of measurement research is the work of Patricia Smith and her colleagues on satisfaction.[7] Researchers who are studying satisfaction are likely to use Smith's measures, not primarily because they are compiled in a compact, orderly, and precise manner, but because of the impressive amount of evidence which is presented regarding the validity and reliability of the measures. This evidence is, of course, obtained as a result of an extensive amount of measurement research. Therefore, it is a secondary aim of this handbook to encourage research on the measures which have been compiled and to develop new measures.[8]

Development of New Measures. This handbook attempts to compile measures for the concepts about which there is the greatest degree of agreement among organizational researchers. No attempt is made to include all the concepts used by organizational researchers because the assumption is that the bulk of the theoretically significant concepts will be indicated by this high degree of agreement. There are, however, six widely used concepts for which measures could not be located: conformity, co-optation, efficiency, ideology, shape, and social stratification.[9] New measures will have to be developed. These concepts will now be discussed.

Conformity is the degree to which performance corresponds to the norms of a social system.[10] Sometimes conformity is defined as the degree of discrepancy between the "real" and the "ideal" and at other times it is defined as the disparity between the "factual and normative orders." "Compliance" and "deviant behavior" are, respectively, a synonym and an antonym for conformity. In this handbook, "norm" always refers to a desired course of action, never, as in psychology, to a statistical average.[11]

Co-optation is the recruitment of social system members with the goal of increased institutionalization.[12] For example, American business firms which operate abroad generally attempt to staff their organizations with personnel from the country in which they operate; the goal of this type of recruitment is increased acceptance of the firm by the population of the country.

Efficiency is the amount of resources used to produce the output of a social system.[13] Many researchers, especially those with backgrounds in economics, refer to "productivity" rather than to efficiency.[14] Efficiency and productivity are different labels for the same concept. Efficiency is often confused with effectiveness (the degree to which a social system achieves its goals). A business firm may, for example, be highly efficient—may have a low unit cost for each unit of output—but, because of extreme market fluctuations, be only moderately effective, that is, be only moderately profitable. Efficiency and effectiveness are probably positively related; however, the concepts are different and should be conceptually distinguished.

Ideology refers to beliefs that are publicly expressed with the manifest purpose of influencing the orientations and actions of others.[15] The "American Business Creed" is an example. This creed is a series of beliefs about the nature and benefits of the American economic system, transmitted through American society with the purpose of gaining widespread support for the economic system. Material relevant to ideology is contained in discussions of organizational "sagas."

Sanctions, in the discussion of distributive justice, are the social resources used by a social system to obtain membership conformity to its norms. Three aspects of sanctions are distinguished: amount, structure, and distribution. This handbook could locate no measure of the amount of sanctions available to a social system. Lewellen's work on monetary compensation is sophisticated and promising, but is much too complex for widespread use by organizational researchers.[16] As previously indicated, distributive justice refers to the structure of the sanction system rather than its amount.

Shape is the degree of distribution of members among the different levels of a social system.[17] Large organizations, for example, are typically thought to be pyramidal in shape, that is, the higher the level, the fewer the individuals located at that level. Material relevant to shape is found in discussions of "flatness-tallness."

Social stratification is the degree of dispersion of the social resources of a social system.[18] Organizations, for example, vary greatly with respect to the equality of their distribution of monetary compensation to their members.[19] Material often discussed under the label of "social stratification" has already been presented in the discussions of centralization (power stratification), distributive justice (a system of social stratification is the means used to obtain distributive justice), and succession (vertical mobility). However, none of this previous material measures the distribution of the sanctions in a social system.

ADMINISTRATION

Presentation of Data. Two suggestions are made for the presentation of measurement data. First, the instruments used to collect data should be included in the research report, whenever possible. Replication is hindered when other researchers do not have the exact instruments used in the original research.

The inclusion of the instruments is more of a problem in articles than in books. Editors of journals, in the interest of economy, often suggest removing an instrument or greatly shortening the amount of space devoted to its presentation—thereby making it impossible for other researchers to use the instrument exactly as it was used in the original research. If an instrument cannot be included in an article, for whatever reason, then the instrument can be filed with the American Documentation Institute.[20] An instrument is more likely to be used widely if its availability depends on the paid services of an organization, such as the American Documentation Institute, rather than on the free labor of a harassed researcher who has long since conducted the research and who prefers to concentrate his time and labor on his present work.

Second, means and standard deviations should routinely be included in all research reports. These statistics provide a base of comparison for other researchers who use the measures.

Compilation of Manuals. The long-run result of a large amount of measurement research will probably be the emergence of one or two very good measures for each concept. The situation that presently exists for satisfaction is a close approximation of the situation that should ultimately characterize all organizational concepts. When this stage is achieved, it will then be necessary to compile manuals for the different measures. The manuals will contain the same type of information as this handbook, with the difference that each will compile research for a single measure and not for a series of measures for an entire frame of reference, such as this handbook. Three examples of such manuals currently exist for satisfaction.[21] This handbook properly concludes by indicating how it can ultimately be replaced.

NOTES

1. There is a large literature on the Ohio State studies of leadership. The best single source of this literature is the *Manual for Leadership Opinion Questionnaire* (Chicago: Science Research Associates, 1969). The address of Science Research Associates is 259 East Erie Street, Chicago, Illinois 60611. The manual has a complete bibliography on the *Leadership Opinion Questionnaire* and the *Supervisory Behavior Description Questionnaire.*

   The problem this handbook encountered with the Ohio State studies of leadership—the lack of conceptual precision—frequently occurs in studies of leadership. Examples are the impressive research conducted by Fiedler and his colleagues at Illinois and a series of equally outstanding research studies performed at Michigan. Most of this research is cited in Fred E. Fiedler, *A Theory of Leadership Effectiveness* (New York: McGraw-Hill, 1967). An excellent introduction to the leadership research conducted at Michigan is Floyd C. Mann, "Toward an Understanding of the Leadership Role in Formal Organization," in *Leadership and Productivity*, Robert Dubin, George C. Homans, Floyd C. Mann, and Delbert C. Miller (San Francisco: Chandler, 1965), pp. 68–103.

2. Edwin A. Fleishman, "A Leader Behavior Description for Industry," in *Leader Behavior*, ed. Ralph M. Stogdill and Alvin E. Coons (Columbus, Ohio: Bureau of Business Research, The Ohio State University, Research Monograph 88, 1957), pp. 103–119 (esp. 108–109).

3. The numbers in this handbook are different from the numbers in Fleishman's article.

4. The situation for consideration is basically the same as the situation for initiating structure.

5. The Ohio State researchers, of course, provide definitions for initiating structure and consideration. See, for example, Fleishman, *op. cit.*, p. 104. These definitions are not precise and vary somewhat in the different studies.

6. Arthur L. Stinchcombe, *Constructing Social Theories* (New York: Harcourt, Brace, and World, 1968), p. 6. Two good examples of the type of conceptual work needed by organizational research are provided by Hickson and Peabody. See D. J. Hickson, "A Convergence in Organizational Theory," *Administrative Science Quarterly*, 11 (September, 1966), 224–237; Robert L. Peabody, "Perceptions of Organizational Authority," *Administrative Science Quarterly*, 6 (March, 1962), 463–482; and Robert L. Peabody, *Organizational Authority* (New York: Atherton, 1964), pp. 15–43. Hickson's research is especially impressive.

7. Patricia C. Smith, Lorne M. Kendall, and Charles L. Hulin, *The Measurement of Satisfaction in Work and Retirement* (Chicago: Rand McNally, 1969).

8. The following sources are additional examples of the type of measurement research needed in the study of organizations: Michael Argyle, Godfrey Gardner, and Frank Cioffi, "The Measurement of Supervisory Methods," *Human Relations*, 10 (November, 1957), 295–313; Michael Argyle, Godfrey Gardner, and Frank Cioffi, "Supervisory Methods Related to Productivity, Absenteeism, and Labor Turnover," *Human Relations*, 11 (February, 1958), 23–40; Melany E. Baehr, "A Simplified Procedure for the Measurement of Employee Attitudes," *Journal of Applied Psychology*, 37 (June, 1953), 163–167; Bernard H. Baum, Peter F. Sorensen, Jr., and William S. Place, "Patterns of Consensus in the Perception of Organizational Control," *Sociological Quarterly*, 10 (Summer, 1969), 335–340; Bernice Eisman, "Some Operational Measures of Cohesiveness and Their Interrelations," *Human Relations*, 12 (May, 1959), 183–189; Neal Gross and William E. Martin, "On Group Cohesiveness," *American Journal of Sociology*, 57 (May, 1952), 546–564; Lester M. Libo, *Measuring Group Cohesiveness* (Ann Arbor, Mich.: Research Center for Group Dynamics, 1953); Martin Patchen, "Alternative Questionnaire Approaches to the Measurement of Influence in Organizations," *American Journal of Sociology*, 69 (July, 1963), 41–52; Martin Patchen, *Some Questionnaire Measures of Employee Motivation and Morale* (Ann Arbor, Mich.: Survey Research Center, University of Michigan, 1965); and Joseph Weitz and Robert C. Nickols, "The Validity of Direct and Indirect Questions in Measuring Job Satisfaction," *Personnel Psychology*, 6 (Winter, 1953), 487–494.

9. The discussion of bureaucracy in the chapter on administrative staff points out that a satisfactory measure could not be located for "impersonality." Impersonality is not discussed at this point because it is not used as widely as conformity, co-optation, efficiency, ideology, shape, and social stratification.

10. This definition is based on Albert K. Cohen, "The Study of Social Disorganization and Deviant Behavior," in *Sociology Today*, ed. Robert K. Merton, Leonard Broom, and Leonard S. Cottrell, Jr. (New York: Basic Books, 1959), pp. 461–484 (esp. p. 462). Cohen refers to "behavior" rather than to "performance" and to "institutionalized expectations" rather than to "norms."

11. This handbook's conception of norm comes from Clyde Kluckhohn, "Values and Value-Orientations in the Theory of Action: An Exploration and Definition," in *Toward a General Theory of Action*, ed. Talcott Parsons and Edward A. Shils (Cambridge, Mass.: Harvard, 1954), pp. 388–433. This handbook's "norm" corresponds to Kluckhohn's "value."

12. This definition of co-optation is adapted from Philip Selznick, *TVA and the Grass Roots* (Berkeley, Calif.: California, 1953), pp. 3–16. Co-optation, as defined in this handbook, encompasses Selznick's data about informal co-optation. For a sympathetic critique of Selznick's definition of co-optation, see James L. Price, *Organizational Effectiveness* (Homewood, Ill.: Irwin, 1968), pp. 95–135.

13. This definition of efficiency comes from Amitai Etzioni, *Modern Organizations* (Englewood Cliffs, N.J.: Prentice-Hall, 1964), p. 8.

14. Solomon Fabricant, *A Primer on Productivity* (N.Y.: Random House, 1969).

15. This definition of ideology comes from Francis X. Sutton, Seymour E. Harris, Carl Kaysen, and James Tobin, *The American Business Creed* (Cambridge, Mass.: Harvard, 1956), pp. 1–15.

16. Wilbur G. Lewellen, *Executive Compensation in Large Industrial Corporations* (New York: Columbia, 1968); Wilbur G. Lewellen, "Executives Lose Out, Even with Options," *Harvard Business Review*, 46 (January–February, 1968), 127–142; and Wilbur G. Lewellen, "Management and Ownership in the Large Firm," *Journal of Finance*, 24 (May, 1969), 299–322. An excellent review of the literature regarding monetary compensation is Edward E. Lawler, III, *Pay and Organizational Effectiveness* (New York: McGraw-Hill, 1971).

17. For discussions of shape, see Morris Janowitz, *The Professional Soldier* (Glencoe, Ill.: The Free Press, 1960), pp. 54–75 (esp. pp. 64–68) and Bernard Barber, *Social Stratification* (New York: Harcourt, Brace, 1957), pp. 87–93. A measure of shape, located too late to be included in this handbook, is found in Herbert Kaufman and David Seidman, "The Morphology of Organizations," *Administrative Science Quarterly*, 15 (December, 1970), 439–451.

18. Helpful discussions of social stratification are contained in Jerald Hage and Michael Aiken, "Routine Technology, Social Structure, and Organizational Goals," *Administrative Science Quarterly*, 14 (September, 1969), 366–376 and Jerald Hage and Michael Aiken, *Social Change in Complex Organizations* (New York: Random House, 1970), pp. 23–25.

19. Some clues for the measurement of social stratification are provided in William M. Evan, "Indices of the Hierarchical Structure of Industrial Organizations," *Management Science*, 9 (April, 1963), 468–477.

20. The American Documentation Institute is used by Forehand. See Garlie A. Forehand, "Assessments of Innovative Behavior: Partial Criteria for the Assessment of Executive Performance," *Journal of Applied Psychology*, 47 (June, 1963), 206–213 (esp. p. 207). The article by Forehand is discussed in the chapter on innovation.

It is also difficult to reproduce instruments in books that are secondary analyses of a series of studies. An example is Seymour Melman, *Dynamic Factors in Industrial Productivity* (Oxford, Eng.: Basil Blackwell, 1956). There is no reason why the American Documentation Institute cannot also be used as a repository for these instruments.

21. Robert K. Burns, L. L. Thurstone, David G. Moore, and Melany E. Baehr, *General Manual for the SRA Employee Inventory* (Chicago: Science Research Associates, 1952); Smith *et al., op. cit.*; and David J. Weiss, Rene V. Dawis, George W. England, and Lloyd H. Lofquist, *Manual for the Minnesota Satisfaction Questionnaire* (Minneapolis, Minn.: Industrial Relations Center, University of Minnesota, 1967).

The compilation of manuals, of course, does not mean the conclusion of research concerning the measures in the manuals. The existence of manuals signifies that an extensive amount of research—both measurement and substantive—has already been performed concerning the measures in the manuals. Even with this extensive attention, the measures will require periodic revision. However, if the initial research on a measure is careful, as is the work of Smith and her colleagues on satisfaction, these revisions should not have to be made too frequently—otherwise the advantages of standardization are lost or considerably reduced. The best strategy is to research a measure carefully before giving it wide use.

INDEX